# The Instructor

You are holding a reproduction of an original work that is in the public domain in the United States of America, and possibly other countries. You may freely copy and distribute this work as no entity (individual or corporate) has a copyright on the body of the work. This book may contain prior copyright references, and library stamps (as most of these works were scanned from library copies). These have been scanned and retained as part of the historical artifact.

This book may have occasional imperfections such as missing or blurred pages, poor pictures, errant marks, etc. that were either part of the original artifact, or were introduced by the scanning process. We believe this work is culturally important, and despite the imperfections, have elected to bring it back into print as part of our continuing commitment to the preservation of printed works worldwide. We appreciate your understanding of the imperfections in the preservation process, and hope you enjoy this valuable book.

THE INSTRUCTOR
THE MAN AND THE JOB
CHARLES R. ALLEN
SECOND IMPRESSION

THE INSTRUCTOR
THE MAN AND THE JOB

A HAND BOOK FOR INSTRUCTORS OF INDUSTRIAL AND VOCATIONAL SUBJECTS

BY
CHARLES R. ALLEN

SOMETIME AGENT FOR INDUSTRIAL TRAINING OF BOYS AND MEN, MASSACHUSETTS BOARD OF EDUCATION, AND SUPERINTENDENT OF INSTRUCTOR TRAINING, U. S. S. B. EMERGENCY FLEET CORPORATION

PHILADELPHIA AND LONDON
J. B. LIPPINCOTT COMPANY

COPYRIGHT, 1919, BY J. B. LIPPINCOTT COMPANY
PUBLISHED JANUARY 25, 1919
REPRINTED APRIL 20, 1919

SET UP AND PRINTED IN UNITED STATES

PREFACE

For a long time men in trades and industries have been imparting what they knew to learners, and in order to do this some sort of an instructing process has been carried on.

It is equally true that for a long time those whose business it was to impart knowledge, have been learning how to teach, that is, they have been learning the principles and practices of the teaching trade.

Since the industrial instructor has usually stuck to his shop and the teacher has stuck to his school, the body of knowledge, experience, and skill in the teaching trade has not been available to the trade instructor, so that, in general, trade instruction in industry and in vocational schools has been carried on without the advantage of the use of the teacher's trade.

Just as in any other trade, there are in the teaching trade "operations," "tools," equipment and methods that have been found most effective in putting things over from the instructor to the learner. Information regarding them has not, however, generally been accessible to the industrial instructor, because it has been confined to professional teachers and embodied in educational publications which are not likely to come to the attention of the mechanic.

Moreover, where such publications have come to his attention he has found them hard to understand and their contents difficult to apply, since they are written for the use of teachers in general schools.

Training courses for vocational instructors where they have been established have aimed at meeting this difficulty by presenting the principles and practices of the teaching trade in such a manner that industrial instructors could apply them in their own special line of instruction, but in many cases trade instructors are unable to avail themselves of the opportunities offered by these courses.

PREFACE

This book is intended, therefore, to serve two purposes—to serve as a handbook to instructors in industrial plants, and also to serve as "instruction notes" in instructor training courses.

The material as presented here has been developed out of notes originally used in instructor training courses and subsequently modified for the training of shipyard instructors in connection with the instructor training work of the Emergency Fleet Corporation under my direction, in which over one thousand instructors have been trained.

The rapid development of trade and industrial training, both in vocational schools and in industrial plants, and the special development of intensive training due to war conditions make the trained instructor of greater and greater value to American industries. It is hoped that this book may contribute to the development of efficient training in our vocational schools and in our industries. If it does, the purpose for which it was written will have been accomplished.

CHARLES R. ALLEN.

October 1, 1918.

INTRODUCTION

THOSE of us most familiar with the work of Mr. Allen have long been anxious that he write for publication so that all those interested or engaged in industrial education might have the benefit of his rich experience and ripened views. This book on the preparation of teachers is the first result. Let us hope it will be followed by others dealing with the problems of the organization and administration of vocational schools with which Mr. Allen has been so closely connected for almost two decades.

There are few, if any, men so well qualified as he by experience and ability to speak with authority in this field. Personally, I owe to the author a debt of gratitude I can never repay for the help he has given me during the past ten years. He has been not only a capable assistant at various times but also mentor and guide upon whose keen analysis of problems and sound philosophy of vocational education I have long relied.

Comparisons are always invidious. Nevertheless, I am of the opinion that this book is the most important contribution yet made to industrial and trade training. It deals with the most vital of our problems—the proper selection and training of competent instructors—without which government grants and imposing equipment are but sounding brass and tinkling cymbals.

While only principles of pedagogy fundamental to all successful teaching are presented, they are applied to the instruction problems of the vocational class with a keenness of analysis, a wealth of illustration, and a clearness of statement not to be found in any other text with which I am acquainted. Recognizing that which the War has made apparent to all, that large industrial plants as well as schools must in the future carry on training for new employes, the text has been prepared so that it can be used equally well in the preparation of instructors for schools or for industrial plants, most of whose teaching problems are common.

INTRODUCTION

The book presents not abstract theory but practical methods based on sound principles which the author developed in his work as a supervisor of teacher training in Massachusetts and worked out in the form here given while he was supervising training courses for shipyard instructors under the Emergency Fleet Corporation of the United States Shipping Board. The plan of training, therefore, is not a dream or a guess but a demonstrated success.

Every one interested in or touching the problems of vocational education, particularly industrial education in any way, needs to read this book. It will help him to think straight as well as to train teachers properly. Indeed, all those engaged in regular education cannot fail to profit by studying the exceedingly clear analysis and discussion of methods of instruction where "pedageese" is avoided so that the text may be equally readable by all.

Employers and foremen will gain from Mr. Allen's exceedingly clear and thorough discussion a conception of the need and possibilities of training the new workers of which most of them have never dreamed. Perhaps most valuable of all, those who believe that regular schools of education can meet the needs of shop instructors by the customary courses on educational philosophy and method given by those unacquainted with industrial processes and vocational schools, will learn from the book that the pedagogy of industrial education has already built up a definite content or courses of its own. Those courses can only be taught successfully by persons familiar with the organization and processes of both industry and the industrial school.

C. A. PROSSER.

TABLE OF CONTENTS

PART I

TRAINING IN THE PLANT

CHAPTER		PAGE
I.	The Principles of Effective Training	3
II.	Methods of Training	11
III.	Training on the Job	23
IV.	Picking the Training Force	31

PART II

THE ANALYSIS AND CLASSIFICATION OF TRADE KNOWLEDGE

V.	The Producer and the Instructor	37
VI.	The First Operation. The Determination of what is to be Taught	42
VII.	The Classification of what Must be Taught	46
VIII.	The Determination of "Blocks"	64

PART III

ESTABLISHING AN EFFECTIVE INSTRUCTIONAL ORDER

IX.	The Determination of Learning Difficulties	77
X.	Establishing a Difficulty Scale	85
XI.	Applying the Difficulty Scale	88
XII.	Getting Jobs into an Effective Instructional Order	92
XIII.	Tying up the Auxiliary Information with the Job Instruction	97
XIV.	Getting the Jobs in more than One Block into an Effective Instructional Order	106

TABLE OF CONTENTS

PART IV
PUTTING IT OVER

CHAPTER	PAGE
XV.—The Trade Instructor	117
XVI.—What Instruction is	121
XVII.—The Instructing Operation	126
XVIII.—Detailed Discussion of Steps in the Lesson. Step 1	132
XIX.—Detailed Discussion of Steps in the Lesson. Step 2	136
XX.—Detailed Discussion Step 3	139
XXI.—Detailed Discussion. Step 4	141
XXII.—Securing Trade Intelligence	143

PART V
METHODS OF INSTRUCTION

XXIII.—Methods for Step 1	147
XXIV.—Methods for Step 2	151
XXV.—Methods for Step 3	158
XXVI.—Methods for Step 4	163
XXVII.—Information and Development. Lines of Approach	165
XXVIII.—The Technical Lesson and the Production Lesson	169

PART VI
LESSON PLANNING

XXIX.—Lesson Planning	177
XXX.—An Illustration of the Planning of a Lesson	184

PART VII
INSTRUCTIONAL MANAGEMENT

XXXI.—Special Problems of the Instructor	205
XXXII.—Organization for Handling Different Types of Instruction	210
XXXIII.—The Organization of the Instructional Gang	219

TABLE OF CONTENTS

CHAPTER		PAGE
XXXIV.—Instructional Conditions as they are Affected by Surroundings and Material		235
XXXV.—How Surroundings Affect Instruction		245
XXXVI.—Handling the Gang for Effective Instruction		248
XXXVII.—Interest and Interest Factors		257

PART VIII

ORGANIZATION FOR TRAINING IN INDUSTRY

XXXVIII.—The Organization for Training		287
XXXIX.—Instructional Bookkeeping		304
XL.—Training Principles and Policies		319
XLI.—Apprenticeship Training		334
XLII.—The "Cold Storage" vs. the Application Theory		336
XLIII.—The Relative Order of Theory and Practice		342
XLIV.—The Short Unit Course		347

PART IX

THE USE OF THIS MATERIAL IN INSTRUCTOR TRAINING COURSES

XLV.—The Use of this Material in Instructor Training Courses		351

APPENDIX

A.—The Use of this Material by Foremen		361
B.—The Use of this Material for Self-Training		363
C.—Some of the More Important Terms Used		365

PART I
TRAINING IN THE PLANT

CHAPTER I

THE PRINCIPLES OF EFFECTIVE TRAINING

This book deals with three factors in efficient production—the instructor, the man, and the job. The instructor, because it is through effective instruction that we can secure efficiency in training. The man, because when properly trained he does the best work. The job, because production efficiency comes from well instructed men doing good jobs.

Therefore it deals with the question of effectively training green men or "learners" and with other forms of training for production work. It points out some ways by which learners can be trained most rapidly and trained to do their work in the best way through the application of definite principles to training problems. One of the most important points in effective training is to see that the men who are used as instructors really know how to "put over" what they know, hence, a considerable portion of this book is given over to a description of how such a man can organize his trade knowledge for effective instruction, how he can effectively plan his instruction work, and how he can best handle his men under instructing conditions. The organization under which such a man can work to the best advantage is discussed and an effective type is described.

To avoid any misunderstanding it should be stated here that this book does not deal in any way with trade processes, or with technical training. It assumes that, whether the training is given in a school shop or in the plant itself, the instructor is thoroughly equipped so far as knowing how to do his job is concerned. It deals solely with instruction, not with production, except so far as effective training functions in better production and greater output—which it does.

An appendix contains suggestions as to the use of this material by men in industry who desire to become better instructors and to those who may undertake to use it in "Instructor Training Courses."

The Possible Field of Training.—In any production plant the product is got out by a number of people who are employed on a variety of jobs. These jobs may range from highly skilled to unskilled jobs. The variety of jobs to which effective methods of training can be applied is much greater than is generally supposed. In the past it has frequently been considered that only jobs in the so-called skilled trades were worth training for. More recent study has shown that there are very few industrial operations or semi-skilled jobs for which definite training is not of value. In general, it may be said that a job is worth training for if it presents these characteristics:

(1) Anybody cannot learn to do the job. That is, in training, it is found that certain natural qualifications count, as quickness, neatness, a good eye, physical strength, weight, etc.

(2) The trade recognizes jobs of different degrees of difficulty in the same line—as, for example, in machine shop work or in making paper boxes there are recognized "grades" of jobs.

(3) There is a best way of doing the job.

(4) It is recognized that an appreciable period of time is required for a learner to reach maximum efficiency—in other words, a man cannot do the job as well the first time as he can after a period of practice.

There are but few jobs that do not meet these conditions. The training discussed in this book has in mind training on such jobs as well as in skilled trades.

The Necessity for Training.—Whether a new man comes into the shop from another shop of the same kind, or from a trade resembling the trade that he takes up, or comes in absolutely green, he needs a greater or less amount of "breaking in"—that is, he needs training. Of course, what he needs and how much he needs depends on what his new job is and how much he knows, already, but he always needs *something* put over to him if he is to do his new job as well as it should be done.

Somebody has to put this over to him, and, to that extent, that somebody is just as truly an instructor, a teacher, as if he were a "regular" teacher in a school. After all, a teacher is only somebody whose business it is to put things over—to teach. Teaching is therefore always going on in any shop. It is a necessary part of the carrying on of the work, because (while it would be an ideal condition if it were possible) it is impossible for any shop to keep going by only employing men who know how to do the work and especially men experienced in doing the work of that particular shop. There will always be some turnover. Men will drop out for one reason or another and other men must be employed to fill their places. So instruction, or training, must go on all the time. In some way, the new men that come in must learn how to do the work, and this training process must be carried on in addition to the production work for which the shop is established and operated.

The Best Situation.—If this training process has to be carried on somehow we would have the best conditions if:—

(1) Each man were trained so that he could do his job in the best possible way.

(2) Each man were trained to do his job in the least time compatible with thorough training.

(3) The experiences of each man during the training period had been such that he stayed through the training period and did not quit when only partly trained.

If he is trained so that he can do a first class job that is evidently the best proposition both for him and for the shop. A man who is thoroughly "onto his job" and knows it is less likely to quit, makes better money, spoils less stock. Whatever time and effort may have been spent in training him is certainly a better investment and is likely to be a more permanent one.

The less time taken to train him, *provided he is well trained*, the quicker he gets up to full production capacity. This again is both to his advantage and to the advantage of the shop.

If his experiences in training are disagreeable, if he is continually "bawled out," if he feels that he is not "catching on," if he knows that he is not "getting on," if he is "guyed" by the regular workmen as a "greenie" he is very likely to quit and hunt another job. In such a case, the shop has not only lost a man, but has lost *whatever training the learner had got up to the time that he quit*. The value of this training lost in the turnover is greater than is generally realized.

Training an Overhead Charge on the Shop.—However it is handled, training costs money. This money makes an overhead charge on the shop. The more this overhead charge can be kept down *and men still properly trained* the better: but this overhead cost cannot be "ducked," it is there whether one sees it or whether one doesn't. The problem is to make this overhead cost as small as possible and still do a good training job. In order to get a line on how to do this it is necessary to know what items affect the training cost.

In many cases both shops and men are losing money because an unnecessary amount of time is spent in training, because the training as given is not scientifically planned and put over, because, under the conditions, much training is lost in turnover, and because many learners never learn how to do a really first class job.

Some Factors in the Overhead Training Cost.—Among the more important factors tending to increase the overhead training cost are:

(1) Turning out second class men because no precautions were taken to see that the learners were trained only by first class men.

(2) Taking too little time to train a man properly because it was nobody's business to follow him up and check him up to see that he was properly trained.

(3) Allowing him to continue in training after he is trained, and knows or thinks that he can do "as good a job as any other fellow"—resulting in discontent and an increased turnover.

(4) Putting improperly trained men onto regular production work because no training standards have been established.

(5) Accepting for training, men who are not fitted for that particular sort of work or continuing to train them after it has become evident that they are unfitted for work in that particular line.

Turning out Second Class Men.—How can a man that does not know how to do a job himself teach another man to do it? How can a man who is only a second class man train a green man into a first class man? It can't be done. In the average run of a shop there are men of all grades: some first class, some average, some hanging onto the pay roll by the skin of their teeth. If the training is "anybody's job" what are the chances for a given learner to get his training from a first class man? Even if the new man starts with a poor man and is later polished off by a good man, say the foreman, how much will he have to unlearn? How much extra trouble will it make? How much extra time will it take? That time and trouble cost money. The cheapest way is to use only good men for training from the start.

If a second class man trains a second class man and he in turn trains a second or more likely turns out a third class man, where is the shop headed? Evidently, so far as skill and efficiency go, it is on the down grade, and the longer this process goes on the further down the grade it goes. The whole tendency is to steadily reduce the level of efficiency.

On the other hand if the skill and knowledge of only first class men is utilized for training, if learners are only trained by first class men, then the tendency is to continually raise the level of the skill and efficiency of the shop.

Turning out a Man before he is properly Trained.—Unless there are definite standards established and somebody sees that a learner is trained so that he can meet those standards before he is turned out from training, the shop is likely to get a good many poor men because they are not fully trained. These poor men will go on causing an unnecessary overhead cost as long as they are employed. After they go out onto regular production work they are not likely to make up what they lack. They are more likely, sooner or later, to quit or get fired. In either case, the value of the partial training that they did get is lost to the shop. If a training job has to be done anyway it pays to do a good job while you are at it.

Keeping a Man in Training after he is Trained.—As already pointed out, training costs money—somebody must give time

—machines and tools must be used in instruction—so long as a training process is carried on in any way. Unless the training is stopped as soon as a learner is trained so that he can do a good job, time and equipment are being spent or tied up for no useful purpose. Where the training calls for putting a learner through a series of jobs from the easiest to the most difficult, it is often thought that it is a paying proposition to keep him on a job after he has learned to do it as well and quickly as he ever can do it, so as "to get some production out of him." As a matter of fact the cheapest thing to do is to pull him off that job as soon as he can do it and put him onto the next one. That is, the cheapest thing to do is to get him into the regular production force as soon as possible. As a regular man on the job he will get at least as much out of the equipment and be a better asset to the shop. If he has been properly trained, so far as he is concerned, the overhead cost for training has been stopped. In other words, it pays to *concentrate* training; get it done; finish the training job as soon as possible and get the training organization and equipment at work on some other man.

Not only does this unnecessarily prolonged training period increase overhead costs as just indicated, but, it also tends to make the learner discontented. Rightly or wrongly he is liable to think that he is being "worked." As a result he is much more likely to quit. This also adds to the overhead cost as already pointed out.

Failing to Establish Training Standards.—Wherever it can be done, failure to establish training standards results in men being put on production work by guess instead of through exact knowledge that the man is competent. This guesswork results either in the learner being held in training too long or not long enough. Whatever may constitute "a fair day's work" by trade standards should be determined and a man trained until he can meet these standards, if the overhead cost of training is to be reduced to a minimum.

Training the Unsuitable Man.—Another serious cause of unnecessary overhead cost is attempting to train a learner without making any attempt to size him up against the requirements of the work for which he is to be trained, or after it has become evident at any point in his training that he is not the man for that particular sort of work. Any man cannot be trained so that he will make a good man on any job. Suppose a man is started in training for a job requiring a high degree of accuracy and it appears that he has not got the "accuracy sense," or the job requires neatness and quick fingers and the learner is not naturally neat and has "butter fingers." (For example, in one concern it was found that only two girls out of three could make fancy paper boxes. Any machinist will say that "you can't make a machinist out of anybody.") In such cases as these (and they will occur) the quicker it is found out the less the unnecessary cost due to useless training.

The Value of Good Instruction in Reducing Overhead Cost—Training Cost.—There is no question that a man who knows how to put it over, who knows the instructing game, can train a learner faster and better than a man who only knows the job even if he knows that job thoroughly. Experience has proved this again and again. If a man who knows how to instruct can train men on a given job in half the time that is required by a man who does not know how to put over what he knows, overhead costs are reduced. A considerable portion of this book is given up to "pointers" on how to put it over, because this is such an important factor in cutting down training costs.

Summary of Conditions for Effective Training.—If a concern must train somehow in order to keep up the effectiveness of its force (and all concerns must) its problem is to secure maximum production and minimum overhead cost by bringing all its force to a point where they can all do their different jobs in the "best" way. Since training, no matter how it is carried on, puts an overhead charge on the business the problem is to train as well as possible but to keep the training cost as low as possible and still train first class men. This is largely a matter of meeting certain conditions among the most important of which are: (1) Training the right people by some suitable method of selection. (2) Conducting the breaking-in process in such a way that the learner will stay through it and then remain with the concern. (3) Establishing standards of good workmanship and training to those standards.

Overhead cost will be cut according to the degree to which the training work is organized and operated according to the definite principles that underlie efficient training work.

CHAPTER II

METHODS OF TRAINING

Methods of Training.—As has already been pointed out, training has to go on somehow in practically all shops. It always has gone on—in some form it always will. At different times and in different concerns training has been carried on in a great many different ways, but all of these ways, or methods of securing training, can be put into one of two classes, which we can for convenience call training by absorption and training by intention.

Training by Absorption.—Where this method is used there are no definite arrangements made for training. New men "pick up" their work as they can. They get what information they can from others who are on the same sort of jobs. Perhaps they find a "good fellow" at the next machine and "get next" to him at the noon hour. "They use their eyes and their mouths." In this way they gradually get so that they can do some sort of a job or else get fired. If they are able to stay on the job they are finally *absorbed* into the working force—hence the name.

Under this method it is absolutely nobody's *business* to help the new man to get onto his job. What he gets he gets himself, either through his own efforts or through the friendly help of other workers or foremen *who are not paid to help him but are paid to get out production*. It is a case of "pushing him off the end of the dock" to sink or swim, and taking a chance that if he starts to drown, and yells for help, somebody will leave his regular job long enough to throw him a line.

For clearness of illustration the case cited above is, of course, an extreme type, but it illustrates the actual way by which a man gets his training in a shop where no definite plan for training is operated. The point is, that the shop, as such, assumes no responsibility for seeing that new men get the training that they need. Getting such training is strictly "up to the man."

A common modification of this method is where a shop allows piece workers to take on learners as "helpers." As an example, suppose a weaver in a cotton mill is running a certain number of looms, say, for illustration, eight. His wife's cousin makes a deal with him to come in as a "helper." Perhaps the "helper" pays for the privilege. With the aid of this "helper" the weaver can run, say, ten looms instead of the eight, so he makes more money. After a while the "helper" thinks that he can run a few looms himself, and when the mill is short on weavers he gets a chance to try it on his own hook. In this way he gradually becomes some sort of a weaver. What training he got, good or bad, he did not get through any training plan operated by the mill. "*Officially*" the mill had nothing to do with it. It did not even know "officially" that the man was in training.

Another illustration of how this method works in practice is when a man "steals his trade." For example, he goes to a machine shop where they work on a lathe job. In a few hours or half a day the foreman finds out that the man knows nothing about his job and fires him. However, he has found out something about the job. He goes to another concern, represents himself as a lathe hand and gets a job on the strength of it. This time he may last a few days. He works the same game again with another shop. Because he knows a little more he may last a little longer. By keeping this game up he may finally become able to do some sort of a lathe job.

As in the other cases, what he got he got by himself, with what help he could get from other men whom he "pumped" as he could, and who were not supposed to help him, but were supposed to work on their own jobs.

Training by Intention.—This method differs from training by absorption in that there is some recognized plan for training new men. Somebody is expected to train them either as all of his job or as a part of his job. Some illustrations of how training by "intention" is carried out in practice would be an apprenticeship scheme; a definite recognition of helpers as a part of the working force; a definite responsibility placed upon foremen to train new men as well as to get out production. Definite training departments, whose sole responsibility is to train, as described in this book, and trade schools, would illustrate training by intention carried to the extreme point of development. In all of these cases somebody is paid to train the new man. It is *intended* that he shall be trained—hence the name.

Characteristics of the Two Methods.—It will be noted that in the preceding description of the two methods no questions were raised as to how well or how cheaply men could be trained by either method. It was only pointed out that by one method somebody is made responsible for training the men, and by the other method nobody is made responsible, and the man is left to get his training as well as he can—it is his job and nobody else's.

The Two Methods Compared.—If the two methods are compared certain facts become evident. By the "absorption" method the length of time required for a man to get so that he can do the job, is a pure matter of accident. If he is a "good fellow" of considerable push, and happens to get in with some other "good fellows" who are interested in him and are willing to show him, the training time will be shortened. If he happens to be timid or shy, or runs up against a bunch of men who "throw him down" or "kid" him when he tries to find out something about his job, the training period will be greatly increased. If he gets jobs of different degrees of difficulty he is likely to get them any way that they happen to come. Since nobody is looking out for him. he is put onto regular work when he guesses that he can do it and can convince whoever is in charge that he guessed right. He cannot be really trained against standards. Nobody really *knows* when he is trained. What help he gets may come from men who are not themselves first class men on the job, so that the way that he learns to do the work may not be the best way. Even if they are good men there is no probability that they are good at putting over what they know to a new man, and he does not get an entirely clear idea as to how the job should be done. All such things make his training long, ineffective, incomplete, and in the end, costly.

Where the plan of training by intention is operated somebody is made responsible for training the man. It may be the foreman, a skilled man in charge of a helper, or an instructor who only trains. Whoever it is, a part of his job, or all of his job is to properly train the man. Under this plan it is possible to see that he gets help when he needs it, and that he does not have to wait for a chance to get it any way that he can. It is possible to see that he gets the easiest jobs first and the most difficult jobs last. It is possible to keep track of his training and know when he is trained enough to meet given standards. It is possible to be sure that what he gets he gets from first class men, and not from anybody that happens to be around. This amounts to saying that by this method the training can be controlled and planned whereas it is accidental and cannot be controlled under the "absorption" plan.

Of course the degree to which training under the intention plan is effective is determined by the extent to which it is organized in accordance with sound principles, and the manner in which these principles are worked out in detail, but the points noted above can be effectively met where training is by intention and cannot be effectively met when training is by absorption.

Training by Intention the Cheaper Plan.—From the standpoint of the overhead training cost, as already discussed, training by intention is the cheaper plan. Many large concerns recognize this fact and operate intentional training schemes. The various conditions that have been pointed out as unavoidable under the absorption plan (unnecessarily long training periods, learning from poor men, loss of partly trained men, etc.) all make for an excessive overhead cost. The possibilities pointed out under the "intention" plan permit of giving the most effective training at the lowest overhead cost. The degree to which the cost is actually reduced depends, of course, on how the training is actually carried out in practice.

Some Ways by which Intentional Training is Carried out in Practice.—Of course intentional training is carried out in all

METHODS OF TRAINING

sorts of ways in practice, and the methods of "breaking-in help" that are usually followed in such schemes for intentional training are well known to shop men, but for purposes of discussion some of the more common methods are given here.

(1) The foreman, in addition to his responsibility for getting out the product, is made responsible for the training of new men. He personally instructs them, keeps track of them, checks them up. Many foremen have been very successful in training men themselves and, in some cases, have developed most excellent methods.

(2) A competent workman (an "old hand") is put in charge of one or more learners. (Helpers, apprentices, green men.) In the old days, under the apprenticeship method, this was the standard plan. Training is, of course, carried on in the regular shop as in the first case.

(3) Certain men are given the exclusive job of training. These men are paid to do nothing else. Men are broken in by them—it is their job and nobody else is supposed to have anything to do with the man until he is trained. Such men are sometimes called *instructing* foremen to distinguish their job from that of production foremen. Under this plan training is also carried on in the shop.

(4) Training is not carried on in the regular shop but in special "training shops," so that men do not get into the regular work until they have been thoroughly trained. Under good conditions the training is given with the same equipment as that of the production shops, and the same sort of work is carried on. A modification of this plan is the trade school shop as it has been developed in some parts of the country.

(5) Distinct training departments are established with distinct heads and instructing staffs. So long as men are in training they are under the authority of the training department and not under the production foremen. When properly trained in the training department they are turned over to the production department as competent men. Training may be given in special shops or in the regular production shops.

Of course, there are many modifications of these five forms. For example, a foreman will often start a distinct training shop for elementary training. This separate training shop may be in some corner of the production shop. After a little preliminary breaking-in in the special "shop," the man's training will be completed in the regular shop. The five examples given will, however, serve as a basis for discussion.

Training by Intention Requires an Instructor.—Before taking up a discussion of the relative advantages and disadvantages of the different typical methods just cited, one important point should be clear. Training by intention, however it may be carried out in detail, always puts the responsibility for training onto *somebody*. That "somebody" is paid for giving part of his time, or all of his time to training instead of giving all of his time to production. That is, *training by intention always uses an instructor*.

This is true because an instructor, whatever he may be called, is somebody who is paid to "put it over": to teach.

In this sense, training by absorption does not assume that any instructor is required.

The Job of the Instructor.—Whenever a man has the job of putting over what he knows to somebody else, whether he thinks so or not, he is an instructor. His job is to instruct or, to use the more common word, he is a teacher and his job is to teach. Men who give shop instruction rarely think of themselves as teachers. They seldom realize that they have the same sort of a job as any other teacher, but such is the fact. So far as the teaching end of it goes, teaching Bill Jones how to set an index head on a universal miller, teaching a new recruit how to handle a rifle, and teaching Bill's son, Sammy Jones, how to solve an algebraic equation are all the same sorts of jobs. Like any other job it can be well done or badly done, but is the same *kind* of a job. Whatever he may be called, a man who has an instructing job is an instructor.

If a man has the instructing job on his hands he naturally wants to do that as well as it can be done. As in all other cases, the best conditions will enable the instructing job to be done in the best way. It is also true that when a job is done in the best way it is done in the cheapest way: that is, in the long run it costs less to do the job in that way, though sometimes, before the matter is thought out it looks as if it was costing more. The following paragraphs discuss the different methods of intentional training that have been given from the standpoint of getting the most effective instruction as well as from the standpoint of cost.

The Different Methods Compared.—If we look at the five methods of training given it is evident that they can be divided into two groups. In examples (1) and (2) the instructor has a *double job*. The foreman, or the breaker-in has to *get out the work and also instruct*. In examples (3), (4) and (5) the instructor has only one job: to instruct. As is pointed out in detail later, this does not mean that men under instruction may not turn out work, and good work, but it does mean that the *job* of the instructor is only that of training. He is responsible for the training that he does. The work turned out, while important, is a "side show." In cases (1) and (2) we have a divided responsibility, in cases (3), (4) and (5) a single responsibility.

The Single Responsibility Plan is Better.—A production force is on the job to get out product. The shop is organized to turn out work; that is what it is there for. A foreman, or other executive or supervisor, is responsible for getting out the maximum product as well and as quickly as possible. Men are employed to do their individual jobs and not to train other men. Anything that interferes in any way with the best conditions for getting out the work, slows up production and puts an unnecessary overhead cost on the production work. The attempt to handle training through the regular production force, not only interferes with production but also interferes with the efficiency of the training. The following paragraphs discuss these points in detail.

Why Training by the Use of the Regular Production Force Interferes with Production.—The general principle involved here is the value of specialization. When it is desired to get a piece of work done as well as possible, the best way to do it is to put someone on that job, hold him responsible and let him give his undivided attention to getting it done. The more he can concentrate on it, the better work he will do. Men who are held responsible for production will do better work if they concentrate their time and effort on production than they will if their time and effort has to be divided between two distinct jobs: training and production.

For illustration, assume that a foreman, as in example (1), is expected to run his shop and also act as an instructor; these are some of the results:

(1) The problems of getting out production are of one kind. They relate to operations, production, speed, getting maximum service out of the equipment. They head up into getting out the product in the necessary quantity, of the necessary quality and with as much speed and as little lost motion as possible.

The problems of training are, as shown later, of a totally different kind. They relate to methods of training. They deal with such questions as, what a man is thinking about while he is being instructed; how to secure and hold his attention; how to be sure that he fully understands; how to find out what he has not fully understood. They head up into turning out trained men as rapidly and efficiently as possible.

Now these two kinds of problems call for two distinct kinds of thinking and for two distinct kinds of training. It is hard for a man who is used to thinking about production problems to shift once for all and think about instructing problems as he does when he becomes a "steady" instructor. This has been the experience of every shop man who has become an instructor. He finds it a hard and a slow process to make the shift. Under the conditions assumed, the foreman who both runs his shop and instructs must make this shift a great many times a day. First, for example, he plans to get out a certain job by ten o'clock the next morning. Then he must think out the best way to instruct a man on a certain job. Next he may have to shift back to another shop problem, then back to an instructing problem and so on. He is in the same condition as a man trying to do a pattern maker's job and a machine shop job

METHODS OF TRAINING

at the same time, or a ball player trying to pitch and cover first base. Mentally he is running back and forth between two entirely different kinds of jobs.

Now such running back and forth means a distinct loss of efficiency. A man cannot thoroughly get "down to brass tacks" on either job. The result of putting this double job onto a man who is responsible for production is to keep him from doing his best on the production job, and that suffers accordingly. Under these conditions production suffers because the man responsible for keeping it up to top notch is bothered with the details of another job as well as those of his own. This is especially true where either job is enough to keep a man busy.

The usual and almost inevitable result is that one of the jobs is neglected. Either training or production suffers. Under ordinary conditions training suffers badly and production is retarded as well. The foreman is bothered, he is interfered with on his main job, and the training is badly done, so that there is a loss at both ends. The above discussion will apply equally well to the case where skilled men in the shop are expected to do their jobs and also instruct. If they do any real instructing they are in exactly the same situation as the foreman—their thinking and attention must run back and forth between the two kinds of problems which they are supposed to handle. This interferes with doing the job, and also interferes with the effectiveness of the training.

(2) The extent to which a combined producer and instructor leaves his production job in order to instruct is so much time lost in production. When a skilled man leaves his job to show a green man how to do something, whatever time he takes is lost time so far as production goes. If this instruction work is divided among a number of men the total time lost amounts to considerable. This of course slows up production to just that amount. The same amount of time concentrated in one or more men who gave their time to instruction only would serve to instruct a considerably larger number of men.

The amount of time and attention that is diverted from

production, under the conditions just discussed, is enough, where any amount of training is carried on, to appreciably affect production efficiency. Men whose job is to get out production cannot work with full efficiency if they have to carry the "overload" of training as well.

Put it in another way. A certain number of men have to be instructed. This takes a certain amount of time and energy no matter how it is done. If this time and energy are drawn from the production force it will require *more* time and energy than if the same number of men were trained by instructors who did nothing else. This saving of time and effort means an increase in production, in addition to the direct saving due to time and energy kept in production where the production force do not have to instruct.

Why the Use of the Regular Production Force Interferes with Effective Training.—If training interferes with production the situation also works backward. It is almost impossible to secure the most efficient training when the same men are made responsible for both maximum production and efficient training work. This is true for practically the reasons given in the last paragraph. Trying to do both jobs cuts down good work on both.

The instructing job, if it is to be well done must be concentrated upon. Learners must not be left standing around for further instructions because the "instructor" has to attend to some production problem at just that time. Neither should they be poorly instructed because the instructor was too hard pushed for time to properly plan the instruction work.

When the instructor comes off a production job and comes on an instruction job he has to make the same "shift" described in the last paragraph, only this time *from* production *to* instruction, and he will not do as good a job of instructing as he could have done had he been thinking of instructing all the time.

The effect of this continual shifting on the efficiency of both training and production is generally overlooked because it is largely a mental question and so is concealed. Often the man who is trying to do both jobs is not aware of the trouble himself. He may be conscious of the "drag" but he does not realize the cause. The great interest that many foremen take in training, and their unconsciousness of the "drag" of the double job, often makes them reluctant to turn training over to a specialist although it really means a relief.

Specialization an Advantage.—Keeping the responsibility for getting out production and for training separate unquestionably makes for the efficiency of both. Men who are to *instruct* should be held responsible for instruction only. Men who are to produce should be held responsible for production only. This is the most efficient organization. Giving both jobs to the same set of men cuts down efficiency on both and is a wasteful organization.

This means that whenever training is to be done, instructors should be employed: men whose sole business is to instruct—and these instructors should be trained for their jobs.

As in any other line of work, instruction will be good or bad according to the degree to which the instructor is "onto his job," according to the degree to which he is an expert in his line. This is as true in the instructing trade as it is in any other trade.

Definitely and Accidentally Trained Instructors.—As in any other trade, an instructor may have "picked up" his trade as an instructor or he may have secured definite training. We may have a trained or an untrained instructor. As in other trades, there are best ways of putting over instructing jobs and a man can get these "points" from a man who knows them. That is, an expert teacher who knows how to teach can show a prospective trade instructor a good deal about "how to put it over," in connection with that man's instructing job. Of course it is plain that such a "training course" would not undertake to teach a man anything about his trade itself, but would only show him how to "put over" to better advantage the trade knowledge and skill that he already possessed.

It is evident that the more a man knows about his job the more time and attention he will put into it, because he *does* know more about it. This is as true of an instructor as of anybody else. The more he knows about the instructing job the more he will feel the "drag" of a double responsibility, the more he will see the loss of efficiency in training due to "shifting." The less a man knows about instructing as a distinct trade the less the double combination will disturb him. This makes it particularly desirable that trained instructors should be only held responsible for instruction.

The Value of the Trained Instructor.—Experience has shown that a trained instructor can do a much better instructing job than an untrained man, no matter how competent that man may be in his trade or on his job. The former can train men quicker, easier and better. He knows how to handle men under good instructional conditions which are often very different from good production conditions. He can plan his work and use the best "putting over" method for a given teaching job. He knows how to inspect his own work and can tell whether his learners thoroughly understand what has been taught them. He can analyze his trade and can determine just what instruction should be given a man for a specific piece of work.

The employment of trained instructors, therefore, adds greatly to the efficiency of any training work, and the cost of properly training them is more than repaid by the increased efficiency that results directly in the training itself, and, through that, in decreased overhead charges and increased production.

Summary.—Training must be carried on somehow. It may be by intention or by absorption. By the absorption plan the concern, as such, assumes no responsibility for seeing that the recruit secures training. By the intention plan it does assume that responsibility. Training by intention is more efficient and cheaper, but requires an instructor. The instructor may be required to attend to both instruction and production or the two jobs may be specialized. Specialization is more efficient and cheaper. It is still cheaper and more efficient not only to use specialized instructors who *only* instruct but to use trained instructors, who know *how* to instruct.

CHAPTER III

TRAINING ON THE JOB

The preceding chapters discussed the value of definitely organized training, described certain common methods by which this training may be carried out, and pointed out the most economical and efficient working conditions. There still remains to be discussed the question of how and where this training is to be given.

This is particularly important, as many training schemes have been less efficient than they might have been because undesirable and inefficient methods were employed.

It is also true, that, for reasons discussed later, more expensive and less effective training methods are quite liable to be employed in industrial plants where those in charge were not familiar with the fundamental principles on which the most effective training can be developed.

The Two Methods.—Whenever practical training is undertaken, it is generally carried on according to one of two methods which for convenience may be designated as training on the job and training by exercises. Whatever the details, in training on the job, the learner, from the beginning, is put directly on actual work. Production starts as soon as training starts. From the beginning of his training, the learner uses the same tools and machines and works up the same stock as would a regular producer on that job. He turns out a product that is of value, although, of course, his productivity is not so great.

In training by exercises, the learner is not put on actual work from the start. Production does not start when training begins but there is a period during which the learner does not produce in the sense that his product is of value. It may be true, that, by the exercise method of training, the learner may use the same tools and machines, or even work on the same stock as a regular man on the job, but his product is not used. It is "junked," or dissembled after it has served its training purpose. The test for an "exercise" is therefore, not how the job is done but what becomes of the product after the job is done.

The Two Methods Illustrated—The Exercise Method.— Take the case of training riveters in a shipyard. According to the exercise method, a green man would be set to driving rivets on some old plates. After he had driven a number, they would be cut out and more rivets would be driven in the same holes. This process would be repeated until he was considered sufficiently expert to "graduate" into real work in the production force. The same old plates would be used over and over again for successive learners.

Another illustration is in the method of training in machine shop work often followed in the shops of technical schools. A series of operations are laid out to be put through by the learner. (Say, rough turning, fine turning, thread cutting) and, after these operations are finished, the final product is "junked." Still another illustration is in training bricklayers; a wall is laid up by the learners and laborers are employed to tear it down.

Another variation of this method is where a learner is put on as an observer and after a while is allowed to "try his hand" on some odds and ends, as in a jointry shop, where, after some observation, he is allowed to try making a joint with pieces of scrap stock.

It will be observed in all of these cases, that between the time that the learner is taken on and the time that he was started in on "work" there was a greater or less period of time when he was of no direct productive value.

The Two Methods Illustrated—The Job Method.—The second method can be illustrated by such cases as the following. In training a riveter in a shipyard, from the start, he is put upon work that has a value. This work, of course, is selected for its simplicity, but, the rivets that are driven stay driven, unless, of course, they are defective, as in the riveting done by any production riveting gang. The parts that are riveted together stay together and go into the ship. In the same way, in jointry work, simple jobs that really count in production, are selected and given to the learner from the beginning. The simplest, roughest jobs are given first and the learner gradually progresses to finer and more difficult work as his training goes on. In training a learner on a special machine, he is started directly on the machine itself without any appreciable period of observation. In all such cases, it will be noted that no appreciable period intervenes between the time that the learner is started in training and the time that he begins to produce.

Theory of the Two Methods.—The exercise method is based upon the theory that a learner must, in some way, secure a certain amount of skill before he can be trusted on actual work. Unless he has acquired this skill he will spoil work, damage machines, spoil jobs. In certain cases, in training for skilled trades, it is also based on the theory that if a learner can be given skill in a series of disconnected operations he can, later, readily combine any set of those operations into the doing of any given jobs.

The method of training on production is based on the theory that, under proper conditions, the "non productive period" is unnecessary, in the great majority of cases. The greater interest of the learner, the value of his product, the added training value to learners in working under actual working conditions more than offsets the chances of the small amount of spoiled work that results where this type of training is carried on under proper conditions.

Since most men in industrial plants have not known how to secure proper conditions and have sensed the dangers of the "jobs" method of training, it is not surprising that they have tried the exercise method to a greater or less extent.

Advantages and Disadvantages.—The advantages of the exercise method may be listed out as follows:

(1) If the learner is thoroughly trained on exercises before he is put to work, the danger of spoiled work is minimized.

(2) Since his work is of no value he does not require as careful watching as if he were on a real job.

(3) Such work has a certain trying out value.

(4) Where definite instruction is planned such exercises can be arranged in any desired order without regard to the requirements of actual work.

(5) In many cases exercises can be so contrived that the learner can be less "bother" around the shop than if he were put onto regular production jobs.

The disadvantages of this method may be listed out as follows:

(1) As already stated, this method calls for a period of non-productive work. In a school, where students are not paid for their time, this is perhaps less important than in a shop where learners are under pay. In the shop this non-productive period adds to the overhead cost.

(2) The training conditions are artificial. Under actual working conditions men are not put on work unless the product is of value to the output.

(3) Experience has shown, especially in shops, that where a learner knows that his product will not have to meet the actual test of use, he is less interested, tends to be more careless in his work and is less anxious to get on.

(4) It is very difficult to apply in many shop operations, especially on automatic or semi-automatic machines and on a large number of semi-skilled jobs.

(5) In many cases, exercises as planned, do not reproduce actual working conditions. In the effort to avoid tying up tools and equipment on non-productive work the tendency to use "artificial" exercises is strong. One illustration of this is the common tendency to consider that any old worn out tool or machine is good enough for training exercises.

The advantages of training on the job may be listed out as follows:

(1) There is no non-productive interval, hence overhead cost is reduced.

(2) The learner's interest is kept up from the start, hence he is much more likely to do his work as well as possible, and to desire to get on as fast as possible.

(3) It is practically the only method that can be used in training on many industrial jobs. (Semi-skilled, automatic, etc.)

(4) All training can be given under actual production conditions.

The disadvantages are:

(1) The danger of spoiling work, if not properly controlled.

(2) The difficulty of securing the right sort of work for training by selecting it only from the work of the shop.

(3) The difficulty of securing suitable work for training without seriously interfering with the regular production work.

Training on the Job the Better if these Difficulties can be Minimized.—It is evident that training directly on productive work is the cheaper and more efficient method provided its disadvantages can be removed. If the period of nonproductive work can be cut out, that is a distinct advantage. If the interest of the learner can be kept up to the highest pitch, the time required for training will be reduced and the learner will be much more likely to stay through the training. As stated, there are many jobs for which it is practically impossible to train on any other basis.

The disadvantages of the exercise method are fundamental in their character. The objections to the job method are not fundamental, but can be eliminated by a proper organization.

Many concerns have admitted the advantages of the method of training on production and, in fact, many have tried it in some cases with unsatisfactory results. This failure has not been due to the insuperable difficulties of the plan, but to the omission of a vital factor, *the trained and competent instructor*. Where such work has been undertaken without such an instructor all the difficulties of this method have been at their maximum. With no instructor (as by the absorption method) where such help as was given was given by other workmen incidental to the doing of their own jobs, of course results were very bad. Machines were smashed, stock spoiled, men injured and discontented, training poor. Even where the foreman has had this additional load put upon him, in addition to his proper job, that of running his shop, similar results have occurred, though it is only fair to say, that many foremen have worked "overtime" and have achieved some measure of success in spite of their double load, especially where such men had some notions as to the principles of effective instruction.

Where an instructor has been employed he has usually been selected either because he was a good production man or as has sometimes occurred, because he was not (the idea being to use a less valuable man on the training work and keep the better men in production). In few cases was he selected because he could *instruct* efficiently, either because he was a natural teacher or because he had been trained as an instructor.

The Instructor and Training on the Job.—As already stated the key to effective training on production is the instructor who can instruct. Such a man knows how to analyze out the different learning processes through which the learner must go in training for each job. He knows how to take the learner through those processes step by step. He knows how to be sure that the learner has got one step before he takes him to the next. He knows how to handle the learner so that he is interested in getting along as fast as possible and in doing as good a job as possible. If in addition, his job is only that of an instructor, he is on the instructing job all the time, preventing mistakes, anticipating difficulties, straightening out the learner as soon as he starts to go wrong. *And he has no other job to think about.* Under these conditions the dangers of job training are reduced to a minimum.

As in all other trades, as a general proposition, a trained instructor can do a better job than an untrained instructor. Hence the better trained the instructor the better the results in job training. An investment in training instructors will be well repaid to any concern undertaking training and is especially desirable when training is to be carried on by intention and on the job.

The Importance of Training on the Job.—As already stated there are very few situations where training on production from the beginning of the process is not the most efficient and the cheapest in the end. This, of course, provided intentional training is used with properly qualified instructors. Experience has shown that, under these conditions it can be carried on without seriously disturbing the work of the production force. This is, of course, largely a matter of coöperation and proper organization.

The adoption of this method makes it possible to train effectively on a large number of specialized and semi-skilled jobs for which training cannot be given in any other way. It is as important that efficient methods of training should be used for training on these jobs as on "skilled" jobs. Many a concern suffers more from lack of first class workers on jobs of this class than from lack of skill in its highly skilled men, who are often relatively few in number. The tendency to concentrate attention on training to the few highly skilled trades that may be represented in the force results in a loss of efficiency. Some large concerns have even found it desirable to train their office boys.

Training on the Job in the Trade School.—A trade school that trains its students on productive work differs in no essential way from a commercial concern so far as training conditions go. The same requirements as to trained and qualified instructors exist here that would be found in an industrial plant training its learners on the job. What has been said applies therefore to such a school as well as to an industrial plant. It is the personal conviction of the writer that exercise training has no more place in an efficient trade school than it has in an efficient plant.

Summary.—There are two general methods of training: on the job and by exercises. The exercise method assumes a period of non-productive training, the job method does not. A comparison of the advantages and disadvantages of the two methods shows that the exercise method has certain fundamental disadvantages and the "job" method certain disadvantages that can be practically cut out by proper organization and right working conditions. Difficulties in carrying on job training have been mainly due to lack of specialized, trained, qualified instructors. The job method is the most efficient and the cheapest, both in industrial plants and in trade schools.

CHAPTER IV

PICKING THE TRAINING FORCE

The final key to the success or failure of any training course is the sort of man that is put in charge of the work. Effective organization is necessary, adequate provision for training is necessary, but these alone will not give effective training results.

The following suggestions may be of value to those who may be interested in manning a training plan, or in selecting prospective instructors to attend an Instructor Training Course.

Trade Experience.—It is useless to look for good instruction unless the instructor is a thoroughly good workman. The notion that "a man that is not good enough for the job is good enough for an instructor on that job" will only lead to trouble. Where foremen or their subordinates are asked to pick out men it has sometimes occurred that they have recommended men that they wanted to get rid of rather than their best men. This may have been natural for men who had no notion of what an instructor's job really is, but these men were of course, really defeating their own ends.

Experience has shown again and again that the only man who is worth selecting for a prospective instructor is a thorough master of his job.

A rough guide is the length of time that a man has worked at his trade. For instruction in skilled trades it should be not less than eight years. For specialized work it may be less, but the tendency is to undervalue a long trade experience, as an asset for an instructor. As already stated he must not only know about the job, but must know how to do it, and his experience must have been sufficient so that he can "hold down his job with any man." He must command the trade respect of the production force.

General Education.—Many concerns have felt that young men of good general education, who had had some contact with the industry in the line in which they were to instruct, were desirable material for instructors, though they had little or no actual trade experience. Often a young man with some technical training who has acted as an inspector or assistant to an executive is selected on account of his education and general ability. Such men are not likely to succeed as instructors and should not be selected. If an instructor cannot "hold up his end" with any man in the shop, if they do not respect him on a production basis, if they do not know that he has "been through the mill," he will not succeed as an instructor no matter how well educated and intelligent he may be. Such a young man may know a great deal about *how* to do the job, but being able to *do* the job is another matter. Intelligence is needed, but it is that of the shop, not that of the school.

Of course the above statement does not mean that the more general education a man has the better, *provided he has his trade*, but the tendency to assume that good education is an equivalent for trade ability is an unfortunate one.

Another mistake sometimes made is in selecting a man who has had a school experience but has either no trade experience or very little. This comes from a confusion as to what constitutes the job of a trade or job instructor. An educational experience is of value, but alone, it will not serve the purpose, for the same reasons given in the preceding paragraph.

Age.—Prospective instructors should not be too young. From thirty to forty is perhaps the best age, but men well over forty have made good instructors when properly trained. A man who takes up instructing has to learn a new trade, the instructing trade. Whatever his age, if he has grown "stiff" he is not likely to pick up and practice the new trade effectively. If too young, lack of trade experience and immaturity will prove handicaps.

Other Desirable Qualifications.—A supervisory experience, such as that of a foreman, is desirable provided it has not been so long that the man has lost the "feel" of the job. Where a considerable period has elapsed since he actually worked at the job himself this is likely to prove a detriment.

The Ability to "Put It Over."—It is commonly assumed that if a man can do a good job himself he can teach a learner how to do it. This is not the case, however. Many men who can do a first class job cannot teach anybody else how to do that job. The two qualities do not necessarily go together. It is true that the better a man is on his job the better instructor he will make, *provided he can teach*. Some men seem to be "natural teachers, but such men are rare. The average good man can acquire, however, the ability to instruct best through an effective training course. This has been very plainly shown where such courses have been conducted.

The Director of Training.—The desirability of putting the training work in charge of a responsible head (a director) is discussed later. In selecting such a man, many concerns have failed to recognize the importance of his job. They have picked out men who were too young. Men without sufficient experience in handling men; men without knowledge of the principles of great training, whose only experience has been in the field of production have been put upon this work. An experience in production, especially in the plant in which the training is to be given, is a valuable asset for a director, but, nevertheless, if he lacks knowledge of the principles of good training and of instructional organization he will be lacking in efficiency. Any director should be as good an instructor as any of his staff.

The director of a training department has a job that is as vital to the success of a concern as the work of any other department. He should be chosen as carefully as any other department head and *paid as well*. He should be given authority commensurate with his responsibility.

Summary.—The best instructor is a man of thorough trade experience, preferably in the plant. He should not be too young or too old. He should be a first class man on his job, but adaptable and able to change from production to instructional conditions. The attempt to substitute men with other types of experience is liable to lead to unsatisfactory results, and to lower the efficiency of the training.

PART II

THE ANALYSIS AND CLASSIFICATION OF TRADE KNOWLEDGE

PRODUCTION AND INSTRUCTION

A Comparison

THE SHOP	THE INSTRUCTOR
Turns out a product.	Turns out an instructed man. (A learner.)
Knows what kind of a product it is going to turn out.	Knows what kind of work he is training the learner for.
Gets out the product from specifications and plans from which parts are made and then assembled.	Works from a planned course of instruction made up from definite teaching units. (Lessons.)
The man responsible for the finished product knows all the parts that go into the complete product.	The instructor knows all the branches and operations of his trade.
The parts of the complete product are assembled in the order that will give the most rapid and easy assembling.	The course of instruction is put over in an order that will enable the learner to get it as rapidly and easily as possible.

CHAPTER V

THE PRODUCER AND THE INSTRUCTOR

Introductory Note.—Parts II., III., IV., contain material especially prepared for the use of instructors or prospective instructors, and for use in Instructor Training Courses. For this reason certain points presented in Part I. are again presented here from a somewhat different angle.

The Producer vs. The Instructor.—All industrial work is carried on in order that a *product* may be obtained; its aim is to turn out some sort of a manufactured product: to "get out *production*." For this purpose workmen are engaged, machines are operated, tools are used. The aim of a cotton mill is to turn out cloth, of a steel mill to turn out steel; of a shipyard to turn out ships. In these or in any other production plant the workman or mechanic by the exercise of his knowledge and skill contributes to the production of the particular article for which the plant is operated. The greater the skill and intelligence of the workmen, the better the equipment, the less stock spoiled by poor workmanship and the more effectively the different jobs are routed and inspected, the more efficiently and cheaply is the cloth, or the steel or the ship turned out. A man who has learned his trade and has practiced it efficiently is therefore an efficient *producer*. He has lived and worked in the surroundings of the production plant; he naturally thinks of his job in terms of *product*.

Training is carried on in any industrial plant in order that people (apprentices, learners, helpers, etc.), that is, people who do not know how to do jobs, may learn how to do jobs. Unless training were in some way carried on in connection with production after a while production would stop because all the people who knew how to do the work had died and there would be nobody to continue the work; so that we should have no more steel, or cotton cloth or ships. The aim of training is therefore not to turn out production but to turn out men who have been given the necessary skill to enable them to weave cotton cloth, or make steel or build ships. Its product is an effective producer, but is not production.

An *Instructor*, by the exercise of his knowledge of instruction methods and his skill in applying them to the work of instruction, produces an efficient workman and makes him out of a man who, before he was instructed, was not a worker at all, or was not a thoroughly efficient worker.

The greater the skill and intelligence of the instructor the better the instructional equipment, the fewer good men or apprentices spoiled by poor instruction and the more rapidly and efficiently the instructional process is carried on, the more efficiently and cheaply are the learners converted into efficient producers.

A competent *producer* who has also been trained to instruct and who on account of that training, "knows his job" from the standpoint of putting over what he knows, is an efficient *instructor*. As an instructor he works on a training job. He naturally thinks of his job in terms of trained learners. He thinks in terms of *training* and not in terms of *production*.

The Producer who Becomes an Instructor.—When a man who has always been a producer, becomes an instructor, he usually gets into difficulties because he does not realize that he has, in reality, changed his job; that he has stopped being a producer and has become a trainer. He attempts to do a training job but he still thinks in terms of a production job. This is why a man who knows his trade usually thinks that he can teach it, and why, when he finds that things do not go right he usually blames it on the men or apprentices he is trying to instruct. Some men are natural teachers; they have, in some manner, picked up more or less of the instructor's trade, but in general, no matter how thoroughly a man may know his trade, or how much experience he may have had in production, he usually "falls down" as an instructor when he first tackles the instructing job because he does not know how to put over what he knows into the head or the hand of his learners. Often he realizes that he is not doing a good instructing job, becomes discouraged and quits, when the real difficulty is that he never realized that, when he became an instructor he really took up a new trade which he knew nothing about and that what he needs is to get hold of the new trade, (instructing) in order to succeed.

Some Common Difficulties.—Among the more common difficulties which the "green" or untrained mechanical instructor encounters are: First, inability to take account of stock as to what he knows; that is, he knows it, but he has never listed it out. He cannot *analyze* his trade. Second, when he has to put over more than one job he does not know how to arrange the different jobs so that each job that the learner masters makes the mastery of the next job easier. He does not know how to arrange his jobs in an effective *instructional order*. Third, he is often unable to distinguish between what must be taught as jobs and what should be given to the learner in the form of information. Fourth, he does not know how to plan so that it will be given to the learner at the time that he must apply it on the job for the first time. Fifth, he does not know how to teach or *put over* any given job rapidly, effectively and thoroughly. Sixth, he does not know how to handle learners under *instructional conditions* though he may know how to handle them under production conditions.

The First Difficulty: Inability to Analyze.—It is one thing to know; it is another thing to know what you know. A man who has learned to do things by doing them is not, as a rule, in the habit of "taking stock" of his trade knowledge. On the job he uses his knowledge and skill so unconsciously that he hardly gives a thought to how he does it or what he does to do it. He works, so to speak, automatically.

When he undertakes to put over to somebody else what he knows, or what he can do, that is, when he becomes an instructor, he must be able to determine what he is going to teach. The learner does not know it; he has got to learn it. The instructor does know it and he must therefore know what he is going to put over to the learner so that he can determine just what the learner must know when he has instructed him.

Of course, the instructor, knowing his trade, has all these

things in his head, but, until such a "stock taking" is carried out the instructor is in much the condition of an old-fashioned country store where all sorts of things are in stock but nobody knows just what is in stock. Just as the up to date store has an inventory, so the instructor must take an inventory of his stock,—what he has to teach.

The efficient workman who becomes an instructor even if he recognizes the necessity of this stock taking cannot usually do it at first, because, as pointed out above, he has never had occasion to look at his work from that angle. He must do what amounts to looking at his trade as an outsider would; he must watch himself at work and note down what he does. He must "watch himself at work." This is a hard thing to do if a man is not used to doing it, and the producer who becomes an instructor has never had to do it, hence he usually gets into trouble because he has not got the *power of analysis* as it is called.

The Second Difficulty: Inability to Arrange the Work in an Effective Instructional Order.—In teaching a trade a great many things must be taught to the learner one after the other. That is, the different things which the instructor wishes to put over must be handled in some order. In a general way almost anybody will recognize the desirability of giving "easy work" before giving "hard work," but beyond that general notion few mechanical instructors go unless they know how to arrange the work in the most effective instructional order. A further difficulty is that, if they do undertake to arrange it in an effective order they usually work it out from the standpoint of difficulty in production, which is all right for a production job, but all wrong for an instruction job, because the instructor must figure his order on the basis of the things which make it difficult for the learner to acquire, which is a very different thing from the question of the difficulties of doing a job. The instructor must determine *learning difficulties; not production difficulties.* Failure to take in this distinction between the two kinds of difficulties commonly results in getting an inefficient instructional order of instruction, when any order is laid out.

Training for the Instructing Job.—People who make a business of teaching have found out how to go to work to get

THE PRODUCER AND THE INSTRUCTOR 41

what they wished to teach into an effective instructional order and how to determine just what must be taught. These methods and rules for going at this job are well known to instructors in schools but, naturally, the man who comes onto an instruction job directly from the trade does not know them and so does not know how to go at this part of his job as an instructor. He really has to learn a new trade with new operations and new tools. He can be greatly helped in getting hold of his new trade if he can learn it with the help of an "old hand" at the teaching trade. Where this can be done the prospective instructor can secure help in getting his instructor training. Where he cannot get such help and must train himself, the job is more difficult but he can get considerable help from the following notes.

This part deals with that side of the instructor's job which concerns itself with the determination and classification of what is to be taught to the learner in a given trade.

Under these conditions the suggestions for self-training in the Appendix will be of value.

CHAPTER VI

THE FIRST OPERATION. THE DETERMINATION OF WHAT IS TO BE TAUGHT

The Trade Analysis.—The first operation in the work of an instructor is to determine what he has to teach to train a learner for the trade that he is to be taught. If only a portion of the trade is to be taught, (as might be the case with a man who partly knew the trade) or where a man is to be trained in some portion of the trade, (specialized operations, for example) which might come up under some conditions, the instructor must determine, out of all the things that should be taught for the complete trade just what things must be taught in that particular case. The instructor must not only be able to take account of stock for the whole trade but must be able to determine what will be required for any part of the trade. If the learner is to be trained for a house carpenter, or a tool maker, or a printer, just what must he know and be able to do when the instructing process is completed? If he is to be trained as a special machine operator, just what must be taught him so that he can do that job as well as it can be done? If in printing, he is to be trained for some special branch of the trade, as compositor or press feeder, what part of the whole printing trade must be put over? If a man is to be trained to make sheet metal pipes and elbows, just what must he be taught out of all that a first class sheet metal man needs to know, before the instructor will "stand" for him as a competent man in that special work? In order to be able to answer such questions the instructor must know exactly what he must put over in each case, and so must take "account of stock." Unless he does this he can, at best, only guess at what the learner should be given to fit the requirements of each case.

Such a stock taking is commonly called *analyzing the trade* and is the first operation which the instructor must take in laying out a course of instruction.

What is Meant by Analyzing the Trade.—Analyzing the trade simply means listing out all the things that the learner must be taught if he is to be taught the complete trade. If the trade is that of a carpenter, the instructor notes down all the different jobs that a carpenter has to do. If it is plumbing, or book binding, or machine shop work, the same listing of jobs must be carried out. If, in addition to the jobs themselves, there are certain special words (technical terms) whose use he must learn, or special tools whose names he must know, or constructions or computations which he must be able to make or special safety precautions that he must take, these must also be listed completely out.

The point in each case is to make a complete list of *all* that the man must know when the instructor has trained him for the complete trade. If less than the complete trade is to be taught then the problem is to pick out what is required in that case from the complete "trade list."

Laying out More than One Course of Instruction.—An instructor in a training department often has to instruct more than one sort of learner. For example, an instructor in printing, if he is competent, may have to instruct one group of learners who are to be compositors, another group who are to be trained for linotype operators, and another group who are to be pressmen. Under some conditions it might be necessary for the same instructor to train different groups in different stages of progress in the same trade; or in different specialized parts of the same trade. In all such cases, a distinct analysis must be made for each line of instruction. Where partial trades are to be taught, a special line of instruction must be laid out, only, as pointed out above, in this case, the special instruction material can be taken out of the course of instruction for the complete trade.

The essential point is that the instructor must first know what sorts of training he has to give and then lay out lines of instruction for each sort of training. In order to do this he must be able to make the necessary analyses.

Where work is carried on by a gang, as in riveting in a shipyard, or in blacksmithing, the instructor should make as many analyses as there are different jobs in the gang, and not make one analysis for the work of a whole gang. For example, in the case of the riveting gang mentioned above, one analysis should be made for the job of the heater, another for the riveter, a third for the passer and a fourth for the holder on. The same method of going at it would be followed for other gang trades.

The Instructor Must Do this Job.—In making these analyses the instructor uses entirely his knowledge of his trade. He simply picks out from all his trade knowledge what he considers necessary to put over for a given instructing job. Evidently this work can only be properly done by a man who thoroughly knows his trade. Only another man who knows as much about the trade as he does can help him in this. The work requires considerable time, because a man, even if he knows the trade thoroughly will seldom list out all necessary points the first, or even the second time.

Summary.—The line of instruction must be based on an analysis of what is to be taught. This the instructor gets at by looking at his trade from the outside and listing all the jobs, special terms, calculations, etc., which he must somehow put over to the learner. Nobody can help him in this; he must get it from his own knowledge of his trade. (He might, of course, get some help by talking it over with another man in his own trade.) If the instructor is to instruct more than one sort of learner, as many analyses must be made as there are distinct lines of instruction to be given.

THE CLASSIFICATION OF TRADE KNOWLEDGE

Man is Paid for Doing

Jobs
- Production Jobs
  - Assembling
  - Shaping
  - Forming
  - Miscellaneous
- Service Jobs
- Technical Jobs:
  - Trade Drawing
    - Sketching
    - Making
    - Reading
  - Trade Mathematics
    - Problems
    - Constructions
    - Special Methods
  - Trade Judgment

Man is not paid for having

- Trade Terms
  - Material
  - Machines
  - Location
  - Operation
  - Special
- Trade Science
- Knowledge of Stock
  - Recognition
  - Working Properties

Auxiliary Knowledge........

but is paid for doing jobs which he could not do well unless he possessed and used auxiliary knowledge.

- Safety First
  - Ignorance
  - Carelessness
  - Accidental
  - Occupational
- Care of Tools and Equipment
  - In use
  - Not in use
  - Prevention of loss
  - Prevention of waste

CHAPTER VII

THE CLASSIFICATION OF WHAT MUST BE TAUGHT. THE SECOND OPERATION IN GETTING OUT A LINE OF INSTRUCTION

Preliminary.—The previous chapter discussed the question of determining what the learner must be taught if he is to be trained for any given trade or particular line of work. For each case the instructor must determine what that learner must know and what he must be able to do when the period of instruction is completed. These various things however are of more than one kind, and the next step is to divide all the things that the learner must be taught into different sorts or classes. That is, the *content must be classified*. This process corresponds to sorting out bolts into different sizes, or distributing type or mail. In a sense we label a set of pigeon holes and sort out what we intend to teach into the different compartments according to the label on each compartment. According to its character this thing goes into one compartment and that thing goes into another compartment.

The Importance of Getting Properly Classified Analysis.—Getting out a correct and complete analysis and then classifying correctly is the key to the whole problem of getting an effective order of instruction. If the analysis is not complete the instructor will omit things that the man should be taught if he is to be completely trained. If it is not correct, the man will be improperly trained and cannot do his jobs properly. If the jobs that are to be put over are not properly classified, the instructor will not know how to choose the best methods of instruction for the different kinds of lessons, he will not know how to choose proper teaching conditions for instruction and he will not know whether what he wishes to give to a learner in any given case should be taught him or merely given to him as information. He will not be able to distinguish between the things that must be taught as a part of the job itself, and the auxiliary material which should not be taught in separate lessons but "hung onto the job" by the method described later.[1] One of the chief reasons for inefficient instruction is that instructors are unable or unwilling to take time to thoroughly work out the classification and analysis of the lines of instruction which they have to teach. They never know exactly where they are. One of the chief differences between a good instructor and a poor instructor is that the former does base his instruction on properly worked out and classified instruction material and the latter does not.

Classification Labels.—The term *job* means anything that a man is paid to do. Reading a blueprint is a job, running an automatic machine is a job, setting type is a job. It should be noted that something may be a job for one man and not for another, according as he is or is not paid for doing it. A blueprint man is paid for making blueprints. That is his job, but it would not be a job for a machinist.

The Different Sorts of Jobs.—If we look carefully at the different sorts of jobs which men are paid to do we find that they are not all of the same kind; one class of jobs such as pattern making, gear cutting, paper box making, type setting, high power machine work require the working up of stock; the stock is in some different shape or form than it was at the beginning of the job, or, after the job was finished, the different parts were arranged in some definite relation to each other that had been determined in advance. We will call such jobs *production jobs*.

Another sort of job, such as reading a blueprint, or making a lay out for a sheet metal job do not themselves result in the working up of stock, but are necessary for the doing of production jobs. We will call jobs of this sort *technical jobs*.

A third sort of job, such as that of the power house man, the steam engineer, the crane operator, while they do not contribute directly to the getting out of the product, make it easier or less expensive. We might operate a heavy shop without power cranes, but we would do it much more slowly

[1] Chapter XIII, Part III.

and it would cost much more. We could, perhaps, carry the material around with gangs of men, but we would lose time and spend more money on the job. We will call such jobs *service jobs*.

Service Trades and Production Trades.—In general, in most industrial plants there are trades that consist of service jobs and trades that consist of production jobs. Under ordinary conditions it seems probable that much more training will be required for production jobs than for service jobs. While the methods of instructional procedure would be the same for both classes of trades, this book deals more directly with instruction for production trades. Such modifications as would be required for service trades will readily suggest themselves to an instructor.

Trade Jobs and Technical Jobs.—In the practice of nearly, if not all trades, both technical and production jobs are called for. In some trades there are many technical jobs, as in sheet metal work, or in mould loft work in a shipyard, in some cases there are none, as in operating special machines or in most textile jobs, such as weaving or spinning. Anything is a job, however, (as defined in this book) provided it is something that a man is paid to do. Whether it is a technical job or a production job is a matter for further classification. The chief value of being able to distinguish between the two classes of jobs is that in instructing, matters of selection of method and determination of the best place where the instruction can be given are largely affected by the class of the job which is to be taught.

Classes of Production Jobs.—Production jobs may be divided into assembling jobs, shaping jobs, forming jobs and miscellaneous jobs. Under ordinary conditions in any plant each trade consists mainly of jobs of one kind, so that we have *assembling, shaping trades and forming trades*. In each of these trades there may be a few jobs that do not agree with the basis of the classification for that trade; that is, in a shaping trade, for example, there may be a few jobs that are not shaping jobs, although they are performed by a man who follows that trade. Such jobs would be classed as miscellaneous jobs for that trade.

CLASSIFICATION OF WHAT MUST BE TAUGHT

Since each kind of trade, under the above classification, needs somewhat different treatment when it comes to laying out a course of instruction, some of the chief characteristics are discussed in the following paragraphs.

Assembling Jobs.—An assembling job calls for the putting together of parts that some other workers have turned out. Such trades as type setting, plumbing, installing, brick laying or setting stone work would come into this classification. After assembling, the parts are just the same as they were before, so far as they themselves go, but they are arranged in certain relations to each other so as to form an assembled product. (A brick wall, a page of type, a shoe, for example.)

It is evident that a man in an assembling trade must know the names of a great variety of parts and must be familiar with a great many names which indicate location, relation to some other part, etc.

As will come out later the assembling trades work out, for a line of instruction, quite differently from the other production trades. Machines and tools are usually simple, skill comes mainly in the ability to adjust parts correctly, or to fasten them properly when they have been adjusted in place.

Shaping Jobs.—In a shaping job the form of the stock is not changed but the shape of it is. Thus, for example, a plumber or a coppersmith, in bending lead pipe changes the shape of the pipe but not its form. A pipe that has been bent into a curve is still a pipe, but its shape has been changed.

Forming Jobs.—In forming jobs the stock is formed by some method, as in the case of the blacksmith or foundry man. A lead pipe when bent could still be recognized as a lead pipe but a piece of bar iron made into a horseshoe would not be so recognizable. The pipe has been *shaped*—the bar has been *formed*. In working with steel these forming jobs often require the use of heat.

The forming job usually requires less general knowledge of locations, but does call for more skill in the use of the special tools of the trade, and often in the application of more auxiliary knowledge.

Miscellaneous Jobs.—As already stated in any trade there are liable to be some jobs that do not agree with the characteristics of the trade or which may even seem to belong to another sort of trade. For example in house carpentry, which is essentially an assembling trade where the stock comes ready milled, it might be necessary to get out some wedges, which would be a forming job. Such a job would be classified as a miscellaneous one for the house carpenter's trade.

Classification of Technical Jobs.—As already stated, a technical job contributes to the getting out of the production job but does not, itself, result in the forming or shaping or assembling of stock. Reading the blueprint for dimensions or shapes would be a job of this character. Figuring the offset for turning a taper would be another. Figuring the gears on a screw cutting lathe would be another. Making the constructions for getting out a pattern for sheet metal work would be another.

Kinds of Technical Jobs.—Almost all, if not all technical jobs require either the interpretation (reading) of a drawing or sketch or call for some form of calculation. That is, they are either jobs in the use of sketches or blueprints or they are jobs in calculations. They are either *trade drawing jobs or they are trade mathematics jobs*. A third class of technical job occasionally occurs in certain trades which calls for knowledge of a condition, such as the job of temperer, judging when a piece of steel is at the correct heat for tempering. Such technical jobs, when they are found, nearly always call for some knowledge of science or for skill and knowledge in the adjustment of parts.

Trade Drawing.—In certain trades such as machine shop work or pattern making practically all information comes from the designer to the workman in the form of the blueprint. Whenever a blueprint is read we have a technical job. Such jobs occur much more often in some trades than in others, for example in the machine shop work as against the work of the anglesmith, working from a templet. The printer has no call to use the blueprint, the roof framer has. In some trades there would therefore be no trade drawing at all, and in others there would be considerable. The instructor must determine in each case, if there are any jobs requiring trade drawing in the particular trade that he has under consideration; if he decides that there are no jobs of that character, he should cross trade drawing out of his "stock in trade," if there are, he must include such technical jobs in the list of jobs that he prepares.

If any drawing is included in the trade the instructor must determine whether it is sketching, or blueprint reading and if it is sketching, whether the demand is for the making of sketches, or the reading of sketches, or both.

Mechanical Drawing.—Outside of the training of draftsmen and others for the drafting room there is little likelihood that there is any demand for the making of regular mechanical drawings in the ordinary run of instruction work in industrial plants. A trade instructor is not likely to be called upon to lay out a regular course in mechanical drawing even in the training of apprentices.

The test, in each case is that the sort of drawing (if any), that is included in the training course is the sort of drawing that the man actually uses in connection with the doing of his job. If he has to read the drawing only, he should be trained only in the reading, if he has to make sketches, he should be trained only in that; if he has to read sketches only, he should be trained only to read them. Under good instructional conditions, the industrial instructor will not waste any time in instructing a man in anything that he will not actually need to use and apply in the work for which he is being trained.

Many shop instructors have a tendency to desire to train in regular mechanical drawing regardless of whether the man will use it in his trade or not. That is, they tend to want to train men out of the shop and into the drafting room; to make draftsmen out of them instead of workmen. While a knowledge of mechanical drawing is undoubtedly of value to any man engaged in mechanical pursuits, work of this character should seldom or never become a part of the work of the shop instructor, since the ability of a man to make a mechanical drawing seldom is a job in his trade. Blueprint reading, and sketching, are much more likely to be included in the work of the instructor. Courses in mechanical drawing are often available in the evening courses conducted in many cities and towns. If a man in the plant desires to put in some of his own time in taking such a course, he might well be encouraged to do so, but his time in the training work of the shop should be spent only on the sort of jobs that are included in the job or the trade for which the training is given.

Trade Problems.—Certain trades require some form of mathematical work in connection with the doing of some technical jobs. Laying off patterns in sheet metal work, is, in reality, a form of geometrical work. The sheet metal worker uses what is known as descriptive geometry in making his layouts, because he lays out in the flat to get a form that is in the round, or square, as a tank or a pipe. The machinist makes certain arithmetical calculations in connection with his work as when he "figures" the offset for turning a taper or works out the data for setting an index head. Even the use of a rule is a form of mathematical work, as when a carpenter measures a piece of stock. In its simplest form even counting is a form of mathematical work.

In listing out mathematical jobs, it must be remembered that whenever measurements or calculations have to be made, or patterns laid out some form of mathematics is used. The instructor must not think of algebra or geometry, as taught in the schools as the mathematics that he is looking for in analyzing his trade. Instructors often fail to recognize the fact that the simple calculations or constructions or measurements which are used in their trade are mathematics at all. They are thinking only of "school" mathematics, and because they do not use algebraic equations or geometrical demonstrations in their work, they will say that their trade uses no mathematics at all.

Special Devices.—In nearly all cases the shop or trade mathematics is worked out by certain special trade processes or with certain special tools or devices. For example, the machinist uses a table of squares or of decimal equivalents for his work, the printer uses the em scale, the steam engineer determines horse power by the use of the indicator card. In only few cases will the "school method" of doing the work be the same that is followed in the trade. This is why the man who comes into the shop from a school generally cannot "figure out" things as they are figured out in the trade. His method, which he has learned in school is often not the method of the trade. This is also the reason why there is little use in teaching the regular "school" mathematics to apprentices or learners.

In general, the trade mathematics for any given trade has been worked out so that as little time as possible is used up in this sort of work. Tables, formulæ, special methods of all kinds are really time saving devices.

The Question of Accuracy.—As just stated trade mathematics is usually worked out by the method that will save the most time. In industry, nobody works out mathematical problems for the sake of doing them, but because the result of the work is needed to do the job. Unlike "school" work, in industry no time is wasted in getting a result that is more accurate than is necessary. The carpenter does not figure stock to 1-1000 of an inch; the templet is not laid out to a small fraction of an inch; in each case the problem is only worked to the degree of accuracy that the job requires, and no time is taken for further accuracy. Methods in many cases are only approximate; they give results near enough for the needs of the job and therefore serve the purpose sufficiently.

Trade Mathematics in Various Trades.—In general, the skilled trades call for more technical jobs in mathematics than the semi-skilled, yet even these vary. Sheet metal work has more jobs of this kind than printing, for example. Paper box making, high power machine work, etc., have few if any technical jobs of this class. Automatic machine work has, of course, practically no jobs of this character.

Analyzing the Trade for Trade Mathematics.—In analyzing his trade for the trade mathematics the instructor should first make sure that there is any mathematics in it, and if there is, look carefully for the sort of technical jobs in which it comes up. He is most likely to omit the simpler jobs because he will not think of them as being mathematical jobs at all.

Auxiliary Material.—In addition to the mathematics and the drawing we have to consider what may be called the auxiliary knowledge or information which the learner must be given in some way. In general this auxiliary material, as it may be called, will consist of a knowledge of trade terms, of a few simple scientific facts, mainly connected with the effects of heat on material, a knowledge of the working properties of stock and the ability to pick out one kind or another, a knowledge of the precautions which must be taken to avoid accidents and the ability to take care of tools and equipment. Information as to such points as are noted above unquestionably contributes to the effective doing of the job, but the *application* of such information by the workman does not constitute either a production or a technical job as defined in these notes.

That is, the possession of information as to the care of tools, and the using of that information so as to save abuse or loss, while a valuable asset to the workman, is not, in the strict sense of the word, doing a job. It is therefore, for convenience, classified as auxiliary material, because, while the application of this knowledge is essential to the doing of the job, the man is not directly paid for having the knowledge, but he is paid for doing the job. For example: A draftsman is paid for making a working drawing. He makes it in order that all necessary information may go to the man who is going to welt in the shop. He is supposed to put all that information on the drawing, but he is not careful to make all his lettering and his figures plain: for example, he does not put the different dimensional numbers on in the proper place or according to the standard usage of the plant. If he does this because he does not know the proper way of making his figures, or the correct method of placing them, or that all figures should be given, he has not got that particular auxiliary knowledge. If he knew how to do it right, but did not do it right, he has failed to apply his auxiliary knowledge. In either case he has not done as good a job as the man who had acquired and applied this auxiliary knowledge, because he has turned out a drawing that is more likely to cause error and waste, and to slow up production. Putting the proper dimensions, etc., on the drawing was one of the operations connected with the doing of the job of getting it out, but *knowing how* to mark it correctly and *marking* it correctly was an application of correct auxiliary information. The man is *paid* to mark the drawing; he is *expected* to know how to mark it correctly. That is, he is expected to possess the necessary information as to the correct method of lettering, location of the different dimensional figures in the proper place, and to apply this knowledge. Doing this is not, however, in itself, a job.

Auxiliary Material: Trade Terms.—By trade terms is meant all the special words that are used in any given trade or occupation in connection with talking about the work or doing the job. Each trade has its own set of such trade terms. (Such terms are often designated as *technical terms*.) Often a man who belongs to one trade will not know any of the terms of another trade, nor does he need to know them so far as following his own trade is concerned.

Classification of Trade Terms.—In general trade terms will relate either to material, machines, locations or operations. There are usually a few terms in any trade that do not come under any of the above classifications and which may be designated as *special terms*.

Location Terms.—In the shipyard such terms as Starboard, Port, Forward, Aft, etc., as used by the sailor, ground floor, second floor, valley, cellar, attic, as used by the house carpenter would be illustrations of these terms. Some trades, as that of the machinist, use fewer location terms than other trades such as shipyard trades, but practically all trades use some special location terms, which the learner must in some way learn how to use in connection with his work, and which must be listed out and provided for in the course of instruction.

Tool and Machine Terms.—Any trade using machines and tools has special names for those machines, for different tools for the parts of such machines. The machinist has the shaper, the planer, the knurling tool. The ship fitter has the templet, the puncher the tit punch, the wood mill man has the pony planer, the buzz saw, the mortiser, the band saw. The pipe fitter has the Stillson wrench. The driller and reamer has the old man. The printer has the stick, the tinsmith the iron.

The learner must acquire the machine and the tool terms for his trade and be able to use them properly.

Operation Terms.—All trades that carry on operations have special names for the different operations. The printer justifies and makes ready. The machinist makes a rough cut, or a fine cut, the jointer takes the wind out of a piece of stock, the pipe fitter makes up a joint. The learner must become familiar with the operation terms for his trade and must connect them in his mind with the operations which they designate. In making the analysis and classification, considerable care should be used to get all terms of this class, since they play so important a place in the giving and understanding of instructions.

Material Terms.—All trades use special terms to distinguish the different kinds of materials with which the work is done. Such terms as snap or flush rivets, phosphor bronze, mild steel, hard pine, ten penny nail, cut nail, channel bar, news stock, soft solder, are illustrations of this sort of term. As in the case of operation terms their use in the giving of important instructions makes their careful listing particularly desirable.

Special Terms.—Terms that cannot be otherwise classified may be designated as special terms for that trade. Terms falling under this classification are usually very few and of minor importance.

Auxiliary Material: Trade Science.—In determining the existence or non-existence of science items in the auxiliary information called for by a given trade a sharp distinction should be made between specific applications of general scientific principles with which the learner must be familiar in order to do the job, and the general principles themselves. The specific facts, if necessary, should be listed, but general principles should not be included in the analysis for shop instruction. Of such specific scientific items probably the electrical and machine shop trades will show as much as any. The instructor will, in general, find little or no science in his trade analysis. It is true that many trade operations involve the application of some scientific principle, but in only relatively few cases will a knowledge of the scientific facts lying back of the operation in any way help the man to do his job. Regular courses in science, such as are taught in the school have practically no value in this sort of work, even in the training of apprentices. An instructor should be very sure that any "science" that he lists down is of actual value in shop training before he includes it in the auxiliary material with which he proposes to deal. There are for example undoubtedly a large number of scientific facts connected with the work of a temperer, such as combustion, oxydation, the changes in properties of metals produced by a rise in temperature, but all that the temperer needs to be able to do is to recognize the right color. A knowledge of the scientific facts mentioned above would not help him to do his job in the slightest degree, hence it would be entirely useless to include them in the auxiliary knowledge that was to be included in a course of instruction for temperers.

On the other hand in machine shop work certain scientific facts such as those relating to friction in bearings, the principle of the lever as it affects the tool in the tool post, have a direct value. A knowledge of the relation of the direction of warping to the heart or sap side of stock is of value to the pattern maker, and such facts would be included in the auxiliary information listed for those trades.

Auxiliary Material; Knowledge of Stock.—All production trades require the working up of stock. In practically every trade there is more than one kind of stock and the workman must be able to recognize the different kinds. The different kinds of stock have different working properties and this fact often requires modifications of operations or different operations according to the particular sort of stock used. Provision must therefore be made to see that the learner is able to recognize the different kinds of stock which he will come in contact with, and that he will be familiar with the working properties so far as they actually affect the doing of the jobs in his trade.

Instructors should be careful to list down only those things relating to recognition of stock and its working properties, which will be of actual value to the man in doing his jobs. Many instructors tend to include in this classification much material which has no value in shop training, because they think that there ought to be considerable material of this sort in their trade when it really is not there, or they think that "it would be nice for the men to know it." As in the case of mechanical drawing, it is undoubtedly true that properly arranged courses in general science (physics, chemistry, applied mechanics) have a value to the mechanic, and where such courses are available in the evening, men may well be encouraged to attend them, but science work of this kind should not be considered as a part of the shop training proper.

Safety First.—In practically all trades there is more or less danger of accidents to the operator, to the machine, to the helper or bystander. Different trades vary greatly in the relative danger to the man on the job and to others. Dangers in the machine shop are confined almost entirely to the operator. In the steel mill, in general, the reverse conditions exist—whether involving danger to the operator, the bystander, or both, in shop training special attention should be given to matters relating to the prevention of accident. Every accident that puts a man or a machine out of business slows up production to that extent so that proper training in "safety first" is an important factor from the production standpoint.

Most accidents are due to the lack of training in habits tending to prevent carefulness or to ignorance. The antidotes therefore are training and instruction, both of which are part of the job of the trade instructor.

Accidents are of two kinds, involving danger to the man on the job or to others. They may be classified as due to any one of four causes, namely: *ignorance, carelessness, accidents, and occupational dangers.*

Occupational Dangers.—There are some trades that cannot be followed without subjecting the worker to danger. After all precautions have been taken, and the workers are fully instructed in "safety first," there still are certain dangers that "go with the job." Operating a circular saw, operating a blast furnace, working in a lead factory, filling shells with T. N. T., marine diving, are instances of trades which involve occupational dangers. Usually occupational dangers involve the worker himself and not others.

Accidental Dangers.—An accidental danger is one that could not be foreseen but arises out of some unexpected situation. If a belt that has been properly inspected breaks causing injury to someone, this is an accidental danger. Such dangers usually involve both the worker and others.

Dangers Due to Ignorance.—A workman on a speed lathe job does not know that if his tail stock center is not properly oiled, it is liable to burn out, letting the stock fly, putting both himself and others in danger. A painter, not knowing how to place the supports under his scaffold properly, tips off from one end, injuring himself or damaging passersby on the ground. A mill man on a buzz saw, does not know the danger of a back snop, and an accident occurs as a result. Such accidents as those just cited can be prevented by training the learner so that he will use the proper precautions to avoid them. They are accidents due to ignorance regarding the precautions that can be taken to prevent them and will be avoided if a man has been properly trained in taking the necessary precautions on the job.

Dangers Due to Carelessness.—If a man has been properly trained in taking necessary precautions and an accident occurs because he does not take the precautions that he was trained to take, if he knew but didn't think, or knew and "took a chance," the accident was due to carelessness. Accidents of this character are much more likely to occur with experienced men than with inexperienced men. In this case as in the others accidents may do injury to the man on the job or to others.

Care of Tools and Equipment.—Wherever tools are used there is always an opportunity for the taking of precautions to prevent loss or abuse. If these precautions are taken the work is speeded up; if they are neglected, the work is slowed up. In the same way, if tools are abused or are so carelessly handled that they are put out of commission, the working equipment is reduced and the amount of the product diminished.

Matters relating to the care of tools and equipment classify in general, into four lists: (1) care of tools and equipment in use, (2) care when not in use, (3) the prevention of loss, and (4) the prevention of waste. In all these cases there is more or less auxiliary knowledge that the instructor should list out and plan to include in his course of training. It is evident that the greater the extent of the equipment, the more expensive the tools, the more delicate the mechanism, the greater the value of such training, but in all cases there is some knowledge that should be given to the learner and which he should be trained to apply in connection with his jobs.

Care of Tools in Use.—Unless specially instructed, the average man, thinking only of doing his job is very likely to be careless in taking care of tools and equipment while in use. Even when he owns the tools himself he is often ignorant of the value of a little care during the progress of the job. Tools are left out over night, or are not put under cover when temporarily out of use; a man attempts to use a tool for something that it was not intended to be used for; he scatters his tools about during the progress of the job and when he wants a particular tool has to spend a lot of time finding it. Of course matters of this kind apply mainly to trades where hand or portable tools are used rather than where machines are the chief portion of the equipment. In operating machines a man will, often, through ignorance or carelessness, run a machine on an overload. He lets it run without proper lubrication. He "jams her through" and strains or in some other way causes an unnecessary depreciation or reduces the working capacity or the accuracy of that particular machine. He may even put it out of commission entirely.

In all of these cases the average man, if his attention has been directed to the results of such abuse, and he has been given the necessary auxiliary knowledge and trained to apply it, so that he thinks about such matters, while he is doing the job, will take precautions to prevent improper running down of the tools or machines or other equipment with which he carries on his jobs. The instructor should carefully determine what points in his trade should be covered in this connection, and should list them out as a part of the auxiliary knowledge in his proposed course of instruction and training.

Care of Tools when not in Use.—Tools and equipment are often seriously damaged while out of use through lack of knowledge of how to protect them or through carelessness. The farmer leaves the mowing machine in the pasture till next year, certain machines in the machine shop are shut down for a period and are not "slushed down," a crane is laid up and is not properly protected, machines temporarily out of use are allowed to stand and rust.

In the case of hand tools the same general conditions will often prevail; jacks are left lying where they were used last until somebody wants them, small equipment units are not turned back to the tool room as soon as they are no longer needed but are left lying around to be exposed to the weather; small tools are not protected as they should be, for example, the tool room boy does not keep the micrometers covered with vaseline, or wrenches are not kept properly oiled when stored in the tool room.

In all such cases the precautions that should be taken to avoid such damage should be listed by the instructor; the necessary information to prevent such abuse determined, and included in the auxiliary material to be put over in connection with the instruction in the trade that is to be handled.

The Prevention of Loss.—As distinguished from the abuse of equipment we have the loss of equipment; this, of course, occurring mainly in the case of hand or portable tools and small pieces of equipment. A man is using a crowbar; in the hurry of getting the job done he throws it down when he is through with it and forgets all about it. It is lost track of and for the time being, so much is gone out of the available equipment. A little later when another job calls for a bar it is held up because they are short on bars, and the whole production program may suffer. The learner must be trained to think of such things; he must be informed as to proper methods of procedure as to turning in equipment when he is through with it and he must be turned out of the training course so informed and trained that slowing up of production and increased cost due to loss will be reduced to a minimum. The instructor must therefore, as in the other cases, list out the cases where tools are liable to be lost in the work of his trade and make provision for including this auxiliary information in his job instruction in his program of instruction.

The Prevention of Waste.—Stock and tools cost money. A man who is careless about waste can easily appreciably increase the cost of production. Multiply the waste of one man by thousands, and you have a large sum. Suppose that one man, through lack of proper training wastes five dollars worth of stock in a week; in a year this means two hundred and fifty dollars. If one thousand men are employed, this means a quarter of a million dollars in a year. As in the other cases the ways in which an untrained man will cause waste and the information that he needs to avoid such waste must be listed out by the instructor and included in his plan for instruction for that trade or occupation.

Some General Suggestions.—Simply telling a man what precautions to take to avoid abuse of tools or waste of stock will do little good. "Bawling him out" when he does fail to take proper precautions will do still less. Abuse and waste will be reduced in proportion as the instructor succeeds in getting the men interested in these points and in bringing about a "state of mind" on the part of the learner so that he will apply the information which is given him in connection with the training work and will apply it intelligently. If the man can be got to see what waste and abuse mean in terms of loss of time, slowing up of production, loss of money that might go to the doing of more work, a great deal can be done by a shop instructor to cut down losses of this kind. Much will depend on the skill and ability of the instructor in handling this problem, but as a starting point he must determine what the "danger points" for waste and abuse are for his trade and get them included in his "inventory."

This Chapter Deals entirely with Classification.—It should be noted that this chapter deals entirely with the classification of the material that the instructor determines should, in some way, be included in the course of instruction and training that he proposes to put over for a given trade. It does not deal with the methods by which any part of this material is to be put over, or how it can be best arranged for effective putting over. These points are discussed in following chapters.

Analysis and Classification on Specialized Work.—According to the trade or job to be taught the analysis may require a great deal of work or very little. Getting out the complete analysis for a skilled trade, such as machine shop work, is a considerable piece of work. On semi-skilled jobs it is very simple, there are few jobs, few trade terms and so on. For automatic machine work the analysis is still simpler. In all cases however the process of analyzing and classifying what the man should know should be gone through. It is as important to do this on single, simple jobs as when instruction is to be given in skilled trades sometimes covering hundreds of jobs. It is not a question of much or little but of knowing what there is.

CHAPTER VIII

THE DETERMINATION OF "BLOCKS"

Preliminary.—In carrying out the two preceding steps the instructor has analyzed and classified the job and the auxiliary knowledge and information which must, in some way, be put over to the learner. What has been done so far corresponds to taking account of stock in a store and classifying the stock according to the kind of goods. Just as a grocery store may have in stock sugar, tea, canned tomatoes, beans, rolled oats, etc., so the instructor has listed out his stock, the production jobs, the technical jobs, the trade terms, the safety first notions, etc., of the trade that he intends to teach. His stock in trade is now inventoried and classified.

The Grouping of Teaching Jobs.—The instruction to be given may include the entire range of a skilled trade, as in apprentice training, or part of a skilled trade, as in training for one branch of that trade (lathe hand, planer man in a wood mill, etc.). It may, on the other hand, only deal with one or more semi-skilled jobs, as in paper box making. It may only deal with one job, as in a munition factory.

Where there is only one job to be taught, and, in general, where semi-skilled trades are to be taught, the question of "blocking," as discussed in this chapter, will rarely come in. In the case of most skilled trades it is an important factor in laying out an effective plan for instruction.

If a learner is to be taught a skilled trade, or a considerable part of such a trade, he has got to be instructed in a considerable number of jobs, and under these conditions it is probable that these jobs can be grouped in in a way that will be most effective for easy progress of the learner.

Where a learner is to be instructed in a certain number of jobs and trained to apply the necessary auxiliary material that goes with those jobs he has got to be "routed" through these jobs in some order. There are three ways of routing him through these jobs: (1) The jobs could be grouped in no determined order at all, but could be given in any way that they happened to be available; (2) The jobs could be grouped according to production difficulties; (3) They could be grouped according to the kind of learning difficulties that the learner would meet during the instructing process. As has already been stated the product of the instructing process is a trained man and not a production job. In the case of a production shop in routing jobs, the same three methods can be followed: (1) Jobs can be put onto any machines that happen to be available; (2) Jobs can be routed through the shop, not according to the requirements for the most efficient production, the saving of the most time, the minimum scrapping, but according to the requirements of some other department, say the shipping department; (3) Jobs can be routed according to the conditions that will give the best and most rapid production. The first method is essentially that of the old fashioned shop. The second method is ineffective because it is based on the requirements of something that has nothing to do with production; the third is the best, because it recognizes the requirements of the particular thing for which the production shop is run, viz.: getting out jobs.

In the same way the instructor has the job of getting out trained men and may follow any one of three methods. (1) He may give his learners any work that may be available, without regard to its difficulties for the learner; (2) He may give his learners jobs in the order required for the most effective production; (3) He may give his learners jobs in an order determined by the difficulties the learner would meet in mastering each successive job. The first method is bad, because it pays no regard to the conditions of efficient instruction; the second method is bad because it is based on the requirements of something that has nothing to do with the instructor's job; (instruction) but is based on the requirements of something else (production) the third method is evidently the best because it is based on the requirements of effective instruction. The shop deals with *production difficulties;* the training department deals with *instructing difficulties,* and must route its instructing jobs according to the best working conditions for that kind of a job, and not according to the working conditions of another kind of a job (production) with which the instructor has nothing directly to do. The problem of the training department is therefore to group its teaching jobs so that the instructional difficulties will be reduced to a minimum, just as it is the business of the shop to group its production jobs so that production difficulties will be reduced to a minimum.

Blocks.—In the case of the grocery store just used for illustration, after the stock has been inventoried and classified, there still remains the question of how this stock can be best arranged for convenient selling. In such a case it is often found that it helps both the salesman and the customer if the stock is arranged by departments, so that all the things that may meet a certain need are put into one part of the store. Thus in the grocery store used as an illustration above, it may be desirable to put all canned goods in one department, cereals in another, etc. This would probably be particularly true in the case of a store carrying a wide variety of stock. Where such a departmental arrangement is made, the classification basis for the department is something that all the goods in that department have in common; this may be a common buying difficulty on the part of the customer, that is, the sort of things that a woman is likely to want to buy together are put in the same department, or it may be that some matter of selling or shipping may determine the department "base."

It may be true on the other hand that in the case of some particular store, say a tobacco store, that there is no need for a departmental lay out because all the stock is of the same kind, though it may vary in quality and price. For example, in a store selling only cigars. So we might say that there are "one department" and "multi department" stores. In arranging his stock for "sale" to the learner the instructor has the same sort of problem to face as has the manager of a store. His "stock in trade" may "sell" well if put into one department, or *block* as it is called, or it may be necessary, for good "selling conditions," (instructing) to lay it out or arrange it in more than one "selling department" or block. Just as the store manager must determine whether his stock is "single department" or "multi department" so the instructor must determine whether his stock in trade, (the instructional material that he has listed out and classified,) belongs to a *single block* or a *multiblock* trade, and, if the latter, what the block bases shall be.

What is a Block?—A block means a group of jobs which all offer to a learner the same *kind* of learning difficulties. All the jobs in a block call for the same *kind* of knowledge, or skill, or call for the use of the same kind of tools, or machines. Such a block may, in itself represent a complete course of training or it may be one of a number of blocks that are included in the required training course. Where blocking is called for and it has been properly done a learner can be carried through any block without having to be instructed in anything that is in any other block. For example, in machine shop work, a learner can be trained on any one of some twelve or fourteen machine tools without being instructed in anything relating to the operation of any machine except the one that he is being trained on. In many of the so-called skilled trades we find that such blocks are found, as in printing, where composition, press work, stone work and machine work are some of the blocks.

In printing, if it were decided that it was not necessary for a man to know anything about composition or stone work in order to do press work, or, that he need not know anything about composition or press work in order to be able to do stone work, or that he need not know anything about either to learn to operate a linotype, we would have more than one block in the printing trade and it would be a *multiblock* trade. On the other hand suppose that it was decided that in house painting or paper hanging all jobs were essentially of the same kind, the difference being in degree of learning difficulties only, (say working conditions, or degree of skill required), then those trades would be single block trades.

A block may therefore be defined as a trade or a part of a trade, that can be taught as if it were a trade by itself. In fact, in many trades we find so-called "special branches" that really are blocks.

For example, in machine shop work milling might be one block, lathe work another, bench work another. A milling machine hand might know nothing about planer work and a planer hand might know nothing about milling, neither man need know about bench work, yet each man may be competent on his own set of jobs. A plumber might know how to handle rigid pipe with threaded joints, elbows and unions, and also how to handle lead pipe with wiped joints, but a knowledge of how to handle lead pipe would not help him to learn how to handle rigid pipe, nor would being able to handle rigid pipe help him in learning how to handle lead pipe. On the other hand, if he knew how to make up iron pipe it would help him greatly with brass pipe. Both iron and brass pipe work would therefore probably belong in the same block, but lead pipe work and rigid pipe work would probably belong in different blocks. A man who could splice manilla could learn to splice wire more rapidly than a man who could not splice at all, both manilla splicing and wire splicing belong in the same block. A knowledge of how to splice either manilla or wire would not help a man to learn how to rig up a three-fold tackle running to a winch, because these operations belong in different blocks of the riggers trade.

A branch of a trade refers to the *practice* of that part of the trade. A block refers to a group of instructing jobs in that branch of the trade. The former is an *operating* term. The latter is an *instructional* term.

What is a Block Base?—What is termed the *block base* is the thing that all jobs in the block have in common which makes them have learning difficulties of the same kind. In printing, the pressman, no matter what particular job he is on always "goes at it" in the same way. It is more *difficult* to make up a form with half-tone cuts than with plain matter only, but it is the same sort of a job: the learning difficulties are different in degree but of the same kind. In this case we would say that the block base was press work. For instructing the machinist, one block base might be the lathe, another the planer, another the shaper, etc., since each machine, in its special construction, operation, special tools, and attachments offers the same kind of learning difficulties, but different jobs on each machine offer these difficulties in different degrees. For a course of training in plumbing, one block base might be based upon work on rigid pipe, another upon work on flexible pipe, another might deal with vitrified pipe, etc.

How the Block Base is Established.—Block bases may be of various kinds. Among the most common are, (a) material, (b) operation, (c) construction.

(a) Material—In certain trades different branches or blocks, depend upon the character of the material used, because the characteristics of the material determines the nature of the operations. For example, iron or brass pipe, vitrified pipe and lead pipe differ so in their working properties that the handling of each forms a distinct branch of the trade, and distinct lines of instruction, or blocks can be laid out for each. That is, the block base, in this case, might be taken as kinds of pipe, and a line of instruction consisting of all jobs on any one sort of pipe together with the necessary auxiliary knowledge to go with that special work, that is, a block, could be established on the base of kind of pipe since all jobs on any particular kind of pipe would offer the same sort of learning difficulties.

(b) Operations—Block bases for some trades can be based on operations.—Here the man works with the same material but the operations are so different that knowing how to carry out one set will not help a man to learn how to go through another set. Thus, in printing, the compositor, the stoneman, the pressman and the machine operator all use type, but a knowledge of press-work is not required for machine operating, or for composition or stone work. In the same way the machinist may work on the same stock with different machines, but the learning difficulties that a learner will meet on these different machines will not be due to the kind of stock to any great extent, but mainly to the construction and operation of the particular machine on which he is being trained, and to the special tools, adjustments, etc.

Lathe hands, miller hands, bench hands, automatic machine operators all work on steel, but knowing how to operate an automatic screw machine would not help a man to learn how to run a universal miller, because he must learn how to carry out certain operations on each machine, and the fact that he works on steel in both cases does not affect the situation so far as learning difficulties and what he has to learn are concerned. So far as these points are concerned, he might as well have snagged castings or learned to chip and file. In such cases it is evident that the controlling factor, or the block base, is operations, since operations is the element that "splits up" the course of instruction into blocks. In a shipyard, while it is true that riveters, bolters up, punch press men, drillers and reamers, all work on steel, the character of the material that they work on is not the important thing, as in the case of plumbing cited above, but the important thing, from the standpoint of blocking, is that the training is entirely determined by the character of the operations with which they must be made familiar and which they must be trained to carry out effectively. In such cases *operations* would determine the block base.

While it is true that miller hands, planer hands, etc., all work on steel, mill men all work on wood, textile operatives all work on cotton or wool, the character of the material that they work on is not the important thing, as in the case of plumbing cited above, but the important thing, from the standpoint of blocking, is that the grouping is entirely determined by the character of the operations with which they must be made familiar and which they must be trained to carry out effectively. In such cases operations would determine the block base.

(c) Construction: In some trades, as in pattern making, the block classification has sometimes been based on some forms of construction. In pattern making, for example, blocks might be based on solid patterns, cored patterns, built up patterns, segmental patterns, etc. That is, in this case, the block base might be neither material nor operations, but the thing in common for a given block (the block base) would be the fact that all the jobs included in a given instruction block would represent the same type of construction.[1]

[1] It should be noted here that the selection of construction for pattern making is only given as a possible way of doing it, and is only given by way of illustration. It is probably not the best way for blocking all that trade.

More than One Block Base Possible for a Given Trade.—It is of course evident that for a given trade there might be more than one set of block bases: one instructor might select one set of block bases and another instructor might "block out" the same trade on entirely different bases, or the same instructor might even block out his trade in more than one way. It would be possible to lay out a line of instruction on either set of block bases, but, as is pointed out in the following paragraph, there is always one way of working out the problem of the selection of block bases that will give the best instructional results.

The Value of Blocking Out the Trade with Proper Block Bases.—Where a modern shop has to turn out a product that is produced by putting the stock through a series of operations, that is, by doing a series of jobs on the same stock, production difficulties are reduced to a minimum by *grouping* the machines that are used so that the stock goes from one machine to the next with the least loss of time and expenditure of power. If the machines can be grouped in such a way that the successive operations can be carried on as easily and rapidly as possible the best production conditions will be met. In the same way, if the training department can group its teaching job in the best way according to the same sort of learning difficulties, the instruction can be carried on with the least expenditure of energy on the part of the instructor and the learner, and the learner will progress the most rapidly.

The Selection of the Best Working Block Base.—As just stated it is often possible to select more than one block base; in choosing between different block bases, where this can be done, the instructor must pick out and use the block base that will give him the best results in instructional practice. Sometimes this can only be determined by trial, but an experienced instructor can generally make a pretty good guess in this matter.

The following suggestions may be helpful on this point. In general, the best block base is the one that enables the instructor to so lay out his instructional order that he gets into one block the greatest possible number of teaching jobs that present the same sort of learning difficulties. Under these conditions, the learner, in progressing through the block will meet the same sort of learning difficulties all the way through, though, of course, these learning difficulties will vary widely in degree as he learns job after job in the block. To put it another way, the less the learner has to "switch" *kinds* of learning difficulties during his progress through a given block the better, the more he gets in the same block all the jobs that present the same kind of learning difficulties, these difficulties differing in *degree* only (not in *kind*), the better.

The condition as to learning difficulties will be best met when the best block base has been selected. When this has been done, the result is that all teaching jobs that present the same learning difficulties will have been got together in the same block and then they can be so arranged by the method described in a following chapter, that the learner can overcome his learning difficulties progressively, working steadily from jobs where the learning difficulties for that block are the least to jobs where the learning difficulties are the most intense. When this has been done the job that would be very hard for him if given him at first becomes easy if given him last, because, in doing the intermediate jobs, he has learned to overcome a considerable part of the learning difficulties that go with the "hard job." On the other hand if he has had to "switch" learning difficulties frequently it is evident that his training in learning to deal with any given group of learning difficulties will not have been so well carried out. Instead of a steady up grade he will have had a series of short "up grades and down grades" during his progression through the block.

Some General Suggestions as to Suitable Block Bases.— The statements given below may be of service in aiding an instructor to determine the block base or bases that will serve him the best in laying out an instructional order that will be most effective.

In case a trade is carried on mainly by machine operations the instruction will deal mainly with the ways of operating these machines because the different machines are differently operated or controlled and therefore the different jobs to be taught will "tie up" to each other (block out) by machines.

That is, a course of instruction on any one machine will present "learning difficulties" different from those encountered in working through a course of instruction on any other machine. In case a trade is carried on mainly by operations carried out by the use of hand tools or simple machines (plumbing, for example) wherein materials (stock) of widely different working properties are used, the jobs to be taught will usually "bunch" for learning difficulties according to material. Where a trade consists of special branches (inside and outside rigging, or printing) where a knowledge of one branch does not help a man in learning how to do jobs in another special branch, the trade will usually block out best by these special branches.

It must be clearly understood that the above statements are in the nature of general suggestions only; each instructor must carefully consider the blocking possibilities of the trade that he is to teach and determine the best block bases for that trade. In this work no general rule will take the place of good judgment and experience. In some cases it may even be necessary to try out several different block bases before the best working block bases can be found.

How to Determine whether a Given Trade Is a Single or a Multiblock Trade.—In order to determine whether the trade which he intends to teach is a single or a multiblock trade the instructor must give careful consideration to the character of the trade with regard to material, operations, etc., as possible block bases. He must first determine whether he has more than one block; if he has, he must decide what the best block bases will be according to his best judgment, paying regard to the suggestions given in this section. If he finds that there seem to be more than one group of learning difficulties he probably has more than one block in his trade.

It will be noted that for the carrying out of this operation the instructor merely decides whether he has one block or more than one block, what the block bases probably are, using all the information at his disposal as to special branches, operations, material, learning difficulties, etc. He does not, at this point, attempt to determine exactly the nature of the learning difficulties for each block, that operation being described in the next section.

Summary.—The first step in setting up the material that the instructor has analyzed out for his trade is to determine whether the particular sort of instruction he is to give calls for training in any considerable number of jobs and if these jobs involve more than one kind of learning difficulty. If he has only a single job, there is no question of job grouping or blocking. If there are any number of jobs to be put over he has then to determine whether all the teaching jobs can be grouped into one block or whether more than one group are called for. This he determines by considering the various factors discussed in this section. He determines his block base if he has one block, and his block bases if he has more than one block in his course of instruction. It is important that this study of "blocking possibilities" be carefully carried out, if blocking is required at all.

Having completed this work the instructor has analyzed what he has to teach, determined the jobs to be taught (if more than one), classified his jobs and the auxiliary material that goes with them and determined whether he has a single or multiblock trade. If he decides that he has more than one block, he has determined his block bases.

He has now got his "stock in trade" classified so that he can use it, and is ready to take up the question of how to determine the most effective order in which the different jobs in any block should be given to the learner.

These questions are discussed in the next part.

PART III

THE ESTABLISHING OF AN EFFECTIVE INSTRUCTIONAL ORDER

CHAPTER IX

THE DETERMINATION OF THE DIFFICULTIES WHICH THE LEARNER MUST MEET IN HIS PROGRESS THROUGH THE LINE OF INSTRUCTION FOR ANY ONE BLOCK. THE FIRST OPERATION IN GETTING OUT AN EFFECTIVE INSTRUCTIONAL ORDER

Preliminary.—If the preceding operations have been properly carried out the instructor has now: (1) analyzed and classified the trade and (2) determined whether it is a multiblock, a single block or a "no block" trade. If the first, he has determined the block bases for each block, if the second, the one block base, if the third, he does not have to consider blocking at all. If he has one or more blocks he has listed out the various jobs that must be taught in each block but has not determined the order in which they can be best given to the learner. Up to this point he has dealt entirely with the classification of his instructional material: first, as between jobs and auxiliary material; second, as, to the proper classification of jobs as technical or production; third, the classification of the technical jobs as mathematical or drawing jobs; fourth, the classification of the auxiliary material under the proper headings, such as safety first, trade terms, etc., and fifth, the jobs that go in each block.

It has already been pointed out in the preceding chapter that where blocking is called for in selecting the best block bases study must be made to determine the best base for grouping the different teaching jobs, so that the learner will, in progressing through any given block deal with the same sort of learning difficulties. Having determined the most effective arrangement so far as blocks go, whether the trade is multiblock or single block, and, if the former, what the block bases are, and what jobs should be included in the block, or in each block, the instructor is now ready to determine the order in which the different teaching jobs that he has determined shall go in any given block shall be arranged so that the most efficient instructional order may be secured.

Operations must be Carried out for each Block.—The operations described in this and the following chapters must be carried out as many times as there are blocks in the trade. Each block will present its own group of learning difficulties, will call for its own difficulty scale, for its own checking levels, and will show its own list of type job specifications. Since the operations are the same for all blocks, though the results are often very different, the following processes are described for one block only.

Securing an Effective Instructional Order for any one Block. —Whatever the instructor intends to put over to the learner must be given to him in some order; it cannot be given to him all at once. This brings up the question as to whether some arrangements of successive jobs are not more effective than others, and whether there is not a *best instructional order* for any given block and, if so, how it can be determined.

Whatever order may be adopted it is evident that if there is more than one job in the trade that the man is to be taught, the successive jobs must be given in *some* order. The learner must be informed at some time as to the necessary knowledge that he must be able to apply to the different jobs that he is to be instructed how to carry out effectively. The instructor must therefore prepare some plan, or "operation sheet" on which he has laid out the order in which he proposes to give the learner the different lessons which it is proposed to teach him, and this must be done for each block of the trade, if the instructor is dealing with a multiblock trade. Such an operation sheet may be called an *instructional order* and the following chapters deal with the methods that should be followed in laying out such an order so that it will represent an effective and efficient line of instruction.

What is an Effective Instructional Order of Jobs?—An effective order of instruction for the jobs that are to be put over in one block presents certain characteristics among the more important of which are:

DIFFICULTIES WHICH THE LEARNER MUST MEET 79

(1) The different teaching jobs in the block are arranged in a definite order.

(2) They are so arranged that, after the first job has been put over each succeeding job extends the learner's knowledge and skill, but does not call for a different sort of knowledge and skill.

(3) Jobs that require the learner to think of the least number of different things at once come first and jobs that require the learner to think of the most different things come last.

(4) The jobs are arranged according to the difficulty of learning how to do them rather than according to the order in which they would be done in getting out a finished product according to a good production order. That is, the order is an *instructing* order, not a *production* order. (Sometimes these two kinds of orders agree—usually they do not.)

An illustration of a course of instruction which does not meet these conditions would be the following procedure in training reamers which illustrates a method of procedure often found when untrained instructors attempt to handle a course of training. Where two rivet holes do not come together "fair" they must be reamed to a common size. This is usually done with a pneumatic or electric drive. The instruction course aimed at training these men to correctly ream any kind of holes where reaming was required. A group of men after having been cautioned as to the control of the machine were placed in compartments of the ship to ream out all holes that required reaming. These holes were of course, of all sizes, fair and unfair (that is, some holes were centered, as punched, or as the plates were temporarily held together by bolts, and others were more or less off center). Some could be reamed in easy positions and some required difficult positions. Under these conditions the learner was immediately put up against jobs of all sorts of difficulty, since he took the holes as they came. He worked in this way until he had learned to ream. Under these conditions the learner had to learn too many things at once, reducing the probability that he would thoroughly grasp any one thing, causing a state of mental confusion and slowing up the learning operation. Taking holes as they came, the learner would very likely first get a very unfair hole to ream, then a fair hole, then a hole of some other degree of fairness. Under a properly arranged order of instruction the work would have been so laid out that holes of different degrees of fairness would have been marked so that the learner first learned to ream the fairest hole, then the next fairest hole, and so on up to the most unfair hole that he would ever have to work on. Moreover it is very unlikely that one compartment would afford enough samples of holes of all degrees of fairness, so that instead of keeping him in one compartment till all holes were reamed, he should have been carried from one compartment to another as the demands of the training required. This would have been equally true of the variations in the working positions on the reaming in different parts of the compartments, top, sides, bottom. Keeping the gang that is under instruction in one compartment till it is all reamed up gives good *production* conditions; such an arrangement is an example of bad *instructional* conditions.

As between the two methods of training given above the latter would train a reamer much faster, make a better workman of him, keep him in a much better frame of mind while he was under training and turn him out with a much better attitude towards his job.

Progression Factors.—It has already been pointed out that an efficient instructional order for the teaching jobs in any one block will present certain characteristics. Any instructor who has any notion of his job at all will attempt to make some sort of a lay out that will meet these conditions and these attempts fall into one of three classes. The instructor who knows the least about his job as an instructor simply guesses at the order in which he will lay out the successive teaching jobs in the block. He "guesses" that a learner should have this sort of a job first and that sort of a job second and the other sort of a job third. He has little or no basis for his guess except, possibly, some vague notions as to what are commonly called "hard" or "easy" jobs in the trade. The instructor who has a better notion of his job as an instructor will lay out the work in a determined order, but he will base his order, not on learning difficulties, that is, not on the difficulties that the learner will have to get over in mastering the successive ideas or operations that he must get, but on the difficulties that he, the instructor, who is himself a competent workman in that trade, would meet in *doing* the different jobs. This sort of instructor fails to remember what he went through when he learned his trade and thinks of things as they are now and not as they were with him when he was a learner.

The trained and efficient instructor will neither guess nor will he confuse *doing* difficulties with *learning* difficulties. He will lay out his order of teaching jobs with regard to the difficulties that the learner will meet in learning how to do the job. He will, in a sense, put himself in the learner's place, and look at the matter through the brain and the hand of the learner who is to be made into a competent workman rather than from the standpoint of the workman who is already trained.

In order to do this, the instructor who follows the "scientific" method of laying out his successive order of jobs must determine what elements, or *factors* enter into learning difficulties. Having determined them he will then arrange his order of jobs so that the learner gradually works, or *progresses* by uniform and gradual stages, from jobs where these factors are the least intense to jobs where they are the most intense. That is, the instructor must determine the *difficulty factors* for the learner for each block of his trade. Since these are the factors that determine the difficulties that the learner must overcome in working or *progressing* through the line of instruction for the block, they are called the *progression factors* for that block.

Progression factors are therefore merely those things that affect the speed, ease and the thoroughness with which a learner progresses through an order of instruction.

The Identification of Progression Factors.—The first step in getting out an efficient progressive order of instruction for any block is to determine the progression factors for that particular group of teaching jobs. In general, it may be said that the instructor must determine the progression factors by making a study of the causes of the difficulties that his learners meet in learning how to do the different jobs in the block. While no general rule can be given the following suggestions may be of service. In a general way it may be said that progression factors affect either "head work" or "hand work." For example, in some trades, the green man is afraid to do certain things; there may be more than one thing that he is afraid of on some jobs and only one thing that he is afraid of on others. Evidently in this case the course of training should be so laid out that he will get first jobs in which he is only afraid of one thing and can get over his fear of that before he is given jobs in which he would be afraid of several things.

In training an anglesmith's striker it was found that he was afraid of letting go of his sledge and hitting somebody, he was afraid of the hot iron, he was afraid that he would not hit what he aimed at and he was afraid that he would not strike "fair." The course of instruction had to be so arranged that the green man did not have to overcome all of these fears at once. In this case fear was therefore a progression factor to be taken into consideration. In other trades there are some jobs in which a man has to look out for only one thing at a time and other jobs where he has to look out for a number of things at the same time, and there are jobs intermediate between these two in this respect. When a crane operator simply lifts a frame he does not have to look out for as many things at once as when he lifts the frame and carries it. In laying out a line of instruction for a crane operator the instructor would arrange the different jobs in such an order that the man would be taught to lift before he was taught to carry. In this case the progression factor might be called complexity and we would say that the progression should be from the least complex to the most complex jobs.

Two Kinds of Progression Factors.—A man who is used to working under production conditions is almost certain to get out production difficulties instead of learning difficulties. When he thinks of the relative difficulties of jobs he is almost sure to think of the difficulties that he, as a competent man, would meet in *doing* them rather than of the difficulties that a learner would meet in *learning how to do* them. His progression factor table will, unless he is very careful, be a *production progression factor table* and not an *instruction* progression factor table.

DIFFICULTIES WHICH THE LEARNER MUST MEET 83

What is a Progression Factor Table?—A convenient device for enabling an instructor to work out his instructional order with regard to progression factors is what is often called a *progression factor table*. In constructing such a progression factor table the instructor, after having determined the progression factors for the block, charts out the progression on paper as follows:

Suppose that there are four progression factors A, B, C and D, and these are accuracy, speed, fear and number of operations. In such a case a progression factor table would look like the sample below.

PROGRESSION FACTORS

TO	Accuracy High	Speed high	No fear	Many Operations	
	↑	↑	↑	↑	↑
	⋮	⋮	⋮	⋮	
FROM	Accuracy very low	Speed very low	Fear high	Number of Operations low	

The vertical lines indicate simply that the learner must progress from jobs where each of the progression factors are at a *minimum* or maximum, as the case may be, through jobs where the factors are of intermediate but increasing or decreasing value. Such a progression factor table should be prepared for each block of the trade for which the instructional order is to be laid out.

Progression Factors May Go Up or Down.—Progression factors may increase or decrease as the learner progresses. Thus, in the sample table given above, accuracy, speed and number of operations went up, but fear went down. So far as fear went the learner had more "scare" in him when he started than at any other time, and the problem, so far as that progression factor goes, is to gradually reduce that scare to zero, and to give the learner a chance to overcome his "scares" one at a time. That is, fear is a *diminishing* factor. The other factors used for illustration start at as near zero as possible. The absolutely green learner has practically no skill, his speed is at the minimum. Numerous operations will confuse him the most at the start, and will bother him less as he gains in experience and skill, hence his first job should call for as few operations as possible. His accuracy is at zero, or nearly so, hence his first job should be the one calling for the roughest work of all the jobs in the block.

CHAPTER X

ESTABLISHING A DIFFICULTY SCALE FOR ONE BLOCK. THE SECOND OPERATION IN GETTING OUT AN EFFECTIVE INSTRUCTIONAL ORDER

Preliminary.—Up to this point the instructor has established his progression factors and laid out a true instructional progression factor table by the method described in the preceding chapter. If his trade is a single block trade, one progression factor table will cover the entire trade; if a multiblock trade, he has laid out as many progression factor tables as there are blocks in the trade. If he is instructing on single jobs of course no question of job progression comes in and he does not have to bother with progression factors at all. The next step is to establish what may be called a difficulty scale for the block under consideration.

The progression factor table as it now stands, merely gives a starting point and a finish, or an outline of minimum and maximum degrees of learning difficulties. The instructor is in the position of a train dispatcher who knows that a train leaves New York and arrives at Boston at given times, but has no knowledge of the position of that train on the route at any intervening time. In order to know approximately how near the train is to Boston at different stages in its progress, the train is reported at definite points between starting point and the finish. In the same way the instructor in order to know how far advanced the learner is, has got to establish a series of checking points between the learner's start and his finish.

The Difficulty Scale.—If a number of horizontal lines are drawn across a progression factor table, each line will represent a stage of the learner's progression through the block, just as the reporting of trains from intermediate stations shows its position between its starting point and destination. We call such lines *checking levels*.

The Number of Checking Levels Required.—The determination of the number of checking levels required is a matter of judgment. Evidently if a block contained a great many jobs, the instructor would want to check up the progress of the learner at more points than he would if the number of jobs were small. The number of checking points would vary also with the character of the trade and the kind of a learner, i. e., in trades calling for a high degree of skill, or if the list of jobs for the block included a good many technical jobs, more checking points would be required than for trades with reversed conditions. Probably more checking points would be required for checking boys than for men.

The object to be accomplished is to enable the instructor to keep a close enough check on the progress of the learner to know approximately where he is between the beginning and end of the block, but at the same time not try to make the thing too fine.

Probably a rough rule would be to establish a checking level for every four to six jobs in the block.

The diagram for a progression factor table when made into a difficulty scale with four intermediate checking levels would look like the figure below:

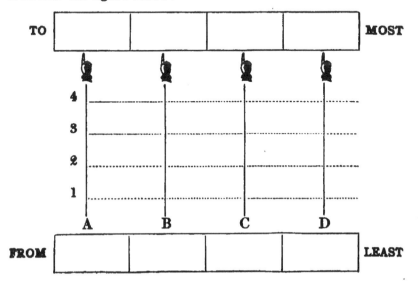

This gives the situation of the learner at six levels, start, four intermediate stations and finish.

Conclusion.—The instructor now has two things, (1) the list of jobs for the block and (2) a difficulty scale for the block. The next step is to use the difficulty scale and the list of jobs for the block so that the jobs can be arranged in an effective order for instruction. The method for doing this is given in the next chapter.

CHAPTER XI

APPLYING THE DIFFICULTY SCALE TO ONE BLOCK. THE THIRD OPERATION IN GETTING OUT AN EFFECTIVE INSTRUCTIONAL ORDER.

Preliminary.—The instructor has now two things to work with: he has a list of the various teaching jobs that he intends to put over in the block that is under consideration and he has the difficulty scale he has worked out for the same block. The next step is to apply the difficulty scale to the list of teaching jobs so that the result will be a lay-out for progression, or *a course of instruction*, that will conform to the standard already set forth in the previous chapters.

When the instructor has done this he has his teaching jobs for the block laid out in an effective instructional order, although, as already pointed out, he will probably find on trial that some modifications will be required as he gains in experience in working through the course with a group of learners.

Checking Level Specifications.—The first step in using the difficulty scale is to take off what may be called checking level specifications. In order to do this the instructor proceeds as in the illustration given below.

Assume for illustration that an instructor in house carpentry is laying out a course of instruction for his trade. He has decided to put into one block all the teaching jobs that he proposes to put over in connection with his instruction on the covering in of a house. He has taken closing in as his block base. He has listed out on cards the following teaching jobs to be included in this instructional block.

CLOSING IN BLOCK

Boarding in	Fancy shingling	Straight gutters
Paper work	Valley shingling	Mitered gutters
Clapboarding	Ridge pieces	Flashings
	Straight roof shingling.	

APPLYING THE DIFFICULTY SCALE

He has determined that this block contains four progression factors: workmanship, accuracy, number of operations and has also decided that the working conditions vary to such a degree for a learner on jobs on different parts of the house that, as between working on the ground and working at an elevation, consideration must be given to the fact that fear will affect the learning conditions.

He has also determined that three checking levels between the beginning and end of this block of instruction will enable him to keep track of the learner's progress with a sufficient degree of approximation for the instructional requirements for this block in this trade.

He therefore has a five degree difficulty scale and a four factor progression factor table. He now places his difficulty scale side of his progression factor as shown in the diagram.

He now prolongs the "degree" lines on his difficulty scale across the progression factor table as indicated by the dotted lines in the figure. Wherever a scale line crosses a progression line we have what may be called a checking point, as indicated by the circles lines in the figure.

Checking Level Specifications.—By reading horizontally along the five scale lines the instructor can now determine the general characteristics of the sort of teaching jobs that would approximately fit into the *specifications* for any degree on his difficulty scale. Thus, in the diagram as given for illustration he might have:

No. 1 Level. (Green learner.) The roughest laying on job that can be found on this sort of work, with the fewest possible operations and working on the ground.

No. 2 Level. (Learner partly trained.) A moderately rough job, requiring some degree of accuracy, calling for a few operations that can be worked on off the ground but not too high up.

No. 3 Level. (Learner about half trained.) A somewhat close job off the ground, calling for several operations. In general, further along than No. 2, but not so far along as No. 4.

No. 4 Level. (Learner considerably trained.) A fairly close job, requiring some fitting, well off the ground, requiring a considerable number of operations.

HOUSE CARPENTRY
CLOSING IN BLOCK

Checking Level Scale	THE BLOCK			
Maximum	Close	Fitting	Roof	Many
5	☞	☞	☞	☞
4	O	O	O	O
3	O	O	O	O
2	O	O	O	O
1	O	O	O	O
Minimum	Rough	Laying on	Ground	Few

No. 5 Level. (Learner completely trained.) The closest job requiring the best fitting, with the most operations of any job that there is on this class of work (closing in), and carried on as high up as is possible.

The instructor now has what may be called *checking level specification*. That is, he has determined the general characteristics of the sort of a teaching lesson that should be given to the learner when he starts, when he is completely trained, and when he has reached three intermediate stages in his progression through the instruction block. It will be noted that these checking level specifications do not refer to any definite job, but only indicate the characteristics of the sort of a teaching job that should be undertaken with the learner at the stages of his progress indicated by the lines on the checking level diagram.

Conclusion and Summary.—By carrying through the operations just described, the instructor has now applied his difficulty scale to his progression factor table and has drawn off the characteristics or specifications of the sort of a teaching job that should be undertaken with the learner at the checking levels on the difficulty scale. It still remains to determine what actual jobs out of those listed out for the block will best fit into the instructional order as prescribed by the progression factor table and the checking level specifications as obtained. This further method of procedure is discussed in the next chapter.

CHAPTER XII

GETTING THE ACTUAL TEACHING JOBS INTO AN EFFECTIVE INSTRUCTIONAL ORDER FROM THE CHECKING LEVEL SPECIFICATIONS. THE FOURTH OPERATION IN GETTING OUT AN EFFECTIVE ORDER OF INSTRUCTION FOR ONE BLOCK

Preliminary.—The instructor in the illustration used in the last chapter has now got his checking level specifications and has the list of jobs that he intends to teach in that block. The next step is to determine in what order these jobs can be arranged to secure best practical instructional order.

Fitting the Jobs to the Progression Scale.—In the case of the instructor in house carpentry already used for illustration in the preceding section, the further procedure would be as follows: He has on cards the ten kinds of jobs that he proposes to teach in the block.

He knows all about these jobs. He selects the job that he thinks will approximate most closely to the number one level on his table. He then picks out the job that he thinks will fit best into the specifications for the number five level, and in the same way he selects three jobs that fit the best into the specifications for levels two, three and four. He has now located five jobs out of the ten on his scale. This leaves five jobs to be distributed between. He does this according to his judgment. To illustrate:

He selects paper work for the first level (minimum) job because it calls for the roughest workmanship of any job on his list; because it calls for practically no fitting, hence no accuracy, it calls for the fewest operations, since it only requires nailing on the paper and cutting it off, and the learner can be given jobs of this character on or near the ground. He selects

EFFECTIVE INSTRUCTIONAL ORDER

a job in paper work where the learner can stand on the ground, because he must consider the fear factor. Thus he secures a job that approximates fairly well to the specifications of the minimum level job.

The number two level specifications call for a moderately rough job calling for some degree of accuracy with two or three operations that can be worked off the ground but not too high up. Clapboarding meets these specifications pretty well and by picking out work where the learner can be put on a staging eight or ten feet from the ground, it gives a pretty fair approximation to the number two specifications.

Specifications for number three level call for a fairly close job, well off the ground, requiring a considerable number of operations. Straight clapboarding near the roof meets these conditions fairly well. On the matter of fear of falling it is fairly good, it does not call for quite enough operations to quite meet the specifications, but it seems about the best choice on the whole. So he takes it.

Specifications for number four level call for a somewhat close job off the ground calling for several operations. He selects for this putting on mitered gutters, since this work must be done up to the eaves of the house (about as far up as the learner can work and have a staging under him) and because, from the standpoint of skill mitering is a pretty close job. There are not quite enough operations, but, on the whole, this job fits the specifications about as well as any.

Specifications for number five level call for the closest job of the list, requiring the best fitting, with the greatest number of operations of any job in the block, carried on under the worst conditions so far as fear of falling is concerned. Several of the jobs on the list meet these specifications to a greater or less degree; putting on ridge pieces is as high up as any, but is rather too simple; putting on flashing around a chimney is better, but on the whole, fancy shingling on the roof would seem to meet the specifications the best, though not the ideal type job for this level. He therefore selects it as his most advanced job. He now has:

Level No.   Job.
   5   Fancy shingling.
   4   Mitered gutters.
   3   Clapboarding on the roof, medium high.
   2   Clapboarding on a low stage.
   1   Paper work on the ground.

The instructor now considers the other jobs on his list. Evidently mitered gutters, chimney flashings, fitting ridge pieces should come in between levels 3 and 4. Boarding on a stage will come after paper work, etc., so that finally the order of jobs might be, with some reason, arranged as follows:

Level No.	Order No.	Job.
5	11	Fancy shingling.
4	10	Mitered gutters.
	9	Chimney flashings.
	8	Fitting ridge pieces.
3	7	Clapboarding near the roof.
	6	Putting on straight gutters.
	5	Clapboarding on high stage.
2	4	Boarding on high stage.
	3	Paper work on stage.
	2	Boarding on stage.
1	1	Boarding on the ground.

The jobs for this block have now been arranged in an efficient order of instruction with regard to the difficulty scale as laid out. The instructor now has his order of instruction for the block.

Type Jobs and Real Jobs.—In the illustration just given it will be noted that in no case did the job selected exactly meet the specifications for the checking level which it was chosen to represent. For convenience we can imagine a job that will exactly meet the specifications of any given checking level, even if no real job does exactly meet them. An imaginary job that exactly corresponds to a set of checking level specifications may be called a *type job*. In selecting real jobs on which to base his different teaching lessons, the instructor, having in mind type jobs chooses real jobs that approximate to the type job that he has in mind when he makes his selection. In this work of approximating he will do good work in proportion as he has the type job specifications clearly in his mind and uses good judgment in "matching up" his real jobs against the type jobs. Of course it might be true that a real job might correspond exactly with a type job, but cases of this sort are so rare in practice that they are negligible.

On the other hand it is not uncommon to find that several jobs all correspond equally well to the specifications of a given type job. So far as meeting the requirements of the teaching job as given on the progression table, one would be as good as another. In such a case it will usually be found that minor variations and the learning difficulties will suggest a most effective arrangement, or, if this is not the case, the jobs in the "bunch" may be assigned in any order as convenience may determine.

Laying Out an Effective Instructional Order in Practice.— An excellent practical method for arranging jobs according to a difficulty scale is to use such cards as are made for card catalog work. Where cards are used the arrangement is flexible, the order of jobs can be easily changed and additional jobs can be readily inserted in the proper place.

The most useful cards for this work are the ordinary size (about 3¼" x 4½"). Guide cards may be used for the type job specifications. Such a guide card might be arranged as shown below.

```
                                              No.____
    ┌─────────────────────────────────────────────────┐
    │                                                 │
    │   Block base_____                          │
    │                                                 │
    │   Checking level specifications                 │
    │                                                 │
    │   _____                   │
    │   _____                   │
    │   _____                   │
    │                                                 │
    └─────────────────────────────────────────────────┘
```

For listing out jobs a card as shown below is about the simplest form.

```
Block_____          Card No._____

Job.................................................................................
_____
_____
_____
_____
_____
_____
_____
```

Where multiblocks are used each block can be indicated by a center guide card of a different color. The guide cards can be arranged in the order of the checking levels that they show, going up front to back. Cards carrying the jobs corresponding to each set of checking level specifications can be bunched behind the corresponding guide card. If they vary much with regard to the specifications they can be arranged in an order working from the specifications on the front guide to the next guide back. Convenient holding cases can be easily procured if cards of standard size are used.

A job card catalog constructed as described is the best form in which to keep an order of job instruction.

If desired further modifications can be developed. Cards can be made to carry additional information, cards of different colors can be used to indicate different classes of jobs, etc. Such an arrangement can be used to record almost any sort of information that may be desired.

CHAPTER XIII

TYING UP THE AUXILIARY INFORMATION WITH THE JOB INSTRUCTION

Preliminary.—The method of securing an effective instructional order that has been presented in this pamphlet has dealt entirely with jobs: production jobs or technical jobs or both. It has been assumed that in listing out the instructional orders the instructor has only dealt with teaching jobs that were to be carried out on actual jobs: that is, on production work.

In analyzing out the trade, however, it was found that there was more or less auxiliary material, largely in the nature of information, that must, in some way, be given to the learner during the progress of his training, and the question of how this auxiliary material is to be handled still remains to be discussed. This question, as a part of the whole problem of securing an efficient order of instruction, is discussed in this chapter.

The Applying of Auxiliary Knowledge.—Whenever a man does a job it is almost always true that, in connection with the doing of that job some auxiliary knowledge will be used or applied. In getting out an operation sheet use must be made of location terms, operation terms, etc. In a technical job, such as reading the blueprint in the shop, some trade terms will come into play and will have to be correctly interpreted by the workman. In using an acetylene torch, or in operating a machine tool the operator must apply certain "safety first" information if he means to do a safe job. In nearly all jobs directions, to be intelligently understood, must use trade terms, and the workman must understand them.

In a previous chapter the method of listing out and classifying this auxiliary knowledge was given, and it is assumed in this section that the instructor has properly listed out and classified all the items that he considers should be included in what he intends to give to the learner as a part of the training course that he has planned.

It has already been pointed out that the passing out of information does not require the use of the instructing process: because straight information is not taught, in the sense in which the term is used in these notes. For example we cannot *teach* trade terms; we can *explain* them, but explaining what the words "diamond point tool," "apron," "bevel gear," "eleven point" and so on *signify* does not mean that we have *taught* them. In such cases there is nothing to teach, because there is no particular reason why these particular terms should carry the meaning that they do. In the same way and for no more reason we call the right hand side of a ship, facing forward, the starboard side, and, under the same conditions, the left hand side the port side. Such terms as mortise joint, bed, justifying, taking out wind, milling, and so forth carry the meanings that they do simply because they are trade terms for certain things or certain operations, and that is all there is to the matter. The instructor can tell what they signify but he does not teach them: that is, he does not put them over by the use of a true instructional process.

As already pointed out an instructor not only has to teach but as a part of his job he must point out certain facts and explain certain terms; he must give certain information. It therefore becomes a part of the problem of an instructor who is planning out a line of instruction to determine how he proposes to "run in" this sort of material, or auxiliary knowledge in the most effective way. If it is not included in his instructional course, the training will be, of course, imperfect. The methods whereby this part of the problem of the instructor can be dealt with are discussed in the following paragraphs.

The Putting over of Auxiliary Knowledge: The Two Methods.—In general there are two methods of putting over the auxiliary knowledge that must be applied to the different jobs in any given block. According to the first method this information is organized into "courses of instruction," and is "taught" that is, passed out, by what is thought to be a series of teaching lessons. This material is divided into different subjects and these subjects are "taught" to the learners at definite times. This is often done by bringing the learners into a room and giving them this information by lectures or "shop talks," before they are instructed in jobs. This method, which we will call the method of *instructing by subjects*, is the usual method that is followed in the regular schools, and is the one that is generally attempted by trade instructors who attempt to follow regular school methods. By the second method this auxiliary material, while it is carefully listed in the instructor's trade analysis, is not brought into "courses of instruction" by subjects, but is "tied up" with the job, by giving it to the learner in small parts, and giving him each part only when it is needed in connection with the job on which he is being instructed. According to this second method the instructor determines what part of the different items of auxiliary knowledge that he has listed out will be called for *for the first time* when the learner has reached any given job in the list of jobs for that block, and plans to give it to the learner at that point. No attempt is made to pass out these different items apart from the jobs with which they are naturally connected. By this method no lectures or talks are used to give the auxiliary material.

The Two Methods Illustrated.—As an illustration of the way in which the two methods would be worked out in practice take the case of the care of tools when in use. According to the first method the precautions that should be taken in looking out for the different tools would be given to groups of men at certain times: a common way would be to bring the men together for an hour or two a week for this information or to attempt to give it in evening classes, which men may attend if they choose. If, for example, a man should know that a certain tool must be kept well oiled, and how to oil it, by the first method he would be given this information at some time during a "course" on the care of tools. If certain precautions should be taken in connection with the use of the tool this information would be given in a "course" on safety first, if certain trade terms were required to be understood, the learner would get these in a "course" on trade terms. Such "courses" would, of course, include similar items for other jobs in the trade. By the other method the particular terms that would come into play in connection with the use of that particular tool, the special precautions that should be taken in using that tool, the special things that a man should know in taking care of that tool would be determined and listed out in connection with the *first job in the instructional course in which that tool came into use*. That is, this information would be given to the learner at the time that he needed it on the job, and not before, and at that time he would only be given the particular items that applied to that particular job.

The two methods may be illustrated by the diagram given below:

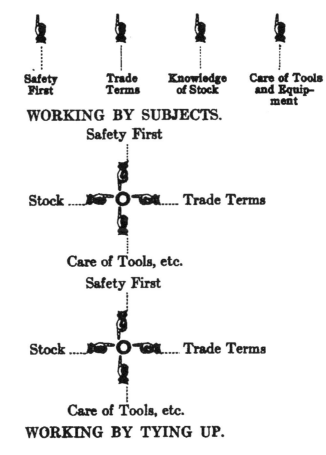

O's represent successive jobs; index lines parts of the different kinds of auxiliary material that should be "fixed up" with each job.

For a more definite example, take the case of the safety first information and the trade terms that would come into the job of operating an air "gun" in riveting. If such a "gun" is started when the die is not pressed against something solid, this die will be "shot" with sufficient force to do considerable damage if it strikes any one. Assume, for convenience, that the terms are trigger, gun, plunger, and die. That the safety first information consists in impressing the learner with the fact that if he starts the gun "free" the tool will "shoot." Assume that this particular operating danger and these particular terms are included in the list of trade terms that the instructor has compiled of all the safety first information and all the trade terms that apply to the trade that is to be taught, in this case, riveting.

By the first method the information about "shooting the tool" might be given as a part of a lecture on safety first at some time before the man had had a gun in his hand, and it would be given along with a lot of other information which would apply to safety in the use of other tools or on other jobs. . So the special terms that would apply to the particular lesson, "trigger," "die," etc., would be given in a talk on trade terms given at a time when the learner was not on the job, and given along with a lot of other trade terms, such as "flush rivet," "snap rivet," "countersunk rivet," etc., that would apply to other jobs in the line of instruction. That is, there would be a "course" in trade terms; a "course" in safety first, applying in each case to the requirements of the riveting trade, each course including all the auxiliary information for that trade under that particular classification.

By the second method the instructor, in laying out his course of instruction, would have looked at his list of trade terms and decided that the terms "trigger" and "die" would come in for the first time in connection with a lesson on the operation of the gun, and would plan for that teaching unit a memorandum that the learner was to be introduced to these particular terms in connection with that lesson. In the same way he would have determined that that lesson was the place to bring up the safety first information connected with the use of the gun, and would have noted that on his lesson plan. Thus the learner would get the special precautions and trade terms that go with the operation of the gun, *at the time that he was first taught how to operate a gun and not at some time before or after he had been taught how to operate a gun.* Naturally this would be a part of his first lesson in riveting.

Untrained Instructors Tend to Use the First Method.—The majority of untrained instructors tend to use the first method; they do this for several reasons among the more important of which are: first, they have the notion that, if the learner can be "instructed," (as they call it) in advance, that is, if he has been *told* the trade terms, precautions, etc., before he is given the lesson on the job, he will *know* and be able to apply these terms and precautions when he is on the job. The theory is that, having been once given them, he will carry them in his head, pick out what he needs to apply on any given job when he needs it, and do it completely and correctly. Second, this method of instruction by subjects is very much the easier method to follow and so appeals to the overworked or lazy instructor. Third, it is the sort of organization of teaching material that the instructor sees in the work of the regular schools, the way that his children are getting their schooling, probably the way that he got his own schooling, and he naturally tends to copy that. Fourth, somebody, not a scientific instructor himself, tells him to do it that way and he follows their advice.

The Right Method.—The method of tying up the auxiliary material with the job has always been recognized by teachers as one that is far more effective than the method of handling this material by the "subject" method. It is the method that has always been followed by the really effective teachers in the regular schools. It does not find much place in the work of these schools chiefly because the work is practically "book work," as it is often called, and not "practical work," or work on production. Teaching conditions in these schools also make the successful use of the tying up method very difficult, but in good schools it will be found in use in such subjects as science and manual training, where real things are studied and handled.

The Advantage of Tying Up the Auxiliary Material with the Job.—In the first place the learner gets the information at the time that he sees some "sense" in it; when he sees that it really comes into the job. If it is given him in advance of the job he has nothing to "tie" it to; it makes but little impression. If it is given him after the job he has not been given it when he has a chance to *apply it*. In either case what "tying" he can do will be either to such a general idea of the situation as he may get from such general knowledge of the job as he may have picked up somehow, or from such a picture of the job as he may get from whatever the instructor puts up, in either case a pretty weak thing to tie to. In the second place, and what is more important, it is of no value to give information on, say, safety precautions, unless the man will take those precautions when he is working on the job. If he knows and does not apply, what good has been done? In order that he shall think of the thing in question when he should, he must have gotten it in connection with some operation, so that, whenever he performs that operation the thing, say "shooting the tool" will come up in his mind in connection with that part of the job. It is the failure to recognize this fact that makes so much "preliminary work in the "fundamentals" of so little value; general talks on safety first are given and then, when the men on the job do exactly what the instructor warned them not to do, he wonders what is the matter and calls them stupid. He puts up lessons on fractions, and then finds that his men do not know how to use fractions on the job; he teaches trade terms in advance of their use and, when they come up on the job, the man does not know the terms. In all these cases the trouble is that the instructor, who has plenty of trade experience to tie to, forgets that the learner has little or none; it is another case of the instructor thinking of the problem with his own brain and not putting himself in the place of the learner.

The Practical Tying Up of the Auxiliary Material with the Instructional Order of Jobs.—An instructor who has arranged his technical and production jobs in an effective instructional order and who now wishes to "work in" the auxiliary material that goes with the trade, proceeds as follows: He takes the number one job on his list and determines what items on his list of safety first material should be given in connection with that lesson; the same for trade terms, for knowledge of stock, etc. He lists these items on the card that carries that job. He does the same with the next job and so on until he has distributed all his auxiliary material among the different jobs to the best advantage, bearing in mind that the job for bringing up any given item for the first time is the one on which the learner will feel the need to use or apply that particular item for the first time.

The Question of General Information.—In what has been said in this section reference has been made only to the course of instruction for some one trade that the instructor has planned to teach. Entirely outside of this there is undoubtedly a large amount of information of a general character that the new man needs to have given him in some way, but which is no part of his special trade training. Whether he is to be trained in spinning, weaving, machine shop work, or any other occupation in the plant, he needs, for example, information as to where and when and how he gets his pay, where the dispensary is, how to get around the shop, etc. Information of this sort should not be included in the trade training course as planned by the instructor for that trade. It is, in fact, doubtful if it is not the business of the welfare department or the employment office to give information of this sort. If the instructor plans to give it it should be worked out as an independent program from that for his "regular job" the occupation for which he is expected to give training. It might be that if this work were a part of the work of the training department, it could be given to one special instructor to work up and attend to before the man was sent to the trade instructor for his trade training proper.

The importance of doing this tying up work well cannot be too strongly emphasized, and it will pay the instructor to give much time and attention to working out this part of his instructional layout. The two important things to accomplish are: first, to run in all the trade terms, precautions and other auxiliary material somewhere in the instructional list of teaching jobs, and second, to be sure that the distribution is such that each part comes to the man when he needs to use it for the first time on the job, *not before and not after*. In proportion as this is well worked out the "tying up process" will be efficient and instructional time will be saved. Under few, if any conditions should the instructor undertake to plan to give any auxiliary material to his men "off the job."

Summary and Conclusion.—In addition to the jobs (technical and production), that constitute the instructional order, or course of instruction for the trade, the instructor, in his analysis has listed out the auxiliary material and classified it under the proper heads. This auxiliary material can be given either by distinct subject courses or by the tying up method. This second method should be followed in emergency training departments because it is much more efficient of the two. Instructors tend to follow the first (subject) method because it is easier and is the method that they commonly see in the regular schools. The instructor should distribute the different items between the different jobs in such an order that any given item comes to the learner the first time that he meets the need for it on the job.

CHAPTER XIV

GETTING THE JOBS IN MORE THAN ONE BLOCK INTO AN EFFECTIVE INSTRUCTIONAL ORDER

Preliminary.—The method of procedure given in the preceding sections has dealt entirely with the case where the trade was a single block trade. As stated, the listing of the teaching jobs, the determination of the teaching difficulties, the establishment of a difficulty scale, the putting the scale against the progression factor table and the getting of the teaching jobs and the real jobs into an effective instructional order must be carried through for each block. When this has been done once for a single block trade the order of instruction is completed, and the instructor is ready to take up active instructional work so far as the arrangement and determination of what he is going to teach is concerned.

Special Problems of the Multiblock Trade.—Where the trade has been determined to be a multiblock trade further complications are introduced into the problem of getting out an effective instructional order because not only the different teaching jobs in the blocks must be presented to the learner in some determined order, but the blocks themselves must also be arranged so that the teaching jobs in all the blocks can be combined into an effective order of instruction. In the case of a multiblock trade we have therefore one more step to take before the line of instruction is completely worked out.

Let it be assumed that an instructor has determined that the trade that he intends to teach is a multiblock trade and that he has worked out his effective order of instruction for each of the blocks. His first problem is to determine the order in which these different blocks should be placed in the course of instruction. That is, the *block order* must be determined.

Independent and Related Blocks.—In general, it will be found that the different blocks are *independent* or *related*. By an independent block is meant one in which the teaching lessons contained therein have no relation to those in any other block. This practically means that it would be possible to carry a learner through any one block without having to refer in any way to anything that was contained in any other block. An illustration may make this clearer.

As already stated, machine shop instruction breaks up into some fourteen blocks, and the general block base is the machine. It is generally held by instructors in that trade that it is perfectly possible to thoroughly instruct a learner in the work that is done on any one machine without being obliged to use in any way anything that he might know about any other machine. This fact is taken advantage of in cases where "special machine operators" are trained: lathe hands, planer hands, shaper hands, etc., are trained so that they are thoroughly instructed in the work on their special machine and may know absolutely nothing about the operation of any other machine.

Where these conditions exist, in instructing a learner on any one machine, the instructor need not in any way assume that the man under instruction has had any experience on any other machine which the instructor must draw upon in connection with the instruction. The complete instructional order for jobs on any one machine can be built up without using in any way knowledge of any other machine. Such a case would probably be equally true in the case of plumbing, for jobs on rigid pipe, lead pipe, soil pipe and so on, and might be true for work in a wood mill in training on the different wood working machines. It might be true in the case of training men in sheet metal work, where the three blocks of reading blueprints, making constructions for pattern lay outs and working the sheet metal, might be found to be independent blocks. This would be the case if it were true that one man could be trained only to read blueprints, another trained only to make constructions and a third trained only in working the metal, and each man could do his job without knowing anything about the other man's job. The test as to whether these blocks (assuming that the instructor had determined that these three blocks did exist in the trade) were related or independent would come in determining whether the instructor, in laying out the work for blueprint reading found it necessary to assume that the learner knew anything about either construction work or about working the metal and whether in instructing the learner in working the metal, any reference must be made to the blueprint reading or the construction work.

Suppose, on the other hand, it were found that, in a certain trade, while the trade broke up in such a way that different block bases were desirable, that is, it was a multiblock trade, what a learner acquired in one block would help him in progressing through another block. Many instructors in pattern making have held that this is true of their trade. Referring to the possible block bases as given already discussed, they have held that, while a segmental pattern offered enough distinctive characteristics to warrant setting up a block on segmental patterns, at the same time this block could best be given to a learner who had already been carried through a block on built up patterns, and that the learner could best be carried through the block on built up patterns after he had been instructed in a block on solid patterns. These instructors hold that learning difficulties would be less in the case of the block on segmental patterns if the learner already knew how to make built up patterns, because a built up pattern differs from a solid pattern only in the fact that for special reasons, it is made in a number of pieces instead of in one piece. On the other hand, these instructors have claimed that work on segmental patterns offered enough special learning difficulties to warrant putting jobs of that kind in a special block.

Possible Arrangement of Blocks.—If a trade is a one block trade there is, of course, no question as to arrangement of blocks, but, if it is a multiblock trade there are a number of possible arrangements. Consider the simplest case first, that of a two block trade. Just as two bricks can be placed in two positions as to each other, one on top of the other or side by side, so the two blocks of a multiblock trade can be placed in *series* or in *parallel*, as shown in the diagram below.

Calling the two blocks A and B we could have:

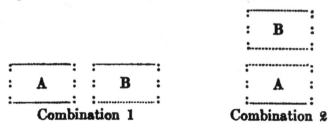

Combination 1   Combination 2

This means that by combination 1 the learner would be instructed in both blocks at the same time, by combination 2 he would be put through block A first and then through block B.

The Case of Independent Blocks.—In the case of independent blocks it is evident that either combination 1 or 2 may be used, but in the case of related blocks but one effective order of block arrangement is possible, combination 2.

The Case of More Than Two Blocks.—Where a trade breaks up into more than two blocks the possible combinations increase rapidly with the number of blocks. In the case of a three block trade with blocks A, B, and C, some of the possible combinations would be as follows:

```
C                         C         B
B
A        A  B  C       A  B        A     C
No. 1      No. 2         No. 3       No. 4
```

With a four block trade the possible combinations would be much more than in a three block trade and so on.

Practical Working Arrangements of Blocks.—For any practical use it is doubtful if any combinations of block other than the straight series or parallel will serve any useful purpose. It may occasionally happen that some trade will call for some modified arrangement of either combination 1 or 2, but the chance is so unlikely that it may be dismissed by merely drawing the attention to the fact that such combinations are possible.

The Relation of the Blocks to Each Other.—The first step for the instructor is therefore to determine the relation of the blocks in his trade to each other. Here he may find any one of three possible combinations:
1. The blocks are all independent.
2. The blocks are all related to each other.
3. The blocks divide into two groups:
   (a) Independent blocks.
   (b) Groups of blocks that are dependent, but which form a group independent of any other block or group of blocks.

The third case is very uncommon so far as practical work goes. While such combinations can be worked out as a rule they run the thing down finer than is necessary for practical working purposes in getting out a line of instruction.

Some instructors tend to go into this matter of block arrangements altogether too finely: the result being a considerable increase in the complexity of the layout with no corresponding gain of importance in the efficiency of the instructional order resulting therefrom.

The Case of Independent Blocks: The Instruction Line.—Assume that we have a block with ten teaching jobs as indicated in the figure below:

A line drawn from the bottom of the diagram, indicates the order in which a learner will be instructed in the different jobs in the block. Call such a line an *instruction line*. Now if we have a second independent block, either the series or the parallel arrangement can be used.

BLOCK A.
10
9
8
7
6
5
4
3
2
1

BLOCK B.
10
9
8
7
6
5
4
3
2
1

BLOCKS A AND B IN SERIES.

BLOCK A.	BLOCK B.
10	10
9	9
8	8
7	7
6	6
5	5
4	4
3	3
2	2
1	1

BLOCKS A AND B IN PARALLEL.

Independent Blocks: Two Methods of Securing an Instructional Order.—Evidently an instructional order can be secured in the case of the two possible combinations given above in two ways:

We can draw the instruction line through the two blocks in series, and get the order of jobs as B1, B2, B3, B4, B5, B6, B7, B8, B9, B10, A1, A2, A3, A4, A5, A6, A7, A8, A9, A10, or the line might be drawn through all the number one jobs in both blocks, then the number two jobs, then the number three jobs, etc., giving us the instructional order of: A1, B1, A2, B2, A3, B3, A4, B4, A5, B5, A6, B6, A7, B7, A8, B8, A9, B9, A10, B10. In either case we have all the jobs in the two blocks listed out in an instructional order, but a very different order. The first order of jobs is commonly said to be obtained by the method of *block progression*, the second order by the use of the method of *spiral progression*.

The Block and Spiral Methods of Progression.—Evidently these two methods of securing an instructional order can be used whenever a trade consists of two or more independent blocks and in that case only. If the blocks are all related there is no question of choice of method: that of series progression must be used; but whenever there are independent blocks the choice between the two methods must be made. While no fixed rule can be given and each instructor must decide for himself, the following suggestions may be of service:

Conditions Indicating the Desirability of the Use of the Spiral Method.—In general it is considered that the spiral method is the best when it is intended to give what is often called an "all around training" for a given trade, that is, when the intention is to start with a green learner and instruct him in the entire trade. Thus, it is generally held that a course of instruction obtained by this method is the best to use where apprentices are to be trained to become journeymen, or in trade schools which aim at the same sort of complete training. It has the advantage that the learner is, at any given point in his progress approximately equally trained in all the different blocks of the complete course of instruction, so that should he be discharged from the training department at any point before the completion of the training course, and go into production work, he can be placed about equally well in any of a number of lines of work. It has, of course, the corresponding disadvantage that he is not so completely trained in any one block, or special branch of the trade. It is also true in general, that the spiral method lends itself to apprentice training in the so-called skilled shop trades, better than it does to so-called semi-skilled trades, where such trades show a multiblock layout, which is, however, not common.

From the instructional standpoint it has the advantage that the learner in his progression through a course of instruction derived by this method gets all the jobs with the least learning difficulties first, those with the next least learning difficulties second and so on.

On the other hand the method of block progression lends itself best to a situation where the line of instruction obtained is to be used where it is desired to train a learner to be able to secure employment as a workman in some special branch of the trade, but it is not desired to train him so that he can start in on any one of as many branches as the length of his training will allow. Evidently a complete training in one block is better for a short time training period than a slight training in several blocks if it is desired that the learner shall make good on production work in as short a period of time as possible.

The Case of More Than Two Blocks.—The case of a multiblock trade of more than two blocks offers no special difficulties in getting out an effective instructional order except that greater complications are introduced by the number of the blocks. The method followed is the same, the instruction line being drawn through the blocks by either the method of the spiral or of the series progression and the successive jobs as indicated by the line being listed down into an instructional order.

Multiblock Trades.—The more highly skilled a trade the more likely it is to break up into blocks. The greater the number of special machines used the greater the number of blocks. The more nearly all the operations of a trade are carried on with the same sort of tools, or the same sort of materials, the more likely it is to be a single block trade. Semi-skilled trades are rarely multiblock. As already stated, single specialized jobs do not bring up the question either of blocking or of instructional order as between jobs.

Value of the Block.—Where blocking is possible it simplifies the problem of getting out an effective instructional order by making a preliminary grouping according to kinds of learning difficulties. Learning difficulties are of different kinds and when of the same kind, of different degrees of intensity. If grouping is first made according to kind of learning difficulties then the only problem inside any one group is degree of difficulty. Especially in highly complicated trades this method makes the laying out of the instructional order much easier than if an attempt were made to handle both degree and kind at the same time.

Conclusion and Summary.—This chapter deals only with the case of multiblock trades. Unless the trade is multiblock an instructor has no direct interest in it. Where we find that a trade is multiblock the matter of securing an effective instructional order that will include the jobs in all the blocks must be considered. The instructor must first consider whether the blocks are independent or related, then arrange his blocks accordingly. If all blocks are independent he must choose between the methods of block progression and spiral progression; if they are all related, he uses only the block progression. There is a chance that some of the blocks are related and that others are independent; in this case a more complicated arrangement of blocks will be required and it may even be true that the spiral method might be used for a group of blocks that were independent while the block progression method was used for that group and for the other blocks. Such complicated arrangements are, however, very unlikely, and are only mentioned by way of possibilities.

PART IV
HOW TO PUT IT OVER

CHAPTER XV

THE TRADE INSTRUCTOR

The Purpose of Instruction—given an instructor and a learner.—The instructor can do something which the learner cannot do, for example, he can set type, or wipe a joint, or run a machine tool, or make a dovetail joint or an arc weld, or he knows something which the learner does not know, for example, how to read a blueprint, or how to get the offset for turning a taper, or how to figure the amount of wire required for an electrical job.

In either case the problem is to impart, or "put over" that skill or that knowledge into the head or the hand of the learner, so that he can do the job that he could not do before, or knows what he did not know before.

To accomplish this result something must be done, some sort of procedure must be followed, that is, there must be some sort of an instructing process.

The Instructing Trade.—A man who knows how to do things but who is paid, not for just knowing them, but for putting them over to other people is an instructor. No matter how much he knows, or how good a workman he may be, his value as an instructor depends on how thoroughly and rapidly he can impart what he knows. (Imparting, not doing, is his job.) It therefore may be properly said that there is an instructor's "trade" just as much as there is a machinist's trade, or a printer's trade; and the instructor will be efficient in proportion as he knows *his* trade, that is, the *instructing* trade.

The Two Factors in Successful Instruction.—It is evident that the man who cannot impart what he knows cannot be a successful instructor. It is equally evident that the man who can impart but has nothing to impart is equally a failure —The successful instructor must therefore, (1) Thoroughly know what he is to teach and (2) be able to impart it effectively.

In industrial training this means that the instructor must know two trades—his own trade and the teaching trade—his own trade so that he will know what to teach and the teaching trade so that he will know how to teach it. Without a thorough command of *both* trades he will be a failure.

Theory and Practice in Teaching.—Behind the practice of any trade or profession lie the general principles of which each practice is an application. Each trade has its own tools, its own processes, its own methods. In proportion as a man knows the tools and processes of his trade and has acquired good judgment in selecting proper tools and processes for a given job he is a good workman and, to a considerable extent, his power to select and choose usually depends on his knowledge of the general principles on which the practice of his trade is based.

To the "rule of thumb" man each new job is a brand new problem, but the man who knows the principles of his trade will recognize that the new problem calls for an application of some general principles and he knows how those general principles should be applied to the best advantage in any particular case. He is therefore less likely to make mistakes and knows why he does that particular job as he does it.

This is equally true of the trade of instruction. The instructor familiar with the principles and methods, or "tools" of the teaching trade and practiced in applying them to given training problems can deal with any given problem (teaching job) much more effectively, rapidly and intelligently than can the rule of thumb instructor. He saves time, he saves energy and he does a better job.

The Trained vs. the Untrained Instructor.—The difference between the trained and the untrained instructor does not lie in the degree to which each has mastered what he proposes to teach. Often masters of their subject have proved to be very poor instructors. It used to be said of one of the greatest scientists in America on the faculty of one of the greatest universities, that he could not teach anybody anything. Thorough knowledge and mastery of what is to be taught is necessary for an instructor, but that alone will not make him an effective instructor. The difference between the individual who knows and the individual who can impart what he knows lies in the ability of the good instructor to teach or put over what he knows, and this in turn rests largely on his knowledge of the principles and methods of the instructing business, just as such knowledge of principles and methods and tools would make a good workman in any trade.

This instructing ability can be secured in various ways. Just as a trade may be "stolen" at the cost of spoiled machines and stock, so an instructor can steal his trade at the expense of his learners. Occasionally an individual seems to have the instinctive knack of teaching in a fairly effective way. In general, however, training shows as in other trades. The trained instructor shows his training in his ability to always use the most suitable methods, to save the most time and energy, and in his ability to organize his knowledge in the best way for instructional purposes. Moreover, the trained instructor, through his knowledge of principles, knows why he does things, and why some methods will work and some will not, in doing a given teaching job. He has the advantage of knowing the theory that lies behind his practice. Hence a competent workman who has been trained as an instructor, on taking up instructing work, is at a great advantage over the untrained individual, who may have an equal command of the trade, because he is able to impart effectively what he knows, as soon as he begins to instruct.

Instructor Training Courses.—The purpose of instructor training courses is not to attempt to teach a man anything about the practice of his trade. His presence in the course guarantees that he knows his job, so far as doing the job is concerned. The purpose of the training is to acquaint the man with the principles, practice, and methods of tools of the new trade which he proposes to follow: that of an imparter, instructor, or teacher, and to give him an opportunity to learn to apply these principles, methods, and practices to the problem of instructing learners in the trade of which he is already a master.

In a number of cases special instructor training courses have been established to train competent mechanics to apply the principles of the teaching trade to the putting over of their own trade, and have been of considerable assistance to instructors in trades and to foremen who had to break in green help. Among the more recent instructor training courses that have been operated have been those conducted by the Emergency Fleet Corporation in connection with the training of shipyard workers.

PRODUCTION AND INSTRUCTION

Purpose or Aim.	To turn out a definite article from a given piece of stock.	To instruct a given individual in a definite thing.
Man Responsible.	Workman.	Instructor.
Material worked upon.	Stock new or partially worked up.	Learner, green or partially trained.
Procedure.	Successive production operations in a determined order.	Successive instruction steps in a determined order.
Means used.	Suitable tools and machines.	Suitable methods of instruction.
Character of product tested by.	Inspection of product.	Inspection of learners' ability to do the thing that the lesson was to teach him.

CHAPTER XVI

WHAT INSTRUCTION IS

Methods of Instruction the Teacher's Tools.—If instruction is a "trade" the instructor must be regarded as a skilled workman whose "job" is to turn out a "product" (men who do know or can do) from "stock" (men who do not know or who cannot do) by an intelligent selection of tools and a skillful use of those selected (methods of instruction). Just as in other trades the sort of material worked upon and the sort of product required has led to the development of tools which the good workman uses with judgment, selecting at each step in his job, and for different jobs, and different kinds of stock, the tool which will give the best results, and always using that tool with skill and judgment, so in the instruction trade there have been developed various ways of teaching or *methods of instruction*, with which the good instructor is familiar and which he knows how to use with intelligence, selecting in each case the particular method best adapted to the particular teaching job at hand and to the characteristics of the learner whom he has to teach.

How Methods have been Developed.—Just as in the different trades it has been found that certain operations performed in certain order with certain tools and machines yield the best results in turning out a certain product from a particular kind of stock, so in teaching, it has been found that certain ways of going at the teaching problem recognizing certain steps in dealing with the ideas to be taught, and carrying out these steps in a certain order, yield the quickest and best results with given kind of learner who is to be taught certain things for a certain purpose.

Without going into details at this stage it is evident that an apprentice greatly interested in trade processes but not in books might need different treatment from one of a "bookish" type of mind—that the problem of teaching trade processes would be a different one from that of teaching abstract mathematics—and that in each case the way in which the teaching work was carried on would be determined by what was to be taught and who it was to be taught to.

Effective Instruction.—Whatever the methods adopted, the measure of the effectiveness of the instruction is determined by—

(a) The fact that at the completion of the instructional process the learner has completely grasped the new ideas, or can do the new piece of work.

(b) The degree to which this result was obtained with the least expenditure of time.

(c) The degree to which this result was obtained with the least expenditure of energy and effort on the part of both learner and instructor.

It is evident that the first condition must be met;—if the learner has not "got" what the instructor intended to teach him, the whole proposition has failed, the instructor has "fallen down on his job," and he must either try it again and stick to it until the man has "got" the thing to be taught or admit that he made a mistake in attempting to teach that particular thing to that particular man at that particular time. On the other hand, the instructor may have succeeded in "putting over" the lesson, yet may have used such unsuitable methods that he may be properly criticized for having used up much more of his time and of the man's time than would be needed had that particular instructing job been carried out in a "workmanlike" manner. Both conditions (a) and (b) may have been met and yet the instructor be open to criticism for having made the instruction unnecessarily "hard" by going at the teaching job in such a way that unnecessary energy has been expended either on his part or on the part of the learner.

One Common Error is to Consider Condition (" a ") Only.— Many instructors feel that if the learner has eventually mastered the subject of the lesson to a reasonable degree the whole matter is settled since condition (a) in the last paragraph has been met. They often fail to regard matters affecting unnecessary expenditure of time and energy, both on the part of the pupil, as being important. It is a fact, however, that the work of a skillful instructor differs from that of a poor instructor largely in the degree to which he is able to "put over" the lesson in the most efficient way; and, in order to do this he must be able to use proper methods of instruction intelligently and skillfully.

Another common error is to confuse certain parts of an instructor's work with instruction proper. This confusion is particularly common in connection with telling, showing, and dealing, which are not, in themselves, instructing, but which untrained instructors often confuse with the instructional part of their work.

Teaching and Telling.—One of the most common errors of the untrained teacher is to imagine that telling is teaching, that if he merely tells a learner how to do something he has taught that man something. Telling is often a necessary part of the instructor's work, but mere telling never constitutes real instruction. If an instructor says to a man, "This is a dog," or "This is a monkey wrench," the man has been *told* something, but he has not been taught anything. It is undoubtedly true, especially in training green men, that a considerable amount of telling is required, but that part of the instruction work should not be confounded with instruction proper. An instructor must do many things beside instruct. One of the signs of a trained instructor is that he knows when he is telling and when he is instructing, and that he knows when to tell and when to instruct—and one of the greatest reasons for poor instruction is that a poor teacher does not know how to make this distinction.

Why Telling is not Instruction.—Instruction is not telling because instruction is always accompanied by some action on the part of the learner. He either *thinks* or *does*. Simply telling him the name of a dog or a monkey wrench, and stopping there does not require any "come back" or, in teaching language, "reaction," on the part of the man. But we can *teach* a man how to use a dog on a lathe job or the proper way to place a monkey wrench on a nut because he can be made to think about the job or to do the job or to think about the job while he is doing it.

Telling is not Knowing.—The converse of the above statement is equally true. The ability of a learner to merely tell about a thing is no evidence that he understands the thing or can do it. Suppose it is desired to ascertain if a man knows a wrench. If the instructor merely says to him "What is the name of this?" and the man tells him that it is a wrench there is no evidence that that man is using any faculty except memory. But if the instructor says to the man, "Pick out a wrench from that kit," and the man picks out a wrench and not a screw driver, we have some evidence that the names are connected in the man's mind with the proper tool, as distinguished from other tools. Untrained instructors frequently say, "Do you understand this?" and when the learner says "yes" the instructor thinks that he has taught something when, in fact, there is no evidence that the learner has been taught anything. The trained instructor is much less likely to fall into such errors because his training helps him to avoid them, and he knows that they are errors.

Drilling is not Instructing.—Drilling in the school sense means requiring a learner to repeat an operation (mental or manual) a considerable number of times with the aim of making that thing an automatic "come back." An instructor for example, requires a learner to repeat the words "The decimal equivalent of an eighth of an inch is one hundred and twenty-five thousandths of an inch" for five hundred times with the aim of getting him into such a mental condition that whenever he heard "an eighth of an inch" he will automatically think "one hundred and twenty-five thousandths." This would be a pure drill process. While work of this sort has its place its value depends largely on the sort of learner and the subject of the lesson—it is doubtful if it has much value in industrial training. It is merely desired to point out here that drill work of this character should not be confounded with instruction. Poor instructors often think that they are teaching when they are merely drilling.

Why Drilling is not Instructing.—Drilling is not instructing because it assures no intelligent thinking on the part of the learner. A parrot could be drilled in the decimal equivalent of 1–8 as well as a learner. A learner could be taught to figure out this value as required, or use a table of equivalents intelligently. The parrot could not.

Drilling and Repetition Work.—Drilling should be distinguished from repetition work, where a man may be asked to deal with a series of problems involving application of the same principle or to make a number of similar articles in the shop. Under proper conditions repetition work may be an important part of the training process, as will be discussed later. Repetition work involves a steady gain by the learner either in mental or manual skill, until he reaches what has been called the "saturation" point: that is, he can do the job as well and as quickly as he will ever be able to do it. Drilling aims at a purely automatic "come back" only, without conscious thought or intelligently directed work.

Instructing and Showing.—The same statement may be made as to the relation of instructing and showing. This comes up particularly in shop instruction. Showing a man how to do a thing, while necessary, is not, in itself instructing that man; though, as pointed out elsewhere, it may, under certain conditions, be made a part of the instructing process. A man who is merely shown does not *have* to think. He may or he may not. The common complaint of the poor or untrained instructor that he showed the learner how to do something and then the fellow could not do it, and therefore is stupid is due to this confusion between instructing and showing. The man has failed to learn, not because he is stupid, but because he has not been really taught, and the blame for the failure rests not on the man but on the instructor.

Why Showing is not Instructing.—Showing is not instructing because as in the case of telling, simply showing involves no necessary activity, mental or manual, on the learners' part. By the use of various devices already described (such as the use of the informational line of approach in certain steps of the lesson), this activity can be secured and telling may become a part of the instructing process.

CHAPTER XVII

THE INSTRUCTING OPERATION

THE LESSON

Preliminary—What is a Lesson.—In its simplest sense a lesson is a teaching job. In teaching practice the term lesson is used to designate the entire procedure followed in teaching or "putting over" some specific thing. This specific thing which is to be taught may be called the "instruction unit," or, more commonly, the "content" or the "subject" of the lesson. The use of these terms is entirely independent of the character of the teaching unit. It makes no difference whether the subject of the lesson or instruction unit is how to erect a perpendicular to a given line, how to set a stick of type, how to set up a job on a machine or how to saw a board off square, there is a teaching unit to put over or a lesson to teach. If any one of these teaching units is to be "put over" to somebody we must have a process of instruction; that is, a lesson must be taught.

If we think of the instructor as a workman, the learner as stock, the steps as operations, and the methods as tools, we have a close resemblance, between the procedure for production and the instructional procedure.

The Aim Must be Specific.—The subject of the lesson determines the whole subsequent procedure and hence must be given first consideration, and must be clearly defined; that is, it must be specific. A failure on the part of the instructor to determine exactly what he proposes to teach, because, while he thinks that he knows what he is going to teach, he has not thought his teaching job through to the point of knowing exactly what he is going to put over is one of the most common causes of inefficient instruction, and the learner is often blamed for not "catching on" when the real trouble lies with the failure of the instructor to definitely formulate the subject of the lesson. A lesson whose aim was "to teach something about something to somebody" will not be effective. Suppose an instructor states that he proposes to teach a lesson on the automobile, but he doesn't know whether it is on ignition, or timing, or starting, or on clutch control. There is little chance that a lesson starting with so vague an idea as to what is to be accomplished will be either profitable or efficient. It cannot be well planned or efficiently carried out. On the other hand, suppose the instructor says "I am going to teach just how to lay off a 90° angle," or "I am going to teach the proper method of starting and stopping an electric drill" he has laid down a definitely specific aim and hence can plan and teach an efficient lesson.

The Learner Must be Ready for that Particular Lesson.—The determination of method, content and aim all center around the man to be taught. The aim of any lesson is determined, in general, by the aim of the course of instruction or training of which that instruction unit is a part. Whatever the aim or the content or the method of a given lesson, it can only be taught effectively at a certain point in the learner's progress and development.

The teacher must therefore be able to "locate" a given teaching unit with regard to what has already been taught and what is still to be taught to make the learner competent in that particular line of work, and see to it that the given unit of instruction comes to the learner at the right point in his training. This part of the instruction problem is fully discussed in Part III.

The Content Must be Teachable.—By this is meant that it must be possible to thoroughly accomplish the aim of the lesson under the proposed working conditions. Thus it is desired to complete the lesson in a certain time or place, or by certain methods. The content must be so selected that these conditions can be met. For example, suppose it were desired to teach a learner how to make a Western Union splice, or how to set up a job in a machine lathe, and it was planned to teach that lesson in five minutes,—evidently it could not be done. Either the time must be increased or the amount to be taught must be cut down. Or it is proposed to teach the same lesson in a room outside of the shop, or without wire and pliers, so that the instructor can merely describe how the job should be done, that is, he can only talk about it. Under these conditions that job must evidently be taught by such a poor method that it is practically unteachable.

Such errors as those cited above are easily avoided, but a much more serious error, common to most new instructors, consists in undertaking to teach too much in one lesson, instead of breaking the content up into a series of sufficiently small teaching units. The angle smith instructor undertakes to teach a green man "how to strike" in one lesson or instruction unit, or "how to run a fire" in one "bite," in one lesson, the result being failure because the instruction unit is too great to be taught in one lesson. Each would involve a series of lessons, each dealing with a small portion of all that the man must be finally taught for example: on firing—No. 1 Building up, No. 2 Cleaning out, No. 3 Operating.

The Instructing Process a Series of "Operations."—The instructing process consists of a series of steps or "operations," carried on in a certain order. In any training process these "operations" are found and they are always in the same order. Regardless of the time consumed, a lesson is not completed until all of these operations have been carried through successfully and in the proper order. A lesson therefore means simply going through all the necessary steps in an instruction process with one instruction unit.

The lesson should not be confused with the fact that men and instructors may, under some conditions, meet at certain fixed times. An instructor may teach a man several lessons during one morning. The two ideas of a working period and a lesson are in no way connected. It is a fact that a good instructor will try to complete any teaching job as a "continuous process" for obvious reasons. He would rather not have the lesson broken into two or more parts with an interval during which his man is thinking of something else, but the continuous lesson is not absolutely necessary, although highly advisable in the interests of efficiency.

The Four Instructional Operations.—Different authorities on teaching have divided the lesson into different numbers of steps, but the following arrangement is one of the simplest for emergency training instruction. According to this plan, each complete teaching lesson calls for four steps, or teaching operations known as step 1, Preparation, step 2, Presentation, step 3, Application and step 4, Testing (or Inspection). These steps, are always carried out in the order given—The purpose of step 1 is to get the learner ready to be instructed, of step 2 to instruct him, of step 3 to check up errors, and of step 4 to give a final inspection of the instruction job.

Who Conducts these "Operations"—The Learner or the Instructor?—In general, under all conditions, the instructor must control and direct the instruction process, but a careful distinction must be drawn between the instructor as a director and the instructor as a demonstrator. As director he occupies much the position of a foreman directing workmen. The foreman does not do the work,—the men do it. In the same way, the instruction will be efficient in proportion as the learners do the work or the thinking. One of the most common signs of poor teaching is that the instructor does the thinking or does the work—the learners passively following. That is, the instructor shows or demonstrates and the learners merely imitate.

The problem of the teacher is to see that each learner performs the successive teaching operations *on himself*. What he gains is by virtue of *his own activity*—mental or manual—and from the manual or mental activity of another he gains nothing.

The teacher, therefore, is not the driver, but the skilled director of the learner's activity. He is skilled in so handling each teaching problem that the learner works and thinks effectively toward the desired end—the accomplishment of the aim of the lesson. In order to do this he must control the situation at each step, but often without the man's knowledge. He must so control situations that the man thinks in a certain way and towards certain points, but he must do that thinking spontaneously and naturally. As will be pointed out in the following pages, in carrying out the instruction process the instructor takes the *initiative* in certain steps and the learner takes the *initiative* in others. The instructor knows this, but the learner often does not.

Concentration on the Lesson.—It has already been stated that the aim of a lesson must be definitely determined. Even where this has been done there is still great danger of lack of *conciseness*. That is, the instructor does not stick to the particular job that he started out to do. Before taking up the detailed discussion, two common errors should be noted:—

In handling a given lesson the instructor does not confine that lesson to the given subject. He starts to teach a certain thing, but somewhere in the lesson he undertakes to teach some other things not included in the particular unit that he is handling. For example, the lesson is on how to sharpen a certain tool, or how to sew on a button. During the progress of the lesson the instructor brings in something about the manufacture of tool steel or something about button holes. This sort of thing is very common with certain instructors and is bad practice; any lesson should be held strictly to its subject. This procedure is sometimes justified on the ground that it interests the learner, but it requires long experience and teaching skill to know when it is safe to do it; in general, it is a dangerous proposition.

In carrying on the successive steps or operations of a lesson, the instructor does not stick to one step at a time—he mixes them up—he tries to teach a learner something new and at the same time attempts to find out if he has learned something which has already been taught. Each step is a teaching "job" and the effective teacher will do one job at a time.

The Methods Must be Suitable.—As is pointed out later in detail various methods have been developed for carrying on the instructional process just as various tools and machines have been developed for carrying out production. Just as suitable tools and machines must be used to get the best results on a given production job so suitable methods will give best results on any given instruction job. One of the chief distinctions between the good and the poor instructor is that the former knows how to select suitable methods of instruction, and the latter does not.

The choice of a given method in dealing with a given teaching problem must rest with the judgment of the instructor. While general rules can be given, they will not take the place of experience. Just as an experienced workman will do a better job than an apprentice, although the apprentice may know all the operations and machines, so with experience in instruction will come a sense of what to do which will gradually develop into what has been called, the "art of instructing," as distinguished from the theory of that profession.

Supervised vs. Unsupervised Training.—If at the end of the period of instruction a man is shot out into the shop without any further assistance, he will get his trade intelligence very slowly and ineffectively, but if he is still under the supervision of a "trainer" the training process will go on very much more rapidly and effectively. Under emergency training conditions an instructor must, in the sense indicated above, be a trainer as well as an instructor. By instructing the learner in the operations and in the technical knowledge and then training for trade intelligence, shop training can be accomplished in less time than by undertaking to depend upon the instructing process alone.

It is evident that in most cases the man must be trained so that he can "pull together" his trade ability, his technical knowledge and his trade experiences to meet the demands of different trade situations. This process of pulling together, or assembling these factors corresponds to what is known, in general school work as the generalization stage of instruction.

One of our greatest educational philosophers has said that a man is educated in proportion as he can summon all his resources and use them effectively in dealing with a given situation. Effective shop training therefore comes through effective *instruction* followed by effective *training*.

CHAPTER XVIII

DETAILED DISCUSSION OF STEPS IN THE LESSON. STEP 1. PREPARATION

Preliminary.—The different steps in the process of instruction have already been pointed out, but for convenience are repeated here.

1. Preparation.
2. Presentation.
3. Application.
4. Inspection.

This section deals with step 1.

The First Step in the Lesson. Preparation.—The first problem of the instructor is to establish what may be called a foundation for the teaching of the new idea which he intends to "put over" in that particular lesson. This is accomplished by getting the learner to think about some things which he already knows which have something to do with the problem which he is to be taught or the job which he is to be taught to do. He has in his mind all sorts of recollections of past experiences and observations, most of which have nothing to do with the subject of the lesson in hand, but, except in very rare cases, he has, among those recollections some which have a bearing on the subject of the lesson. Thus suppose the lesson was on the operation of the brakes of an electric car. In almost any community it could be assumed that the learner had seen a car, had seen it stop and knew that the motorman did something to stop it. By getting the learner to think about the problem of stopping the car as a job that somebody had to do somehow and for which some provision must be made in the mechanism of the car, his attention could be centered on that particular set of observations (relating to the stopping of the car) and he could be prevented from thinking about a lot of other things which he might know about the car but which have nothing to do with the stopping of a car, and which the instructor knows have no bearing on the aim of the proposed lesson.

By *preparation* the Instructor therefore, in some way, makes the learner think about certain particular things which will aid him in comprehending the particular new thing which is to be taught. This may be called a process whereby the learner is led to establish in his own mind "contact points" between what he already knows and the new ideas which the instructor plans to have him add to what he knows through the lesson that is to be taught. It will be noted that, in carrying out this first step, it is assumed that somewhere in his past experience, the learner has had some kind of an experience or has some knowledge which can be used as a foundation for building up the proposed lesson. It should also be clear that, while the instructor knows, in a general way, what he can get from the learner, and selects those ideas which he thinks that he can best use for a teaching base, the learner is himself usually unconscious of the relation of what he finds himself thinking about, to the subject of the lesson which the instructor has planned to teach.

The problem of the instructor in this first instructional operation or step is, by the use of some suitable method, to start the learner thinking about something which he knows and which the instructor can "tie" the lesson to. Even in the simplest form of instruction on semi-skilled work the need for this step exists and its omission will increase the difficulty of instruction, and usually renders it inefficient.

Elementary and Derived Lessons.—Where the ideas which the instructor uses for the teaching base must be drawn from what the learner has picked up in his life outside of anything that the instructor may have taught him, (and so has to guess that he has it) we have what may be called an *elementary* or *primary* lesson. Where the ideas for the teaching base can be drawn from something which the instructor has taught the learner, usually in some primary lesson on the same line of work, the new lesson will "mesh" into the old, the instructor will not have to guess as to available ideas for the teaching base and the lesson may be called a *derived* or *secondary* lesson.

Preparation Must be Completed before Presentation is Started.—The success of the following steps in the lesson is dependent on this first step being thoroughly carried out, and the instructor must be sure that this is the case before proceeding farther. One of the most common errors in teaching is the failure to thoroughly prepare the learner for the additional material to be put over in step 2[1] (Presentation), and is usually due to the fact that the instructor is in too much of a hurry; he "skimps" this step. As a result step 2 fails, this comes out in step 3, and the whole job has to be done over again. It pays to make a good job of step 1.

No standard rule can be given for determining when learners are prepared. An experienced instructor can tell—an inexperienced one had best err, if at all, on the safe side and, if anything, over-prepare.

Preparation Gives no Additional Information.—It should be clearly understood that, in the work of preparation as commonly carried out, no new ideas are added to those already in the learner's mind, and in no case are any of the new ideas which are to be taught in the lesson touched upon at this stage. The instructor does not undertake to add any new ideas to those already in the learner's mind. He does, (often by skilful questioning) lead the learner to select from all the ideas in his mind certain particular ideas which he has consciously or unconsciously "picked up" at some previous time. These ideas are those which the instructor has determined to make the teaching basis of the lesson in hand.

Exceptional Instances.—In rare instances when there is absolutely nothing that can be used as a teaching base the instructor must provide something that can be used for that purpose. Experience has shown that this is rarely necessary in trade training especially if the instructor is experienced and ingenious. When a teaching base cannot be found the learner must be given an experience which can be used. Until this has been done it is practically useless to try to teach the lesson. Of course when an instructor is forced to create a base, additional time and energy are consumed.

[1] See table, page 148.

In this Step the Instructor Takes the Initiative.—In step 1 it will be noted that the instructor takes the initiative. He knows what he wants to get the man to thinking about, and he so directs the man's thinking that he does think about these things to the exclusion of all other things. But the learner cannot be made to think of these things merely by commanding "Think about so and so." These things must be *suggested*. This is where the skill comes in in this step of the lesson. The man must be stimulated to think or to recall previous knowledge or experiences, and his mental activity directed by a method which makes him unconscious that he is being directed. The most usual method of accomplishing this result is by a certain kind of questioning which may be termed "suggestive questioning," whose purpose is not to secure information, but to arouse and direct the learner's thinking. Sometimes the instructor will use some incident or tell some story as a part of this step. This latter method of stimulating and directing the thinking of an audience is often used by public speakers to good advantage. A man is speaking on juvenile crime, and he begins "This morning I saw a boy arrested for stealing apples. What are we going to do with him?" his object being to get his audience to thinking about the subject on which he is going to speak.

CHAPTER XIX

DETAILED DISCUSSION OF STEPS IN THE LESSON. STEP 2. PRESENTATION

Presentation. Step 2 in the Lesson.—Having brought a learner to the point where he is thinking about such portions of his previous experiences or knowledge as will be of value in teaching the proposed lesson, according to the teaching plan, the next step is to lead him to "get" the new ideas which the instructor desires to "tack on" to what he already knows, and this step is now carried out by the use of some suitable method.

The Function of Presentation is to Add the New Ideas to those Already in the Learner's Mind.—If the work of preparation has been properly carried out, the man now has in his mind certain ideas or certain pictures which the instructor, in planning the lesson, determined would serve him best as a base for teaching the subject of that lesson. The next step is therefore, by the use of a suitable method, to add to the ideas which are in the learner's mind the new ideas embodied in the subject of the lesson. Various methods of instruction are discussed in detail later, but it is necessary that a method of instruction suitable to the subject of the lesson be selected: For example, if the aim of the lesson were to teach a man to think intelligently about the subject of the lesson, it is evident that a different method would have to be employed from that which would be used if the aim of the lesson were merely to instruct him in the correct method of doing a job, where no thinking or judgment was required. A skilful instructor, out of his experience, will always select a method which is best adapted to the aim and the subject of the lesson.

The distinction between the aim of step 1 and step 2 must be clearly understood. As already pointed out, step 1, Preparation, does not aim to add anything to the man's knowledge or skill, but merely to get him to thinking exclusively about certain things which the instructor has already determined can be best used for a teaching base. Step 2, however, has for its aim the imparting of additional knowledge to the man or giving him additional training. At the close of step 1 he knows no more than he did at the beginning of the lesson. At the close of step 2, the teaching unit should have been put over. At this stage in the process of instruction there is however no evidence that he can either apply what he has learned or that he has thoroughly grasped the subject of the lesson. In fact, it may be safely assumed that he has not; that there are certain weak points where the teaching has not been entirely effective. To leave the teaching operation at this stage would mean that the instructor would neither know that he had taught efficiently nor that the man could apply what had been taught effectively; hence the necessity for the remaining steps in the lesson.

"Sticking to the Job" in Presentation.—As already pointed out, the whole organization of the lesson is determined by the character of the instruction unit. The method of instruction is determined by aim, subject, and characteristics of the individual to be taught. While on the one hand all that it is proposed to present to the learner in the way of new ideas or new knowledge is given during this step in the lesson, the succeeding steps being devoted to what may be called "checking up and inspecting," it is necessary that this should be a clean cut piece of work and that nothing should be considered during this step which is not included in the instruction meant to be taught in that particular lesson.

Some illustrations may make this point clearer.—For example, consider the case of instructing a green man in the care of the fire in the blacksmith's shop. The instruction unit is on building up. The instructor in presenting this lesson brings in a lot of discussion about operations in heating the iron, which belongs in another instruction unit. He has not stuck to his job, and to that extent has messed things up.

Effective Order in Presentation.—In this step of the lesson a series of ideas must be presented to the learner, and these ideas must be successively presented in the most effective order, this order having been previously determined. An efficient teacher will pay a great deal of attention to using an effective order in presentation and the failure to do this is a very common error of untrained instructors.

The Question of Emphasis.—Among the ideas or operations which are to be taught during this step of the lesson, some are unquestionably more important than others, and the efficient instructor will recognize this by emphasizing the more important ideas more strongly than the less important points. For example, in training a heater boy the necessity of picking out a rivet at the right heat would be emphasized more than the proper method of picking it up with the tongs.

Effective training requires skill on the part of the teacher, in properly analyzing the teaching unit with regard to emphasis, and considerable practice is often required before it can be done effectively.

Limited Content.—Almost all instructors err on the side of trying to include too much in the subject of one lesson. If a given thing is to be taught, it is far better to cut it up into a series of small lessons than to undertake to teach one elaborate lesson; for example, if it were desired to teach a man to operate an electric drill it would be far better to plan one lesson on stopping and starting, one lesson on catching the drill point in the prick punch hole, one on what to do when the drill sticks, etc., rather than to undertake to teach the whole job in one lesson.

CHAPTER XX

DETAILED DISCUSSION OF STEPS IN THE LESSON. STEP 3. APPLICATION

Preliminary.—If step 1 be considered as putting in the foundation and step 2 as building the house on that foundation, this third step may be thought of as equivalent to a builder's inspection. So far as anybody knows the house is all right but before turning it over to the owner it is carefully inspected, defects or omissions noted and corrected, inspected again, and this process is carried on until the builder is sure that everything is according to the specifications.

In the same way, in carrying out the instructional process, the instructor has laid the teaching base in step 1, he has presented the new material in step 2. So far as he knows he has done a good instruction job, but in this step he puts the learner through a trial inspection that is, he puts the man at work on whatever was given in step 2, and checks up along two lines—(1) Does he know it, and (2) Can he do it.

This step therefore serves two purposes.

(1) Since what the man has learned is of no value to him unless he can apply it, and since power to apply a thing is different from simply knowing it, he must be trained in actually applying, or putting into practice what was presented to him in the preceding step of the lesson, application.

(2) A second, and equally important purpose to be accomplished by this step is to check up the degree to which the learner has grasped all the points in the lesson which has been taught, whether processes or ideas. From this standpoint this step, application, corresponds to a road bed inspection on a railroad whose purpose is to detect "bad spots" which should be fixed. In the same way, no matter how carefully the man has been taught, there will be some "weak

points," some "holes in the road" which must be located and made good before going any further. A common illustration of this would be an arithmetic lesson on interest at six per cent. After the teacher has presented the method of doing it, he will then have the pupil solve a series of problems in interest at six per cent. If the lesson were on figuring the offset for a taper, the learner would then be given a series of problems in figuring offsets. If the teaching unit were on how to correctly mark templates, the learner would be given a template to mark. If it were on bolting up, the man would be given a bolting up job. During this process of application, however, the instructor watches the man while he is working at the job, notes where he fails to grasp some points in the problem, or has not "caught on" to some part of an operation, and gives him additional instruction on that part then and there.

The instructor is therefore using this application step not only to give the learner training in applying, but also to find weak points in the man's knowledge or comprehension of the subject of the lesson. At the close of this step the instructor should be sure that the man has thoroughly "got" the lesson which is to be taught. The carrying out of this step effectively requires care and skill on the part of the instructor to determine just when to assist the learner and just how to assist him; but in no case should the instructor do the work for the man. Of course he might show him some particular step in the process which he did not understand, but the man should be required in this step to go through the whole job and to go through it a sufficient number of times so that the instructor is reasonably sure that all points have been mastered.

CHAPTER XXI

DETAILED DISCUSSION OF STEPS IN THE LESSON. STEP 4. TESTING

Preliminary.—As already stated the purpose of this step is to afford an opportunity for a final tryout or inspection. The instructor should regard the result of the test as more or less a failure if the learner fails to do this work unaided. It indicates that the teaching process was not well carried out, that the instructor's judgment was incorrect and the teaching must be repeated. While this will often occur in practice, it is nevertheless true in theory that if the lessons were perfectly planned and perfectly taught inspection would show that all learners could successfully meet the test with one hundred per cent. efficiency.

Each step must be complete before the next step is started. In carrying out the three teaching steps just discussed, any failure on the part of the instructor to complete one step before he takes up the next step results in an accumulation of difficulties. If the men are not properly prepared in step 1, they will not be properly taught in step 2. If they do not come up to step 3, thoroughly taught, the process of application will require too much time and too much energy. If application has not been properly carried out the men will fail in final test step 4. The instructor should therefore be as certain as is possible to see that each step has been thoroughly carried out before he starts the next one.

The Aim of this Step.—If the instructional process has been properly carried on up to this point the instructor is ready to take a chance that the learner has been properly taught, and if he is right the teaching job is finished, the learner is instructed, he can do what the instructor intended that he should be able to do or he knows what the instructor intended that he should know. The teaching unit has been put over and the teaching process is at an end. But while the instructor may feel sure that this is the case he does not know it because this fact cannot be assumed. During the preceding step he undoubtedly found many cases where additional instruction on some parts of the lesson was necessary, and he therefore has assisted or directed the man more or less during that step. Although he carried on this phase of the instruction process until, in his judgment, the man had got the entire unit that was to be taught, nevertheless he has been going over it piecemeal, and not as a whole.

He cannot, therefore, assume that, unaided and undirected the man who is under inspection can apply intelligently the subject of the teaching unit. That unaided, and absolutely on his own feet he can go through the whole process correctly.

This step, therefore, may be regarded as fulfilling a function strictly comparable to that of final inspection. The instructor must now stop being an instructor and, becoming an inspector, proceed to inspect the results of his teaching by testing in some suitable way, the ability of the learner to do the entire job alone.

CHAPTER XXII

SECURING TRADE INTELLIGENCE

Completing the Training Process.—The proceeding sections dealt with the four instructional steps which must be carried through in order, in putting over any given teaching unit, such as, how to know when a rivet is heated to the right temperature. Each lesson should have been based upon some specific unit. If the instruction has been properly carried out the learner has been taught all the specific things that he needs to know. When this point is reached the *instruction* process is completed but the *training* process is not completed. The learner is in the same condition as a thoroughly equipped shop having all necessary equipment. All of the material, tools and equipment would not be required for any one job, but it is all required for all the jobs that the shop has to do. For any particular job a selection must be made from all the equipment of the special machines, tools, etc., that would be required on that particular job.

The properly instructed learner, in the same way, has at his command all the things which he has been taught, for the doing of any job in his special occupation. Just as the material and equipment for a given job must be picked out, so the properly trained man must be able, to pick out from all the things that he knows about his trade certain particular things that he knows or can do that will enable him to do a given job correctly: that is, he must be able to select intelligently.

Evidently this power of intelligent selection of the certain parts of his knowledge and the certain portions of his skill could not be obtained by teaching the man any number of specific teaching units. The instructing process has done all it can do. This is where it "gets off." The learner is still to be completely trained.

The ability to pick out the proper material and equipment for a given job does not come from simply knowing what material is on hand and the uses of this material; but does come from a wide shop experience. Jobs differ. The man who makes the selections must be *trained* through shop experience as well as instructed.

In practice all jobs are not standardized. That is, under working conditions varying situations arise that require more than a mere knowledge of how to perform the operations. In the case of the bolter-up, no two plates can be handled in the same way. One plate springs one way and another a different way. The crane operator meets new situations continually.

In connection with trade development modifications are continually being introduced. It is practically impossible to instruct a man in the exact way in which he should deal with every situation that will come up in his occupation. This would mean an endless instruction job.

Training vs. Instruction.—Through *instruction* the learner is equipped as thoroughly as is practicable with the things that he needs to know and to be able to do. His *training must be completed* before he can intelligently do the various jobs connected with his occupation. He lacks power to select or to pick out from all the skills, knowledge, etc., in which he has been instructed, and from past experiences, those which he must use in dealing with those conditions which surround the doing of the job itself.

This power to intelligently select, or to "use your head" is often called *trade intelligence* and can only be secured through a training process; not through an instructional process.

A man is trained by going up against a series of situations which must be dealt with by exercising this power of selection. Some men are trained more than others and are the sort of men who are characterized as "using their heads on the job."

This training can only be secured through experience—that is, by doing a lot of jobs under varying conditions.

PART V
METHODS OF INSTRUCTION

CHAPTER XXIII

METHODS THAT CAN BE USED IN THE FIRST STEP OF THE LESSON

Preliminary.—The preceding part described the four instructing operations and explained the use of each operation, or, as they are commonly called, steps. There are various *methods* or ways of putting over each of these steps. Each step can be put over in more than one way—that is, different methods can be used for each step just as different tools might be used to carry out a given operation in the shop. In putting over any given lesson an instructor uses for each step the method that he judges will give the best results under the circumstances. The kind of a lesson, whether technical or production, the type of the lesson, whether elementary or derived, the kind of learner, the instructing conditions, the proposed line of approach, all must be taken into account in deciding what method to use in putting through any step in a given lesson. This part describes the various methods that may be used for each of the four steps in the instructing process.

The names of these methods are shown in the table on page 148.

METHODS THAT MAY BE USED IN STEP 1

Preliminary.—In the preparatory step the following methods are common teaching practice:

(1) The method of suggestive questioning.
(2) The method of the suggestive illustration or demonstration.
(3) The method of giving the learner an experience which will direct his thoughts to the ideas which the teacher wishes to make his teaching base.

POSSIBLE METHODS FOR DIFFERENT STEPS IN THE INSTRUCTING PROCESS BY THE LINES OF APPROACH

	Development.	Informational.
Step 1. Preparation. Foundation.	The suggestive question. Demonstration. Illustration. Experience.	The informational question. Demonstration. Illustration. Experience.
Step 2. Presentation. Putting over.	Demonstration. Illustration. Experiment.	Demonstration. Illustration. Lecture.
Step 3. Application. Checking up.	On the job. Discussion. Recitation. Written Test. Examination.	On the job. Recitation. Written Test. Examination.
Step 4. Inspection. Final Test.	On the job. Recitation. Examination.	On the job. Recitation. Examination.

Method of Carrying Out this Step by the Use of Questions.—A common method of carrying out this step is by the use of questions. Those questions may be so framed that the learner in answering them, is led to think of whatever ideas the instructor intends to use in this step. Such questions may be called *suggestive questions*. When suggestive questions are used they are based upon what is known as "suggestion" that is, if individual A says something, individual B will think something. If A is skillful in what he says he can make B (so long as B is unconscious as to what is going on) think of what A wishes him to think. For example, if A says "I just saw a cow," if B has ever seen a cow a picture of a cow will flash up in B's mind. The part of the sentence which made B see a cow in his mind was the one word "cow," so that we may say that the key idea in this case is "cow." In instructing, the stimulating sentence is usually put into a question. Instead of saying "I saw a cow" the instructor might say, "Can you tell a cow from a horse?" or "Can you milk a cow?" because when put in the form of a question it makes a sharper appeal; but in either case the "key idea" which gets the learner's mind to work is "cow." The rest of the sentence is really an excuse for bringing in the key idea.

Another kind of question does not depend on suggestion but on memory. If a person is asked to tell something that he already knows, as a result of trying to remember, that something will be brought up in his mind. An instructor, preliminary to presenting a teaching unit on the use of a crosscut saw to a learner who knew how to use a rip saw, might ask the learner to tell what he knew about a rip saw. There would be no suggestion, the learner would simply be asked for some information that the instructor knew he possessed. Where the lesson to be taught is an extension of what the learner already knows, the instructor may ask what was taught in the preceding lesson. The effort required to remember this brings it back fresh to the learner's mind. To distinguish them from suggestive questions we may call this sort of questions *informational* questions.

Of course questions may be asked in connection with an illustration or demonstration as described below and may take either form.

When the method of questioning can be used it is the quickest and most effective way of putting over step 1. If there is nothing that can be suggested to the learner or he has no information that will serve to refresh his memory, that will give the ideas on which the instructor wishes to base this step then other methods must be used. These are, an illustration or a demonstration that will give the learner something to start on, or to let him run up against some sort of a problem or experience that will have the same effect.

The Suggestive Illustration or Demonstration.—When the learner has absolutely nothing that the instructor can use for the teaching base it is sometimes necessary to develop the teaching base by using some form of demonstration or illustration, as where the instructor does some piece of work, performs some experiment, shows some model or uses pictures, charts, or diagrams. For example, suppose it were desired to put over a lesson on how to rig a boat to a learner who had never seen or heard of a boat, or anything like a boat. There would be absolutely nothing to "tie" to. Such cases are very rare, but, assuming that this was such a case, the instructor might find it necessary to show the learner a real boat, or a model or picture of a boat in order to get a start. In teaching geography in schools photographs or lantern slides are sometimes used when the lesson deals with something the class has never seen, as the action of ice on a mountain when taught to children who have never even seen a hill, or have never seen ice, as in some parts of the tropics.

The Suggestive Experience.—A teaching base can, in some cases, be established by having the learners do something—giving them a certain experience which the instructor considers will make them think about the things that he wishes to use for his teaching base. For example, suppose, in a training camp it was desired to instruct recruits in the proper way of holding a rifle to the shoulder so as to minimize the kick. Assume that the learner had never fired a gun, and had absolutely no notion of kick. The instructor might give him a suggestive experience by letting him fire a rifle as a green man would, get a sore shoulder by doing it that way and so lead up to a lesson on how to fire a rifle and not get a sore shoulder. A visit to a place where the complete job could be observed as carried out in practice might be used in this way in certain cases.

Summary.—Where there is anything to go on step 1 can be best carried out by the use of questions. This might be called the "standard method." It is the quickest and the easiest to use whenever its use is possible.

Where questions cannot be used one of the other methods must be. Where it can be used the suggestive experience is the better of the two alternate methods. Illustration is the poorest method of all.

CHAPTER XXIV

METHODS THAT CAN BE USED IN THE SECOND STEP OF THE LESSON

Preliminary.—As in the case of step 1 there are several methods that may be used. Those suitable for job training are four in number.

Various Methods of Presentation.—There are four common methods or teaching tools, used in presentation. These are:

(1) The method of demonstration, (2) The method of illustration, and (3) The lecture method. (4) The experimental method.

The Demonstration Method.—This method consists essentially either in showing the man how to do the thing or what the thing is with the actual tools, machines, or conditions under which the problem is to be worked out or the job is to be done. Thus, for example, an instructor in printing may operate the press in instructing a man in starting and stopping it. He may use it on an actual job in instructing a green man in the proper way of doing the job. In instructing in assembly jobs he may use the bolts, wrenches, etc., on a real piece of work. In teaching how to lay out a printing job, he may lay out an actual job that is to be printed.

Provided a real job is done the demonstration can be carried out either by the learner or by the instructor. When the learner does the job under the supervision and direction of the instructor, he is the demonstrator. He is demonstrating to himself. This is as true when he follows directions on paper.

The point of the demonstration method is that whether the instructor does it, or the learner does it under direction of the instructor, the presentation is carried out with the same tools, machines, etc., as would be used on the actual job. In this method no substitutes are used for the real thing.

Where the Demonstration Method Can be Used to the Best Advantage.—While the demonstration method should always be used wherever possible, it can be used to the best advantage under the following conditions:

(a) On the job with group instruction in the shop or the yard.
(b) On the job with individual instruction in the shop or in the yard.
(c) Off the job, when the necessary demonstration material can be secured from the shop or elsewhere.

Where Some Other Method Can be Substituted with the Least Disadvantage.—Where the demonstration method cannot be used, other less effective methods can be substituted. For example: In teaching advanced men, where demonstration materials are not obtainable. The more experienced the man in a particular line of work the less likely is the demonstration method to be the only one that can be used with a reasonable degree of effectiveness. Under the above special conditions the method of illustration can be used with a reasonable degree of efficiency and a considerable saving of time; a very important factor in shop training.

In balancing up the relative values of different methods for a given teaching job, when it is very difficult to use the demonstration method the method of illustration can often be used with advanced men. Under such conditions a good illustration may be better than a poor demonstration.

The Method of Illustration.—This method of presentation consists essentially in putting up to the men not the actual things with which the instruction deals, but things which resemble them sufficiently to serve the purpose. Examples of the method of illustration would be:

(1) In teaching the parts of a steam engine, whereas by the demonstration method it would be necessary either to take the learners into an engine room or to have in the classroom an actual steam engine, by the illustration method there might be used a wooden model with sections cut away to show the construction. As a matter of fact, if men had already run an

actual engine, this method would probably serve the purposes of this problem better, since the internal construction and the relative operations of parts could be shown in a cross section model where they could not be shown with the engine in operation. The method of illustration can be carried out by means of models, pictures, diagrams, sketches, and in short, by a large number of devices which are available in teaching practice and a number of which are discussed elsewhere.

Advantages and Disadvantages of the Method of Illustration.—This method evidently is inefficient in that it substitutes, for the real thing, something which more or less approximates the real thing, and hence requires a certain amount of mental picturing on the part of the learner, or as it is sometimes called, a "carry-over" from the model or the diagram or the picture to the thing itself; that is, the men, while seeing the illustrative material, models, pictures, sketches, etc., must *think* of the actual thing. Green or only slightly trained learners can rarely do this. In proportion as men have come in contact with the real thing, and possess considerable trade experience, they can look at the illustration and think the real thing itself. Hence the method of illustration should not be attempted with learners who have had no experience with the actual thing which is being illustrated. Thus, for example, many instructors fail in the method of illustration, especially in using blackboard diagrams, because the men have not had sufficient contact with the actual thing which the diagrams represent, so that while looking at the diagrams they do not see the thing itself. The method of illustration on the whole, therefore, is not well suited for the more elementary courses of training in any lines of shop or mechanical work.

On the other hand, this method has the advantage of enabling the instructor to control the conditions under which the lesson is given. He can bring a group together in a room, can free them from distractions and can keep their attention fixed upon the matter in hand. The degree to which the method of illustration can be used efficiently would depend largely on the character of the problem, the degree of experience of the men under instruction, and on the judgment of the teacher based upon experience.

Where the Method of Illustration Can be Used to Best Advantage.—If the things to be illustrated are simple and require little "carry-over," the method will be successful. In proportion as the things to be illustrated are complex and require much "carry-over," it will not be successful. In proportion as the men have a large amount of actual experience behind them, this method can be made successful. In proportion as they have not, it will be unsuccessful. For illustration, in steam engineering it is proposed to teach the idea of the cut-off, and it is desired to use a method of illustration which is based upon the use of blackboard diagrams. This could probably be successfully worked out in a course for firemen or engineers who had behind them considerable experience in the engine room. It would not succeed at all with a class of boys who had never seen an engine and did not know what the cut-off was. If for the diagram was substituted a small steam engine with sections cut out of the sides of the cylinder and steam chest, this work might be successfully done with a class of boys who had a sufficient experience in the engine room to know the general operation of the slide valve and the fact that the eccentric controlled the cut-off. In the same way, suppose it were desired to illustrate the method of drawing an object by projection and the point was to give the man the notion of the three points of view. If the illustration used was that of a rather elaborate drawing and the man had had no experience in reading such drawings, this method would probably fail. If it were desired to introduce him to this idea by the method of demonstration, the instructor would be much more likely to succeed if he started in with a brick and got the man by squinting around it to see what it looked like on end, side on, and from above.

Dangers of the Method of Illustration.—The great danger in the use of this method lies in the fact that it is easier for the instructor than the demonstration method, and a lazy instructor continually tends to use it when, with a little more energy and ingenuity he could use the method of demonstration.

The use unquestionably saves time and energy in many cases *where it will work*, and the only ground for using it is that the instructor knows that it will work for the particular men he is instructing on a particular instruction unit, or that the demonstration method is, under the conditions, impossible, and so a choice of a less effective method must be made.

The Lecture Method.—This method of presentation consists essentially in simply passing out the information required. Under a strict informational or lecture method of presentation, no attempt is made to illustrate or to demonstrate. The instructor simply tells the men what he wants them to know, and this method is often the method of the college or the technical school. It is based upon the theory that the lecturer knows something which the students do not know and that the students are capable of securing the information or learning how to do the thing by simply listening to the lecturer.

Where the Lecture Method Can be Used to Advantage.—The lecture method can be used to advantage only in the case of very advanced students who have themselves so much knowledge of the subject that they can easily follow and understand the lecturer. It has little place in shop training work. Thus for example, a corporation lawyer might lecture on corporation law to a group of lawyers or to advanced students in a law school; a specialist in medicine might lecture on his specialty to the members of a medical society; but even at best the lecture method is inefficient, and as a matter of fact, for all ordinary shop training it may be regarded as the last resort of a poor instructor.

Where the Lecture Method Might be Used to Advantage.—Outside of the regular work of instruction in the training scheme there is always a field for the development of general interest, and the lecture method can be used for that purpose. Thus, a lecture by an instructor on his past shop experience, how he got his different jobs, and what sort of work was done in the different shops in which he worked, while it would have no value as an instruction proposition, would undoubtedly, have value in arousing general interest on the part of the group of men that he had under instruction. In the same way, a lecture on various methods of doing a particular job in the shop would undoubtedly arouse interest and might be of value. It should be clearly understood, however, that a lecture given for this purpose is not a part of the regular training work as discussed here, and the men should not be held responsible for any direct "come back" on work of this character. Thus the ordinary practice of giving a lecture under the impression that it is a teaching lesson, requiring the men to keep notes, to write up these notes, and subsequently examining them, is a relic of barbarism from the standpoint of efficient teaching and should not be used in industrial training.

On the other hand, the bringing together of men from time to time for a lecture whose purpose is to stimulate general interest, but from which no direct and specific "come back" is either expected or required, undoubtedly finds its place in training instruction of any grade, from the elementary school to the college.

The Experimental Method.—In the three methods already discussed the work of presentation is, in a way, directed by the instructor. He at least exercises a general control over the carrying out of this step. The instruction unit, as presented, is correct. However it might be worked up, if the instruction unit were on the method of doing any given job the presentation would embody the correct method.

It is, of course, possible to lead up to the problem and then turn the learner loose to discover correct practice by the method of doing it wrong until he discovers how to do it right. That is, he may learn by experimentation. Most boys in a seaport learn to swim and to sail a boat in this way. They get pushed off the end of the dock; they go out in small sailboats and capsize until they have learned to keep a boat right side up. They learn by the method of experiment.

Advantages and Disadvantages of the Experimental Method. —Evidently a learner taught by this method is never likely to forget what he learned, and this is the chief value. On the other hand much time is consumed, the learner is liable to become discouraged and is likely to spoil much material.

Under the conditions which exist in shop training it is not probable that this method would find much place. In the case of a particularly intelligent man on advanced work it might be desirable to let him "dope it out," but such cases would be relatively rare.

Since this method is a possible one and finds a use in certain schools, it has seemed advisable to include it in the list of possible methods for step 2 in the instructing process.

Summary.—Step 2, or presentation, is the part of the lesson in which the addition is made to what the man knows. Where the new stuff is put over. It is in this step that the instruction, as such, is given.

The instructor has as tools four methods at his command—Demonstration, Illustration, Lecture, and Experiment. He chooses his method with regard to the requirements of the particular teaching job that he proposes to carry out. Under emergency training conditions the most effective method is in most cases, demonstration, with illustration as a second choice, and when demonstration is difficult or impossible. The more advanced the men the more likely the possibility of effectively using illustration in place of demonstration. The other two methods probably have little or no value in work of this character.

CHAPTER XXV

METHODS THAT CAN BE USED IN THE THIRD STEP OF THE LESSON

Preliminary.—This step of the lesson is, as described in the preceding part, a means of finding where the learner has not fully grasped the work of step 2 or has still to apply what he got in that step. The choice of a suitable method for this step is particularly important since so much depends on being sure that all the weak spots have been located and fixed up.

Methods for Carrying Out the Application.—Four methods are available: (1) Direct application or trying out on the job. (2) The recitation. (3) The discussion. (4) The written examination. As in the other steps the choice of method is determined by the character of the teaching unit and the sort of learner to whom it has been presented.

Application on the Job.—The most efficient method of determining the degree to which a teaching unit has been effectively "put over" in step 2, is to put the man who has been instructed up against the actual job which he is supposed to have been taught to successfully perform.

This method can be used on any job and is always the first choice of the instructor.

It is generally recognized as giving the most satisfactory results under modern teaching conditions and since it permits of checking up the power to do and to apply rather than the power to talk about how to do, or how to apply (and many men can *do* a good job who cannot tell *how* they do it), it is preëminently the method by which the application step should be carried out in industrial training.

Why Application on the Job is the Most Effective Method.—The efficiency of a man in a working plant depends upon what he can do. If the instructor gives him a chance to show what he can do he has the most direct check on the completeness with which he has put the lesson over. The other methods described substitute talking about the job for doing the job. They are described here because it is sometimes necessary to use one of them in place of the more desirable methods, and also because many individual instructors tend to use them altogether too much, largely because they were the methods by which they themselves were taught in school or because they are easier.

The Recitation.—When using this method the instructor asks a series of questions for the purpose of ascertaining how thoroughly the learner has "got" the lesson, and for uncovering weak points. In proportion as the learner answers all questions correctly the instructor assumes that he can do the job. If he fails to answer some questions correctly this is assumed to show where the weak points are.

The difficulty with this method in connection with practical instruction lies in the fact that the man must go through the various operations *in his mind* and describe them, in order to answer questions correctly. Many men who can do the job all right cannot carry it through in their minds when away from the job, and even if they can do this, the necessity of putting what they see in their minds into words adds an additional complication. The result of this is that a glib talker who has the sort of mind which can form a picture of the job in operation, but who cannot do it well often show up better in a recitation than a man who does know how to do the job but lacks ready speech and imagination.

This misleads the instructor who confuses inability to express with inability to do. Hence in any practical work this method is somewhat dangerous especially in the hands of inexperienced instructors.

It is chiefly of value where what has been taught is purely informational in character and hence finds a large place in the work of regular schools. Since the purely informational side of industrial training work is comparatively small, the recitation can only be effectively used in a few cases.

It is also a fact that the recitation is much easier for the teacher than the method of putting the man on the job, and hence a lazy instructor tends to use it, of course thereby doing a poor instructing job.

The Instructor's Job and the Learner's Job.—It should be noted that whereas the statements made above apply to the case of a learner the case is entirely different with an instructor, who must be able to see the job without actually doing it, must be able to analyze and must be able to talk clearly about the work, in order to carry on the instruction process.

The Discussion.—In the recitation the instructor asks questions and the learner answers the questions. The relation at any given time is always between the instructor and one man. It is quite possible however to set up a discussion wherein various members of the group ask questions, both, of other group members and of the instructor. By watching and sometimes guiding such a discussion the instructor can often check up the degree to which the men have been thoroughly instructed, so that the discussion may, in certain cases, become a method for carrying out the Application Step. It is possible to use the discussion when working with one man but, under these conditions, it is obviously less effective than when working with a group of men who are being simultaneously instructed in the same teaching unit.

Conditions under which the Discussions may Best be Used. —The discussion, considered as a method for checking up, is most likely to be of value when the instructor is dealing with a group of advanced men, or men with considerable experience behind them. It is not likely to be of much value when working with men of little experience, nor is it likely to be of much value in individual instruction.

The Written Recitation or Test.—It is quite possible to substitute written answers to questions for spoken answers. This modification of the ordinary spoken or oral recitation is sometimes called a written recitation. As compared with the oral recitation the written recitation has the advantage that questions can be more carefully answered.than in group instruction; one man cannot take his cue from another; and answers can be more carefully examined and criticized by the instructor. It has the disadvantage of taking much more time for the answering of a given number of questions. All members cannot hear the answer of any one man and cannot get the benefit of the instructor's criticism on each man's answer.

It is also true that many men find even greater difficulty in expressing themselves in writing than in expressing themselves orally so that all the objections which apply to the spoken recitation apply even more strongly to the written recitation.

The Examination.—An examination may be either oral or written. It differs from the recitation mainly in that it uses what may be called the method of sampling. An illustration of the theory on which examinations are conducted would be the method of taking a sample of wheat out of a car which was loaded with wheat, taking this sample at random from any part of the car, grading it, and then assuming that all the wheat in the car was of the same grade as the sample taken. Whereas in the recitation the questions would be "bunched," that is, the instructor would attempt to hit all parts of the teaching unit, in an examination the questions are scattered. It is like the difference between the rifle and the shot gun. Certain questions are asked at random and it is assumed that, if the learner answers these "sample" questions correctly he could answer any others correctly, and so has "got" the teaching unit.

The Value of the Examination as a Method in the Application Step. Evidently the examination is of little value as a method for checking up and for assuring the instructor that the man has got the lesson. The method of sampling must leave large gaps in the checking up process and fail entirely to bring out the points on which the learner needs straightening out. It also has all the undesirable features of the recitation as outlined under that heading. As a method to be used in the application step in industrial training it has practically no value and is only given here because its use in regular schools is so common that industrial instructors are liable to think that it can be used effectively in this sort of work.

How to Know when Step 3 is Completed.—In this the instructor must depend upon his judgment and experience. No set rule can be given. Whatever the method used, the operation is continued until the instructor is satisfied that the teaching unit has been completely put over. Wherever he finds a weak spot the instructor goes over that part of the preceding step which covers that particular part of the teaching unit, in this way filling up the gaps. Sometimes he has to change his method because it is evident that the particular method used for step 2 has failed to work with a given man. However that may be, he finally comes to a point where he is willing to take a chance that the man has "got" the thing that was to be taught.

This step may be compared to trying out an assembled machine, where the machine is run under careful observation. Any imperfections are noted, and faulty parts replaced until the adjuster is ready to O. K. it, that is, he is ready to take a chance on its being right. Instructors are very liable to be in too much of a hurry in carrying out this step and to let a man go onto the final step, or test, before he is ready for it. The adjuster who lets imperfect machines go out of his department has done a poor job and the same may be said of the instructor who lets the learner out of this stage, before he is ready.

Summary.—The third instruction step or application is the part of the instructional process wherein the effectiveness of the work done in step 2 is checked up and defects located and corrected. Of the four possible methods, application on the job is the most effective in industrial work. The recitation or discussion is the second choice; and the examination is of practically no value. The instructor must learn to use his judgment as to when this step is completed. He is likely to err on the side of not doing enough. The more experience and good judgment he has the more likely he is to do a good job in this stage of the instructional process.

CHAPTER XXVI

METHODS FOR CARRYING OUT STEP FOUR IN THE LESSON

Preliminary.—This step is where the instructor puts on the final test. Where the work of the three preceding steps "comes out in the wash." Hence it is very important that the best methods should be used in each case.

Methods for Carrying Out this Step.—Since step 4 like step 3, is an inspection and differs from step 3, only in that during this step the instructor gives the learner no assistance at all, the same methods can be used as in step 3, and the same suggestions as to relative desirability would apply. It is, of course, possible to use a different method in this step than was used in step 3. This is a matter that must be determined by the judgment of the instructor.

The Value of Testing Work.—It should always be borne in mind that the object of the final test is to enable the instructor to determine how well he has succeeded in imparting the thing he set out to teach. The simple fact that a man has failed to do a piece of work successfully is in itself of value only so far as the test is conducted under such conditions that the teacher can determine why he failed. Failure may be due to four causes: a poor learner, a poor instructor, poor teaching conditions, or a poorly conducted lesson; and it is up to the instructor to find out which of these four causes or any combination of them may be the cause for failure. This is the only way in which he can gain experience which will increase his teaching ability.

Most failures in the instructional process are due to the fact that the instructor was not "on to his job." When an instructor states that a learner cannot be taught it is "up to him" to prove that he was "on to his job" before his statement can be accepted as final.

Where the results of the test show that the lesson has been a failure, the first thing for the instructor to do is to consider why.

So far as the poor teacher is concerned, this simply means that he does not know his job as an instructor. So far as a poor learner is concerned, investigation may show that he is incapable of getting that particular lesson at that particular time or possibly of ever getting it at all. So far as poor teaching conditions are concerned, such a state of affairs is due to poor management on the part of the instructor. So far as a poorly conducted lesson is concerned, that of course is due to poor selection of method, poor handling, or some other failure in the actual process of "putting it over." In such cases the instructor will probably find that the difficulty is due to one or more of the errors which are listed below, in the order in which they are likely to occur in the work of an inexperienced teacher:

(1) Teaching too much. (Too large a teaching unit.)
(2) Adopting an unsuitable method.
(3) Failing to complete each step before starting on the next.
(4) Failing to include all steps in the lesson.
(5) Failing to distinguish step 1 from step 2, and step 3 from step 4.
(6) Failing to take sufficient time to teach the lesson.
(7) Lack of patience and tact in teaching the lesson.
(8) Undertaking to teach the lesson under unsuitable teaching conditions.

When the instructor has failed to put over the lesson, he has got to find out *why* he failed and then replan his lesson and teach it so that he will not fail the second time. The more care an instructor uses in planning his lesson, and the more skill he uses in putting it over, the less likely is he to get into this situation.

CHAPTER XXVII

THE INFORMATIONAL AND THE DEVELOPMENT LINES OF APPROACH

Two Methods of Approach.—Whatever may be the nature of the teaching unit and whatever methods may have to be used in carrying out the various steps in the instructing process there still remains to be considered what may be called the instructor's "policy" or method of approach in handling the lesson as a whole. There are two such general methods available which may be designated as the informational method and the development method, or the informational approach and the development approach.

The Informational Line of Approach.—In using this line of approach the whole instructing operation is conducted on the basis of the instructor's giving information to the learner or the learner giving information to the instructor. When the instructor asks questions they are of a kind that calls for information from the learner. When an instructor handles a lesson in this way the chief faculty exercised by the learner is memory.

The entire lesson or any one step in the lesson can be handled in this way according to the judgment of the instructor. An illustration of the presentation step in a lesson handled by this method would be where the instructor gave the rule and required the learner to work from it.

The Development Line of Approach.—In handling a lesson by this line of approach the instructor makes the learner think out the proper procedure. He leads the learner to think out the problem and the method of solution, guides the thinking and aids the learner when he is "stuck" by suggestions, and stimulating questions. He is all the time aiming at making the man do the thinking. Under this method questions asked by the instructor are so framed that the learner must think in answering. A series of questions may be asked which leads the man to think through to a correct method of solving a problem or a correct method of procedure.

The Development Approach Good Instruction.—The object of the development line of approach is to train the man to think intelligently about his job. Its object is to start with what he knows and to lead him by successive steps to reason or think through to the desired results. This is essentially a training process, and for the purposes of many sorts of industrial training it is as important to train the learner to think for himself and use his own ideas, that he should know why as well as how, as it is to train him in proper methods in the doing of the job itself. Every time a lesson is handled by the development line of approach, something has been added to the learner's capacity to attack new problems intelligently, to "think on his job." The result of a course of instruction in which the development approach has been used wherever possible will turn out a man with ability to tackle a new problem and to think it through correctly. The power to do this is, of course, generally recognized as a very desirable quality in many industrial lines, hence the use of this method of approach in industrial training has great value in much of the instruction work in all trades. It is therefore, in general, the first choice of an instructor, and should be used by preference, unless it is evident that the other approach is clearly the most effective for instructing in the particular teaching unit under consideration.

The Use of the Informational Approach.—The informational approach is chiefly valuable where the teaching unit deals with simple operations in which there is only one way to do it and where but little trade intelligence is required. This might be true, for example, in teaching a man how to start an electric motor. It is more likely to be of service with advanced than with green men, and in instructing in simple shop operations rather than in technical problems, or complicated jobs.

Advantages and Disadvantages of the Two Methods.—A good example of the informational method will be found in the ordinary engineer's handbook. This book is prepared for a man who has a considerable experience in the practice of his trade, and whose aim is to get results as rapidly as possible. Usually he is not concerned with the "why" as much as with the result which is required. Often he is not equipped to reason out the rule or the formula for himself, yet he wants the result in his business. Under these circumstances the method usually followed in these handbooks lends itself well to the needs of the men for whose use they are prepared; they are not, however, intended to give training in thinking out the problem. A man instructed under this method would gain but little in power to work out the correct rule for a new problem; if it was not in the handbook he would be stuck.

On the other hand, a person trained by the second, or development approach, would be able to tackle a new problem and work out the rule for himself.

It is therefore evident that for training the man to reason and think in connection with his work the development approach is the better; for rapid results, the informational approach is preferable.

Choice of the Two Lines of Approach.—Evidently each lesson will put the instructor up against the problem of determining which of the two possible lines of approach he will use. In making his decision he would be guided, as suggested above, by the sort of unit that he had to teach: by the sort of man he was going to teach it to. Judgment based on experience is the only guide in this case. It might be pointed out, however, that it is often possible to use the development approach on a lesson where all things considered, it will not "pay" to use it. It may take too much time with respect to the "yield" of intelligence gotten out of it in that particular case, or it may result in distracting the mind of the man from the requirements of the actual job. An instructor must take all these points into consideration in determining the line of approach which he will use in any given case.

Line of Approach as Distinguished from Methods.—A distinction must be clearly drawn between the two *lines of approach* as discussed in the preceding paragraphs and *methods of instruction*. As already stated, the former refers to what has been called the *policy* of the Instructor in handling the lesson or any step in the lesson. The latter refers to the particular devices which may be used under either line of approach in the carrying out of the instructional process.

It is, of course, possible to use different lines of approach for different steps in a lesson, but such practice is extremely unwise and dangerous. It requires a going back and a patching up of the continuity of the instruction process, it tends to confuse the learner, it is liable to break up the conciseness. Where the situation changes radically and unexpectedly during the progress of the lesson a very experienced instructor may save the situation by changing his line of approach. It is better for the inexperienced instructor not to attempt to save the situation, but to begin all over again with a line of approach which will be effective under the new conditions.

CHAPTER XXVIII

THE TECHNICAL LESSON AND THE PRODUCTION LESSON

Preliminary.—While the general steps which have been given in the section on the instructional process would be followed in putting through any lesson, a number of the details, especially as to selection of suitable methods for the various steps, line of approach, and determination of the best teaching conditions, would vary with the kind of the teaching unit, especially as to whether the subject of the lesson (the teaching unit) should be classed as a trade technical or a production unit. The following paragraphs discuss the general effect of the kind of the teaching unit on the planning of the lesson.

Explanation of Terms.—The term *job* as used in these notes means anything that a man is paid to do, whether it does or does not result in the actual working up of stock. If it does result in the working up of stock we will call it a *production job;* if it does not result in the working up of stock but is a necessary step in the getting out of the product, we will call it a *technical job*. That is, a technical job calls for the possession and the use of technical knowledge. It does contribute to the turning out of the job, for example, laying off the sweep or template preliminary to bending a frame is a technical job, but the actual bending of the frame is a production job, because in this latter case the result of the job is a properly bent frame. Knowing how to place a properly heated rivet the right way in the right hole is a technical job, but driving the rivet is a production job. Reading a blueprint is a technical job, but making the article as shown on the blueprint is a production job.

Characteristics of the Trade Technical Job.—In general this sort of a job presents these characteristics:

(1) It is not a direct production job.
(2) It requires the exercise of trade intelligence and judgment.
(3) It contributes to the getting out of production, although it is not a production job.
(4) It need not be done where the production job to which it contributes is done.

The Technical Job Makes no Demand for Product as a Direct Result.—In getting out a piece of work there are usually a number of "jobs" which have to be done but which do not require the direct working up of stock. For instance, a blueprint must be read, or a pattern maker must make a layout, or a printer makes up a dummy.

The Technical Job Calls for Trade Intelligence and Judgment.—The majority of technical jobs call for the exercise of intelligence and judgment. Often there is more than one way of doing the job and the best method must be selected. The particular method followed must often be worked out in a special way to meet the requirements of the special production job to which it contributes. Sometimes the workman must use specially trained judgment. In few cases are technical jobs carried out in a purely automatic way.

The Technical Job Need not be Done where the Production Job is Done.—Since the technical job does not deal with the material itself, it can be carried on anywhere, or in some special place provided for the purpose. It need not even be carried on inside the plant. In many plants special rooms are provided for this class of jobs, such as in the case of mold loft work, in a shipyard or where the foreman takes the blueprint into his office and there reads it and marks out cutting slips.

The Trade Technical Lesson.—This class of lesson deals with ideas instead of material. As a rule the learner must work with his head rather than with his hands. He must be able to carry through a series of mental operations or "thinks." He often has to work with signs that stand for things or ideas included in the lesson. Such as Str. for straight, Dr. for drill, Z for Z bar, I for I beam. He must often use a certain amount of mathematics. He must often express himself in trade terms. He must often be able to read a drawing.

The Teaching Unit is Determined by Trade Practice.—Trade practice has usually established the easiest and most rapid methods of solving such trade technical problems as come up in the direct connection with production. These methods have been developed by the trade with regard to shop conditions, the saving of time, and often with no more regard for accuracy than is necessary for the purpose in hand.

The sheer or body plan is laid out according to the special methods which have been adopted in the ship building trade and might be unintelligible to a machine shop draftsman. Template marks can only be interpreted by a man who knows ship work.

With what Degree of Accuracy should Trade Technical Problems be Worked Out.—A man should be taught to work out a trade technical problem only to the degree of accuracy which would be called for in the trade. Thus, for example, a man laying out a patch plate will not work to the same degree of accuracy as a machinist who is laying out a drill jig. The efficient instructor will waste no time or energy in training a learner to a higher degree of accuracy than is required by the trade.

Lines of Approach for the Technical Lesson.—As already pointed out the technical lesson deals with ideas and signs which stand for things (symbols)—rather than with tools, stock, and operations. It calls for thinking. Hence in general the development line of approach is the proper one to use.

Selection of Methods for the Technical Lesson.—Many lessons of this type require very careful selection of method since they deal so much with ideas or symbols rather than with things. The preparatory step often requires more careful working out than in a lesson on a production job. Probably many more technical lessons are spoiled by careless preparatory work than are lessons in production work. Great care must be taken to avoid "skimping" the preparatory step, and the instructor must be sure that the object of this step has been attained before he proceeds further with the lesson.

In planning step 2, it may be said in general that a greater use may be made of the method of illustration than in instructing in production jobs. In some cases the demonstration method cannot be used under the conditions under which the instruction is carried on, especially where the instruction is given outside of the shop. For example, the problem of laying out a display form, in printing, might be worked out by diagrams on a blackboard, or on paper. The same might be true in instructing in the method of figuring the horsepower from the indicator card.

The discussion can also be used to more advantage than in instructing on production work, and even the lecture method may in a few cases find a place in instructing in this class of teaching units, as in a lesson in a system for template marking.

In steps 3 and 4 it is also true that the recitation can sometimes be used in place of putting the learner in the job. Of course, this method is always a second choice, but sometimes it is the only method available under the instruction conditions.

As in other cases judgment and experience will aid the instructor in selecting the best method for "putting over" this type of teaching unit.

The Lesson in Production Work. Preliminary.—The preceding paragraphs have discussed the question of teaching of trade technical problems. The lesson on a production job, while the general principles of good teaching will apply, offers very distinct characteristics as compared to the lesson on trade technical work as already discussed. Among the most important of these are (1) the aim of the instruction is always to train the men to correctly perform an operation or do a job; (2) the problem is always a specific one, and deals with a definite product; (3) it calls for mechanical intelligence and judgment in the use of tools or the operations of machines; (4) it calls for a sufficient amount of skill to do the job up to the required standard.

Characteristics of the Lesson in Shop Work.—In general, therefore, a lesson of this class presents these characteristics:—

(1) As a result of the lesson, however it may be given, the learner will have learned how to do some sort of a production job, or how to perform some operation, resulting in the production of a real product which can be handled.

(2) The doing of this job will call for the use of machines or tools in a workmanlike manner, according to trade methods.

(3) It calls for the intelligent use of such machines and tools as are necessary.

The result is something that can be seen and handled. As a result of the work of the instructor in instructing and of the learner in doing, some piece of work is completed, or some operation is correctly performed.

The Production Job.—As distinguished from the trade technical job, the production job is always worked out with real stock, real tools, and ends with a real result, whereas the trade technical job ends with an arithmetical answer, a piece of written work, a sketch or a drawing, which, while they contribute to the getting out of the product, do so only indirectly. The real and practical nature of the work involved in doing a production job, therefore, affects the character of the methods of instruction used, especially in that it substitutes operations performed upon a piece of stock for mental operations or ideas as they would be developed in any trade technical jobs.

The Lesson on the Production Job Deals with Training in how to Make Something.—In doing a production job, the learner is working with actual stock, actual machines, actual tools, and is following trade processes. There is little or no requirement that he should think in abstract terms. At every step in the process he has before his eyes the job on which he is working in the form which it takes at that particular stage; hence it is easy for him to connect the various processes and to grasp the necessity of properly completing one process before he undertakes the next one.

The Lesson on the Production Job Calls for Training in Mechanical Intelligence and Judgment.—While the trade technical unit calls for intelligence and judgment in the use of arithmetical processes and other educational "tools," the shop job calls for the intelligent use of actual tools and machines. These are real things, the learner can see them and handle them, whereas, in the lesson on a technical job he can only deal with ideas or mind pictures.

Lines of Approach for the Lesson on a Production Job.— There are in general two conditions under which the informational line of approach can be used effectively in instructing on a production job. The first is where the job is simple and easy to understand. The second is where the man is already well advanced and has reached a point where he has had sufficient experience to be able to think and reason for himself. An illustration of the first case might be the method of starting and stopping a machine. An illustration of the second case might be a lesson in roof framing given to a house carpenter or in stair building given to a jointer. In the same way there are certain kinds of jobs which can be best handled by the development line of approach. It should, in general, be used in instructing green men especially at the beginning of their training or, in the case of experienced men who are to be instructed in new methods or in the use of new materials. It is also at times the line of approach where the instructor wishes to make a particularly strong impression on the man as to the necessity of performing some operation in a certain exact way. The first case might be illustrated by a lesson in making a dovetail joint. The second might be illustrated by instructing a blacksmith who had been used to using an oil furnace and had been changed over to a gas furnace.

It is evident that as in all other cases discussed no hard and fast rules can be given. According to the character of the teaching unit, the experience of the man to be taught and the particular results which the instructor wishes to accomplish, he will select the most effective line of approach in handling a given instruction job on production work. As in other cases, as he gains in experience and acquires the "art" of instruction, his judgment will be good in this respect.

PART VI
LESSON PLANNING

CHAPTER XXIX

LESSON PLANNING

The Lesson Plan.—Whenever something is to be taught, the plan for instruction can be worked out on paper, and is usually designated as the "lesson plan." Such a lesson plan corresponds to a planning or "operation sheet" in a factory, which gives the details as to successive operations and as to the character of the product desired. Where such a plan is completely worked out it requires three steps.

1. (a) The getting out of a *skeleton plan* covering the analysis of the teaching unit into the successive teaching points that are to be put over arranged in an effective teaching order.
    (b) The determination of a suitable J. O. P.
    (c) The layout for step 1, giving the successive ideas to be used in leading up to the J. O. P.
2. The preparation of a *general operation sheet* from the skeleton plan. This sheet gives such data as the type of the lesson, the line of approach, methods to be used in each step, teaching conditions, etc.
3. The preparation of a *detailed operation sheet* in which the exact details as to just how each step is to be carried out are set forth in full. On such a sheet the instructor notes down, *in full*, just what material he will need, just what questions he will ask, and just what he proposes to say. If a method of illustration calling for the use of diagrams is to be used, he sketches those diagrams on his sheet. A complete general operation sheet would correspond to a full description of all that was used, all that the instructor did, and a stenographic report of all that he said.

The Instructor Prepares his Lesson Plan before he Puts Over the Lesson.—All lesson planning is done before the instructor meets the learner to put the lesson over, just as an "operation sheet" is prepared before the job is started. Its purpose is to enable the instructor to do his thinking before he has to actually put over the instruction.

Unless an instructor is a very experienced teacher if he undertakes to do his planning and his putting over at the same time, he will make a poor job of the lesson. According to his experience he can work from a skeleton plan, a general operation sheet, or a detailed operation sheet—the less experience he has the greater detail he should go into in planning his lessons. As he gains in experience he can cut out more and more detail, but, no matter how experienced he is he should have at least a skeleton plan for each teaching unit that is included in his instruction work.

The Order in which an Operation Sheet is Worked Out.—The subject of the lesson being determined what goes into the teaching unit is fixed. The instructor can determine *how* he will break it up into teaching points, but he has no choice as to what to put over. That is fixed by the aim of the lesson.

The instructor therefore begins by laying out the teaching points in *step 2*, then determines on his J. O. P., then makes his layout for step 1, this completes the "skeleton plan," which consists of:

(a) The analysis of the teaching unit into the successive teaching points.
(b) The proposed J. O. P.
(c) The layout for the proposed Preparation.

That is, he starts with the teaching unit, gets his J. O. P. from that, lays out his preparation from his J. O. P.

In Planning the Instructor Works Backward.—It should be noted that in planning a lesson the instructor lays it out in exactly the reverse order to the instructing order. He teaches step 1, J. O. P., step 2. He plans step 2, J. O. P., step 1. In teaching he leads up to the teaching unit in planning he works out from the teaching unit.

Making the Analysis of the Teaching Unit.—As stated above the first step in getting out a skeleton plan is to analyze out the teaching points and arrange them in a suitable order for presentation. Here it is important that the lesson, as planned, should not contain too many points. Too much should not be included in one lesson. A rough rule is that, a good lesson should not contain over eight teaching points. If the unit as originally determined shows, on analysis, more than eight points, it is better to divide it and make two or more lessons out of it.

There are a number of advantages in working with small teaching units, especially with green or immature learners. A series of short lessons given in a good progressive order will get a learner along faster and better than one long lesson covering the same ground.

There are two common difficulties in getting out a good analysis of a teaching unit. First, the instructor does not select good teaching points, so that each point deals with some one part of the instructing job. Second, he does not "bunch" his instruction properly around the teaching points. Each point should be "cleaned up" as the lesson goes along and, having once covered a point it should not, in general, be necessary to touch it again during presentation. The general rule to be followed here is that the more general and more simple ideas should be presented first, the more specific and more complex ideas should be presented later.

Getting Out the " J. O. P."—In planning a journey there must be a point of departure, but the point of departure may vary, and different individuals making the same journey may often select different points of departure. In the same way, in planning a lesson, it is necessary that the instructor should determine what ideas or picture in the learner's mind he proposes to take as his point of departure at the close of step 1, that is just what he intends the learner to be thinking about when step 2 is started. This point of departure may be called, for convenience, the "jumping-off point" since it is essentially the point at which the learner jumps from what he knows to what he doesn't know and is to be taught. It is often true that a great variety of "jumping-off points" may be selected by the instructor. There will undoubtedly be in the learner's mind hundreds of ideas which might bear upon the teaching unit to be handled in step 2. Certain of these ideas could be grouped together to get one "jumping-off point"; but other groups of ideas could often be brought together to get another "jumping-off point." In no case would it be necessary to utilize *all* of the available groups of ideas in the learner's mind.

Judgment Must be Used in Selecting the J. O. P.—In selecting a suitable J. O. P. there is no guide but the judgment of the instructor. While it is, in general, determined by what is in the teaching unit, different instructors would be very likely to use different groups of ideas for the J. O. P., according to their knowledge of their learners and their particular way of working up a lesson. One or two suggestions may be of value. A common form of J. O. P. is to get the learner so that he knows what the lesson is about and wonders how the job is done. This, "I know that somebody can do this job and I wonder how it is done" attitude of mind on the part of the learner often forms a very good J. O. P. especially in instruction on production jobs. A good illustration of this sort of a J. O. P. would be where the teaching unit was on the proper way to stop an electric car so as to get on it, given to children who knew that there was a regular procedure but did not know what it was.

Another type of J. O. P. is a "mind picture" developed in the learner's mind. Thus, for example, if the teaching unit were on a *modification* of a job that the learner had been already taught he can be made to see himself doing the job that he knows how to do as a J. O. P. for the lesson on the new job. An example of this sort of a J. O. P. would be where the teaching unit was on taper turning in the machine shop and the learner already knew how to do plain turning, or where a man knew how to operate a hand lawn mower and the teaching unit was on the operation of a power lawn mower.

A third class of J. O. P. is where the "mind picture" is made up from the learner's past experiences entirely outside of anything that he has been taught, but which call for ideas something like what is in the teaching unit. An illustration of such a case would be where the teaching unit was on riveting and, to get a start, the learner was led to think of a shoe lacing, or of two pieces of cloth sewed together. This, of course, would give a start because the shoe lacing or the thread hold together two pieces of material. The thread idea would be the better since the two pieces of cloth overlap as two riveted plates do.

The above statements are, of course, merely suggestive. An instructor must learn by practice to use effective J. O. P.'s. The more skillful he is in this, the better lessons he can plan.

Making the Layout for Step 1.—Having determined on an effective J. O. P. the next step is to determine what ideas are to be used to lead the learner up to that J. O. P. Here again the skill and judgment of the instructor come into play. A few general suggestions may be of value. In any case it is true that the particular ideas which he would lay out in the lesson plan for step 1 would have to be absolutely determined by the particular "jumping-off point" which he had selected. This explains why it is quite possible that in step 1 the lesson may be carried out effectively by different teachers with the use of very different ideas. Probably a successful lesson could be conducted by various instructors with different bases. The putting over of the notion of a lap joint in boilermaking might be based upon the notions of clapboards on the side of a house, or on the idea of a lap strake boat, or on a picture of shingles on a roof. It should be noted, however, that the idea which the instructor would select to bring the preparatory work to the "jumping-off point" cited above would be largely if not entirely different from those which would be selected for any other "jumping-off points."

Working Toward the Objective.—The efficient traveler, in making a journey will see that every step that he takes brings him nearer to his goal; and in proportion as he side-steps or goes out of the direct line of progress he is less efficient in accomplishing his aim. In the same way, in the planning of a lesson, the instructor must see to it that the different ideas used in the carrying out of step 1 are so presented to the earner that each idea gets him thinking directly toward the redetermined end,—which is, in step 1, the particular "jumping-off point" as determined in advance by the instructor.

The layout for step 1 therefore consists of:—1st, certain ideas arranged in a certain order that the learner may be brought to the "jumping-off point" selected; and 2d, of a group of ideas or a "mind picture," or recollection of something which he already knows which represents the content of the "jumping-off point" selected.

The layout for this step will be efficient in proportion as certain simple rules are followed. Among the most important of these are: (1). Use as few ideas as possible and get the J. O. P. (2) Make the ideas "focus." (3) Make the ideas simple.

(1) Step 1 takes time during which the learner gets nothing new under ordinary conditions. The quicker he gets to the J. O. P. the more time saved, both to learner and instructor. The fewer the ideas used, *provided they work*, the "neater" job the instructor will have done in step 1. A long drawn out preparation will "kill" any lesson.

(2) The ideas used should steadily "drive" the learner toward the J. O. P.: they should "focus." The most general idea should come first, the most specific last. Thus in the lesson given in the next chapter we have (1) a rivet; (2) a *hot* rivet (not all rivets are hot); a hot rivet *just hot enough*. (All hot rivets are not just hot enough)—so that the three ideas "focus". on the J. O. P. of "How can one tell when a rivet is just hot enough."

(3) The more simple the ideas used the quicker this step can be put over and the less danger of confusing the learner or of getting "side tracked" during this step.

A regular layout form such as is shown on page 187 is a great advantage in getting out a "skeleton plan."

The General Operation Sheet.—The general operation sheet is got out from the "skeleton plan" which gives ideas and teaching points only. It is the "skeleton" with the "*how*" added. For each kind of lesson and for each step in the lesson there is a best method under the given teaching conditions. The instructor gives careful consideration to these points and lays out his general operation sheet accordingly. Here again no general rules can be given. Judgment and experience are the only guides.

A standard form for general operation sheets is a great advantage. A suggestive form is shown on page 188.

The Detailed Operation Sheet.—Where used, this sheet is developed from the general operation sheet and calls for no special discussion. An inexperienced instructor will derive great advantage from working out a number of such detailed operation sheets. He probably will not use them in actual shop instruction, but if he has planned and thought out even the least details in advance it will enable him to do much better work on the instructing job.

Planning vs. Instruction.—When the instructor has completed his lesson plan he still has the problem of putting it over to the learner, the group or the class. The planning problem is solved but the instructional operation is still to be carried out. He must now face his class or his group or his individual learner and by the exercise of what has been called the *art of teaching* must skillfully put over the teaching unit. His success in doing this will largely depend on his instructional management as discussed in the part following.

CHAPTER XXX

AN ILLUSTRATION OF THE PLANNING OF A LESSON

This chapter gives an illustration of how the operations described in the last chapter could be worked out on a given teaching unit.

The teaching unit selected is on how to pick out a rivet at the right temperature.

In explanation it may be stated that, in riveting, the rivets are driven hot. They are heated in a small portable furnace or forge. A part of the job of the "heater boy" is to pick out rivets at the right heat for driving. If too hot they are "burned" and should not be driven. If too cold they will not drive properly. This particular job would therefore be included in a course of training for heater boys, and, owing to its simplicity serves well as an example for planning. It is, of course, one of the few jobs that call for judgment. The heater boy is paid for knowing *how* to pick out a rivet at the right heat.

Points to be Considered.—In planning a lesson the instructor has three questions to answer. 1st, What are the ideas to be put over in the teaching unit? 2d, What is the teaching base or "jumping-off point" (J. O. P.) that is proposed to be used? 3d, What ideas already in the learner's mind does the instructor intend to utilize in carrying the learner up to the J. O. P.? Of course it is evident that the instructor who knows what he is to teach will in working out his plan, follow exactly the reverse order from that he will follow in carrying on the lesson with the learner.

Analyzing the Lesson Content.—The instructor must determine the ideas he must put over in the teaching unit, which in this case would be as follows:

The appearance of the rivet varies with the heat.
The rivet must be at a certain temperature.
The rivet must be at a white heat.

Sequence of Ideas Required. Determining the Order of Operations.—Having analyzed the instruction unit into the different ideas of which it is composed, the next step is to arrange them into an instructing order, that is, the order in which they must be put over. This is again identical with the yard problem of making out an operation sheet for determining the order in which the successive operations required for a given job are to be put through. It is evident that the successive ideas must be arranged in such an order that each successive idea when put over, will naturally lead up too, or suggest, the next operation or idea that is to be taken up. The skillful instructor will take into consideration, in laying out his operation sheet, such factors as the previous experiences of the group, how much they already know, what arrangement will best appeal to interest, and any special characteristics of the learners,—just as a planning board would take into consideration the particular kind of stock to be used, the capacity of the different machines in the shop, the particular machines available for the particular job, etc. *Therefore, after having analyzed the teaching unit into its constituent ideas, they must be arranged in some progressive teaching order before a teaching plan or operation sheet can be laid out for step 2.* While experience is the best guide, a few general rules can be given.

Work from the qualitative or general notion to the quantitative or exact notion, always ask "how" or "what" before asking "how much." For example the idea that the rivet must be hot enough should be presented before the idea that it must be at a certain color.

General ideas should be presented before specific ideas. For example, the idea that the rivet must be at a certain heat to be right will be put up before the idea that the right color is just under a white heat.

The Ideas Arranged in a Correct Teaching Order.—Taking into consideration such general rules as the above we might have the following arrangement for a correct teaching order:

The rivet must be at a certain temperature.
The appearance of the rivet varies with the heat.
The rivet must be just under a "scaling" (white) heat.

The above ideas arranged in the order given constitute the teaching unit which is to be put over in step 2.

Determination of the "J. O. P."—In order to put over these ideas the learner must be made to have in his mind a certain group of ideas or a picture to serve as a foundation for the building on of the new idea contained in the teaching unit. In this particular lesson, a good J. O. P. is to have the learner thinking of the problem of knowing when a rivet is hot enough.

Thus we have,

J. O. P. How do we know when a rivet is just hot enough?

Developing the J. O. P.—Having got the J. O. P. the next question is to determine how this picture will be developed in the learner's mind. As in all other cases experience is the best guide. In the case of this lesson the following ideas will probably serve the purpose, if as stated in the teaching conditions, the learners were familiar with a rivet and have the idea of hot and cold, and some general notion of the riveting process, having picked these ideas up somewhere.

We therefore take for step 1,

First idea, a rivet.
Second idea, a hot rivet.
Third idea, a rivet heated enough.

This gives the skeleton plan, and if entered on a suitable form, as suggested in the preceding chapter we would have a skeleton plan like the following. Note that in making out his plan the instructor works *from* the analysis of the teaching unit, through the J. O. P. *to* the layout. In *using* the plan he works in the reverse direction, from the top down.

AN ILLUSTRATION OF THE PLANNING OF A LESSON
SKELETON PLAN FOR LESSON

Teaching Unit....To pick out a rivet at the right heat.....

Primary or Secondary....Primary.....

Learner gets it this way.

Step 1

First Step	A rivet
Second Step	A hot rivet
Third Step	A rivet heated just right
Fourth Step	
Fifth Step	

Layout.

J. O. P. How do we know when a rivet is just hot enough?

Step 2

First Point	The rivet must be at a certain temperature
Second Point	The appearance of the rivet varies with the heat
Third Point	The rivet must be just under a "scaling" (white) heat
Fourth Point	
Fifth Point	

Analysis of the Teaching Unit.

THE INSTRUCTOR

The General Operation Sheet.—The instructor must now determine how he will answer three questions. First, What line of approach he intends to use; Second, What method he proposes to use in carrying out each instruction step; Third, Just how he proposes to carry out these methods in actually putting over the lesson to his learners. In order to answer these questions he first prepares a general operation sheet. For the lesson under consideration this would be as follows:

This particular lesson is on a technical unit in trade science. The development line of approach can be used effectively because the ability to pick out a properly heated rivet calls for judgment, and development of this power of judgment in the learner can only be secured by making him think about the various factors that determine the necessity for picking out a rivet at the proper heat.

Since it is assumed in the teaching conditions that the learners have been given no previous instruction on this subject, this lesson is an elementary, or primary lesson. Under the proposed line of approach the method of the suggestive questioning will be effective, and should be used in step 1. The method of the development demonstration will work well in step 2—steps 3 and 4 could best be handled by testing on the job. The general operation sheet would then be laid out somewhat as follows if laid out on a suitable form.

GENERAL OPERATION SHEET

Teaching Unit.... To pick out a rivet at the right heat.

....

Primary or Secondary (check) Why?.... Because this lesson is to be taught to green boys with no previous experience in this line of work except that they have casually seen riveting going on.

Technical or Production (Check) Why?.. Because stock is not worked up, but heating to correct heat is a necessary step to the production job of riveting.

STEP 1

Line of Approach.. Development.

Reasons.. Calls for training in judgment.

Method Adopted.. Suggestive questions.

Reasons.. Easiest method and can be used.

Teaching Conditions.. On the job. Four boys. Group instruction.

Reasons.. Can be done under the conditions. Is always the best method when it can be used.

Material Required.. None.

STEP 2

Line of Approach.. Development.

Reasons.. Same as in Step 1.

Method Adopted.. Development demonstration.

Reasons.. Develops intelligence on the job.

AN ILLUSTRATION OF THE PLANNING OF A LESSON

Material Required. Furnace connected, and ready to operate, fired up, 25 7/8" rivets; Air gun and air jam connected and ready to operate—Two plates bolted up for riveting tongs, etc.

Teaching Conditions. On the job.

Reasons. Most effective way.

STEP 3

Line of Approach. Development.

Reasons. Must train in intelligence and judgment in making corrections in parts of lesson not fully understood by the learner.

Method Adopted. On the job.

Reasons.. Only way to be sure they can do it.

Material Required.. Same as in Step 2.

Teaching Conditions.. As in Step 2.

Reasons.. Application on the job the best method when it can be used. It can be used in this case.

STEP 4

Method Adopted.. Testing on the job.

Reasons.. Can be done and is best method when it can be done.

Material Required.. Same as before.

AN ILLUSTRATION OF THE PLANNING OF A LESSON

A form like that given below is a great convenience in laying out auxiliary material against the different jobs in the training course.

STEP 2 TEACHING POINTS	TRADE TERMS	SAFETY FIRST	CARE OF TOOLS AND EQUIPMENT	SCIENCE	STOCK
First Point					
Second Point					
Third Point					
Fourth Point					
Fifth Point					

The Detailed Operation Sheet.—As developed from the general operation sheet the detail might be laid out as follows:

Step I. Preparation

First Idea. (A rivet.)
1. Have you ever seen a rivet?
2. Can you tell a rivet from a bolt?
3. Did you ever see any riveting?
4. Is a rivet alike at both ends?
5. Is a rivet round or square?

Second Idea. (A hot rivet.)
1. Could you pick up a rivet that you found lying around the yard?
2. If you saw a rivet on top of a hot stove would you try to pick it up?
3. Why would you take a chance in picking up the first rivet but not on picking up the second?
4. Could you tell a very hot rivet from a cold rivet without touching it?

Third Idea. (A rivet heated enough.)
1. Can a rivet be heated to different heats?
2. Would it make any difference what heat a rivet has, provided it is hot?
3. Hasn't the heater boy got to know somehow when the rivet is at the right heat?

J. O. P. How does he know when a rivet is just hot enough?

Step II. Presentation

First Point. The rivet must be at a certain temperature to work right. (Memo. Head up cold and hot rivet.)
1. Which rivet takes the most time to head up?
2. Which rivet, hot or cold, makes the best head?
3. If you were paid for the number of rivets driven, which would you prefer, cold or hot rivets?
4. If rivets with well finished heads only were accepted, which would you prefer, hot or cold rivets? (Memo. Drive an over-heated rivet.)

AN ILLUSTRATION OF THE PLANNING OF A LESSON 195

5. Does this rivet head up right?
6. Would you rather be paid for driving over-heated, or properly heated rivets?

Second Point. (The appearance of the rivet varies with the heat.)
1. Can a rivet be too cold for the job, or too hot for the job? (Again head up an under-heated rivet and an over-heated rivet, directing the attention of the boys to the appearance of the rivets when they are taken from the fire.)
2. Could you see any difference between the two rivets?
3. Could you pick out an under-heated rivet? An over-heated rivet?
4. How would you do it?

Third Point. (The rivet must be just under a "scaling" (white) heat.) (Memo. Head up a properly heated rivet.)
1. Has this rivet worked right?
2. Could you tell a rivet that would work right from one that is under-heated or over-heated by looking at it?
3. How would you pick out a properly heated rivet?

Step III. Application

(Memo. Place rivets in fire.) Have each boy pick out correctly heated rivets, meantime asking such questions as are suggested below, of the other three boys.

Bill, Pick out a correctly heated rivet.
Sam, Did he do it?
Jack, How do you know he did it?
Tom, You pick out a rivet.
Jack, You watch him.
Sam, Pick out another one.
Bill, That wasn't right, was it?
Jack, Pick out a burnt rivet.

(Memo. Carry on work of this kind until satisfied each boy knows a properly heated rivet.)

Step IV. Testing

(Memo. Proceed to rivet and say:)
Now I'm going to riveting and am going to use each of you boys in turn as a heater boy to pass me ten rivets. If all ten are at the right heat I'll O. K. you to the foreman for a job. Go to it, Sam. You other three fellows don't mix in, give him a show. You'll get your turn. Watch me rivet.

Use of Other Methods.—Other methods *entirely unsuited for* teaching a lesson of this type, and one of which would probably be selected by a poor teacher, but which a good teacher would never use for this sort of lesson, are illustrated in this paragraph. Had the informational line of approach been selected, the questions in step 1 would have been so framed that the answers would require no thinking by the boys.

The instructor might hold up a rivet and say, Is this a rivet?

Is it a hot rivet?

Is riveting done with hot or with cold rivets?

Do the rivets have to be at any particular heat?

Same conditions are assumed as in above lesson, that is, boys have seen riveting.

In the next step the instructor might head up three rivets, one under-heated, one over-heated, and one correctly heated.

As he picks out the under-heated rivet he might say, "You see, this is dull red. It will not do a good job. I'll prove it to you" and then demonstrates, proceeding in the same way with an over-heated rivet and a correctly heated rivet.

In step 3, where a boy picked out a rivet at the wrong heat he will either tell the boy it was wrong or point out one at the right heat.

If the recitation method were used in step 3 the instructor would be prepared with a set of "cross examination" questions, such as,—Must a rivet be heated at the right temperature?

How can you tell an over-heated or under-heated rivet, etc. (informational approach) or, by the (developmental approach), "Why isn't an over-heated rivet just as good? Why isn't an under-heated rivet just as good?" etc.

By the examination method a few questions selected at random would be given. Under either approach the instructor would, by giving additional information or by suggestive comment, straighten out any points he found needing it.

If the lecture method were used the instructor would proceed somewhat as follows: "You boys have seen a rivet, you know that rivets may be heated and that the rivet heater has to know when a rivet is at the right heat. In doing this he goes by the color. If the rivet is red hot it is too cold, if it is too hot it scales, so the way to know a rivet at the right heat is to pick out one that is just under a good white heat, but not to let it get so hot that it scales."

The last two steps of the lesson would probably, in this case, be handled by the recitation or examination method, although, of course, any method could be used.

The Experimental Method.—This method could be used very effectively in step 2, but is not selected in the lesson plan as given because it was not considered it would "pay" in this particular lesson. By this method the instructor would head up rivets passed him by the boys making no comment but calling attention in each case to the character of the resulting job. He would keep this up until the boys had discovered by this *experimental* method the proper color for a rivet that will do a good job.

The Results of Experience.—As an instructor gains in experience he will learn how to select methods and lines of approach best suited to a given lesson. As he becomes experienced he will also gradually get so that he will not find it necessary to work out each detail of the operation sheet as fully as in the sample given in this section. The proper questions, etc., will come naturally to him as he carries on the lesson. He will "follow the class" as is sometimes said. With practice he will even go from step to step automatically, so that he will finally cease to need an operation sheet on lessons with which he is thoroughly familiar. A good instructor will, however, always work from a lesson plan. He will always make his analysis. A collection of such lesson plans for all the lessons that he has to teach is the most important part of the instructor's "kit of tools," and the possession of a "kit" and the ability to use the "tools" in it is one of the indications that show that an instructor is not an instructional "butcher."

Use of a Form for the Detailed Operation Sheet.—A regular form made out for detailed operation sheets is a convenience where much work of this sort is to be done. A sample of such a form filled out for a simple job is given below.

☞ Italic is printed part of blank. ☜

Name: John Smith.   *Trade:* Pattern Making.
Subject of Lesson: Laying up Stock for Gluing.
Type of Lesson: Trade Technical. Derived.
Date: Dec. 21, 1915.
Class: Boston. Section II.
Director: Allen.
The Teaching Conditions.—The lesson is to be taught to a group who have already had the following experiences. (This may range from nothing up to certain lessons in the same unit.)
Class of 10 men who know the principles of warping and why boards warp as they do with reference to heart and sap sides.
The Line of Approach, Development.

STEP 1. PREPARATION

The Analysis for the Teaching Basis.—Out of all the ideas in the minds of the pupils it is proposed to develop the following as a preparatory basis, and to bring them out in the following order:—
First idea: What is the use of gluing?
Second idea: At least two pieces of stock will be required.
Third idea: These two pieces must be put together, face to face.

Method: Suggestive Questions

Proposed Order of Procedure.—It is proposed to develop these ideas in the order given above by the following questions:

First Idea

Is it ever necessary to fasten two pieces of wood together? What do you do it for? What are some different ways of doing it? Have you ever seen a case where nails were not used? What method was used? When would you use glue instead of nails? Why? Name some cases where you have seen glued joints.

Second Idea

Can you imagine one piece of stock? Why not? At least how many pieces would you need? Can you glue up more than two pieces? Could a pattern be built of parts glued together?

Third Idea

Could you glue two pieces of stock together by the corners, and get a strong joint? Why not? Could you glue two balls together and get a strong joint? Why not? What must you have to get a strong joint? What would determine the strength of different joints with same glue? Which would be the stronger, two $1\frac{1}{2}''$ surfaces or two $\frac{1}{4}''$ surfaces glued together? Why?

J. O. P.

TWO PIECES OF STOCK CAN BE PUT TOGETHER IN THREE WAYS—HEART TO HEART, SAP TO SAP, SAP TO HEART.

STEP 2. PRESENTATION

Analysis of New Ideas to be Presented and Determination of Order of Presentation. The new material which is to be "put over" (taught) consists of the following ideas or steps which it is proposed to present in the following order:—

First Point

Are all three ways equally good, and why?

Second Point

Which method is right, and why?

Method of Presentation

The various ideas or steps in the determined order must now be presented by some determined method. As a preliminary the following questions should be answered: based on the following table of possibilities.

Some Possible Methods of Presentation

Development Approach.
  (a) *Experiment.*
  (b) *Demonstration.*
  (c) *Illustration.*

Informational Approach.
  (a) *Demonstration.*
  (b) *Illustration.*
  (c) *Lecture.*

What method do you intend to use?
Development—Demonstration.

Reasons for Selection of Method

Lesson is to be taught in the classroom and demonstrations on material can be easily brought into the classroom in any desirable quantity.

Write out in full how you would carry out the method, describing any demonstration material used, any questions that you would ask, or statements that you would make. Use diagrams or sketches if required. Give full details of the whole process of presentation.

Demonstration material: Several short lengths of wood showing end grain clearly.

Have a man put two pieces together, with ends toward the class. Have a man sketch the ends as they show upon the blackboard.

Have another man make a different arrangement of the two pieces. Have this sketched on board. Have this also sketched and compared as to appearance of end grain. Then try for a third method. Again sketch and compare. Designate these as sketched on the board as A, B, and C.

"John, do you think that you can show me which is the heart side of any of these pieces of wood I have here? Which way have all these pieces of wood warped? If you were to glue two of these pieces together with their heart sides facing the same way do you think they would have that tendency to warp that way? What do you think would be a good way to place those two pieces to overcome that tendency to warp? Sam, would you place the heart or the sap sides together? Why the sap sides? Then it would be better for that reason to place the heart sides out, would it not? Can anyone give me another reason that has to do with the warping tendencies that would also make this method of arranging the stock desirable?

STEP 3. APPLICATION

Distribute among the men a number of blocks of wood, several to each man. Require each man to designate heart and sap sides of each block. Get each man to put the blocks together properly, aiding him by suggestive questions if necessary.

INSPECTION AND TESTING

Require each learner to arrange the blocks distributed to him in the proper manner for gluing, giving no assistance. Inspect each arrangement when completed.

PART VII
INSTRUCTIONAL MANAGEMENT

CHAPTER XXXI

SPECIAL PROBLEMS OF THE INSTRUCTOR

A. PRELIMINARY DISCUSSION

Preliminary.—Any plan for training is carried on in order to render a certain service to the plant. The maintenance or engineering department keeps the plant and equipment in condition to do work. The shops turn out the product. The training plan, whatever it may be, also has its definite job, that of turning out men who are able to work in the different production departments, and able to do their jobs efficiently and rapidly.

This chapter deals with some of the problems that confront a shop instructor in dealing with the men that he has to train, and points out some of the differences between handling men under production conditions and under instructional conditions.

The Place of the Instructor.—The instructor in any industrial plant is one of the staff; as such he must work under the general conditions that are determined by the organization. To this extent he must adapt himself to conditions that, in a sense, are outside of his control. On the other hand, he is charged with the responsibility of training the men that are assigned to him, and, under the general working conditions as set up by the general organization, he must work out his own methods and his own instructional management. As one of the force he must work in coöperation with the other members of the force; with the other instructors; with whoever may be his superiors in the training work. If in a definitely organized training department he must work with the other members of the staff. If he is working as an individual, say as an instructing foreman or as a production foreman training his own force in his own department, he must handle his own men so that his job is well done, under the particular conditions that come out of the special nature of the trade that he teaches, the special purpose for which his men are to be trained, and the type of men that comprise his instructional group.

Some Things that the Instructor Needs to Know.—In general, an instructor needs to possess two kinds of knowledge, he must know how to handle his gang effectively, how to work out an effective instructional order, how to put over the various teaching units that comprise that instructional order, how to analyze and classify his trade knowledge so as to be able to secure that effective instructional order. This sort of work pertains directly to the instructing job. In addition to what may be called this special "job" knowledge he must also be familiar with the general organization in which he is working, with its special aims (the particular sort of a job that it is trying to put over), and with the relations of the training work to the other departments with which it must work. (The employment department, the production department, etc.) Unless an instructor is so informed he will be unable to work in coöperation with the other members of the organization, will not be able to work in harmony with them, and will be unable to do his part in making the training organization a smoothly running machine, doing its work efficiently, rapidly and smoothly.

The General Proposition.—In general any training plan must be organized with regard to the factors of speed in training, efficiency in training and number of men to be trained. Thus we have a speed organization, a quality organization and a quantity organization.

The Speed Factor.—The plant must not only turn out its product but it must as quickly as possible, therefore any men that must be trained to bring the working force up to full production strength must be got onto regular production work as soon as possible. If it is the job of the training organization to supply any deficiencies in skill that may exist in the men that are hired or in men already employed, the sooner

SPECIAL PROBLEMS OF THE INSTRUCTOR

these men are got out on production with that additional skill, the greater the efficiency of the production force. The training organization must therefore not only train its men *well* but it must also train them *as quickly as possible*. If, by the use of the most scientific training methods, a ship riveter or a paper box maker can be trained in three weeks, and if by less effective methods it takes six weeks, the three weeks gained mean just so much more production. If, by good methods of instruction, a machine hand can be trained in two months, and by poor methods it would require a year, the ten months gained represent just so many more machined parts turned out and production has been speeded up to that extent.

The Efficiency Factor.—These men must not only be trained in as little time as possible but, whatever work they may be trained to do, when they complete the training they must know how to do that work as *well as possible*. They must know how to do their jobs right; they must make few mistakes; they must spoil little stock. They must be trained so that mistakes and poor methods will not reduce speed of production.

The Quantity Factor.—Enough men must be trained to do the job and, whatever the number required the training organization must be able to take care of them and get them trained by the time that they are needed. It cannot wait until the men are needed in production and then train them but the men must be trained in advance to meet the demand when it comes. This problem must be provided for in the organization, for, if the men are not ready when they are needed, production will be held up accordingly.

B. THE JOB OF THE TRAINING PLAN

Preliminary.—It is the job of the training plan to fill orders for its product, and its product is training. The employment department knows how many men are required to keep the work up to full speed in any given line; it secures the necessary men. If these men are already skilled in the trades that are called for they are sent directly to the department where they are needed; if they are only partially skilled, or unskilled, they are put under training to acquire skill before they are put into the production work as competent men. The job of the training plan, however it may be organized is therefore to take the men that are sent to it and provide training so that each man, when discharged from training, can go into regular production work so trained, that his skill will enable him to do the most effective work.

The training scheme therefore takes in men who cannot do jobs and turns them back to the employment department able to do jobs. Effective production requires men, skill and materials; the training makes up any deficiencies in skill that any given man may need before he goes into production. Its product is therefore *training*, and it will do its work well in proportion as it trains well, trains rapidly and trains by the use of the best instructional methods.

Effective Management.—Whenever work is to be done there is always a best way of doing it; if the work is production work there is a best order of operations, those operations can best be carried out by the use of certain machines or other equipment units, and there will be certain types of equipment units that give the best service under the given working conditions. The general problem of studying such a production problem and determining the conditions as to layout, equipment, selection of equipment units, etc., that will enable the factory or the shop to turn out the best product in the least time with the least waste of power, time and stock, is the problem of the efficiency engineer.

In the same way the trainer has the problem of getting out his product (training), as rapidly, as can be done and still do a good job, with the least turnover (waste), and with the least expenditure of energy both on his part and on the part of the learner. In general, his problems are similar to those of the production engineer, he endeavors to reduce the expenditure of time and energy to the minimum by using properly worked out orders of instruction, by setting up the best teaching units, by selecting the most efficient methods for each lesson that he puts over, and for each step in the lesson; he holds his turnover down to the minimum by effective handling of his gang. Where the efficiency engineer determines that a certain order of operations will give the best results, the instructor determines what order of instruction will give the best instructional results; where the production engineer decides, that for the doing of a certain production job certain machines should be used, the trainer decides, that, for the effective doing of a certain training job certain methods and lines of approach will best serve the purpose.

The trainer is therefore essentially an *instructional engineer* and must attack his training problems in the same way that the production engineer attacks his problems. In the same way the whole problem of training is essentially one in training engineering, such a department is a training *engineering department*, and in its organization it will provide for the best means of working out its training engineering problems.

Instructional Management.—Just as we have employment management, or production management, so we have instructional, or training management, the term meaning that sort of planning and arranging and organizing for effective instruction and training that the other departments do in their respective fields for their respective purposes. That side of instructional management that deals with the handling of the group under instruction is discussed in a later chapter; the questions that apply particularly to the work of the director of a training department, where such a department is established, are discussed in other chapters; this section deals with the general principles of organization as they affect the instructor so far as they affect his own work with his own men.

CHAPTER XXXII

ORGANIZATION FOR HANDLING THE DIFFERENT TYPES OF INSTRUCTION

Preliminary.—As discussed elsewhere in more detail any plan for training men in an industrial plant may have to deal with any or all of at least three distinct training problems, training the green man, training the competent mechanic who only needs to be given such training as will enable him to "convert" his trade into a new trade and training the man already employed who needs more training in the line of his trade in order that he may do a better job or do work of a higher grade.

Since the general principles laid down in this chapter apply to the trade or industrial school with the same force that they apply to the industrial shop, no distinction has been made between them in the discussion.

For convenience we will designate the first type of man as a green man, the second type as a conversion man, the third type as a trade extension man. Each type must be handled through a distinct type of organization.

Organization for Handling the Green Man.—Under ordinary conditions it is probable that the green man will be mostly trained for the simpler trades or for the simpler lines of work in the trades. As a practical matter it is not probable that, for efficient training work, an attempt would be made to train an exsalesman for a tool maker, it would take too long.

However that may be, the organization for the training of the green men should provide for handling them in sufficiently small groups for effective training, for admission into the group at practically any time, for individual instruction while in the group, for instructional hours that are the same as the working hours in the plant and for training on production work.

Sometimes there is a tendency to carry on training for less than the regular working time unit, the reason given being that it is training work and not production work. This is, of course, no reason at all; the notion of the shorter working unit generally comes, in fact, from the fact that the regular schools operate a smaller number of hours per day than do the industrial plants. This is true and there are some reasons for it that do not apply to training department when carried on in a trade school or in the plant. In the first place most of the regular school work is "book work" rather than work in which the learner is doing something; so that the fatigue factor comes up in less time than in work where the thinking and the doing are combined. In the second place most of the regular school work is carried on inside of buildings where the air is often none too good, a condition very different from that existing in outside production work or even in instruction work in the shop. In the third place the learners in the regular schools are mainly children and those in the training organization are men. In the fourth place there is no particular reason why the regular schools cannot operate more hours a week than has been the custom and some are now doing it. In the last place, even if all other conditions were disregarded, the time required for training should be kept down to a minimum because the man should be got into production work as soon as he can be effectively trained, and the more hours a day that can be put onto training, the fewer days will be required for the completion of the training course.

Organizing for Individual Progression.—Not only should the training work be so organized that a man can be admitted to an instructional group at any time but the organization should be such that each man can progress through the course of training required for his particular case as rapidly as his individual capabilities will admit. A "bright" man should not be held back by men who are less "bright" nor should a "slow" man be speeded up in an attempt to make him keep up with the fast man. Each man should be allowed to travel at his own best gait.

In order to do this it is evident that there can be no class organization, as discussed in Section D and seldom even group organization, but practically all the organization must be on the basis of individual instruction.

Organization for Discharging the Man from his Group.— Just as the organization must provide for individual admission, and individual progression, it must also provide for individual discharge from the instructional group and so from the training work. If men are to be admitted at all times and are to progress each at his own maximum gait, evidently there can be no "graduation day" for the group, but each man will come up for discharge in a time determined by his rate of progression and at a date determined by the date of his admission and by the speed with which he has progressed through the instructional course. Any other organization, especially one modeled on the procedure of the regular schools, where there are fixed times of admission and of "discharge" would defeat the ends of efficient training and are out of the question.

Proper Organization for Training a Green Man.—An efficient training organization should therefore plan for the training of green men on a basis of individual admission, individual progression and individual discharge.

Organization for Handling Conversion Men.—The conversion man differs from the green man in that he already has a trade which, to a greater or less extent, already fits into the requirements of the trade or the job to which he is to be converted. He therefore differs from the green man in two ways, first he is a mechanic; he has a trade experience behind him; second, it is probable that he knows more about the production jobs of the new trade to which he is to be converted than he knows about the technical jobs, or than he is posted on the auxiliary knowledge. It is not improbable therefore that he may be handled in two ways according to special circumstances. On the production work the organization should be such that he can be taken care of as if he were a green man; on the side of the auxiliary knowledge it is not improbable that, under some circumstances, use can be made of the group or even of the class organization.

The organization for handling conversion men should therefore provide for individual work, as for green men, and should also provide for class or group work.

The tendency will be to attempt to do too much work with conversion men on a class basis; the value of such work is limited to certain special cases, but the possibility of those special cases coming up is sufficient to warrant provision for class work in the organization.

Organization for Handling Trade Extension Men.—These men offer entirely different characteristics from the other two groups of men, especially, of course, the green men. They are likely to need either special individual instruction in certain operations, as when the machinist wants to learn the use of the index head, or they want training in the technical jobs of their trade. Under these conditions it is sometimes possible to make good use of the class organization. In general, the organization for dealing with this class of men should include both provision for class work, and for individual work.

Organization for Handling Green Men.—In practically all cases the organization for training green men should be for training them on production, not on exercises. The distinction between those two methods of training is discussed in Part I. The organization should be such that production is a *by product* of training or the training will not be efficient. This point is very important, because, if, under this method of training, the "production" idea "runs away" with the "instruction" idea, the efficiency of the training is very seriously impaired.

Production Work a By Product of Instruction.—The purpose of turning production jobs over to the training organization is, of course, to give that organization an opportunity to train the man on a real job, not as an immediate reason to get the work done, but, as a *result of the instructional process the job is done as a by product*. The instructor is thinking of *training* the man and the man is thinking of *learning* how to do the job, but, nevertheless the job is done.

What is Meant by a "By Product."—In manufacturing, a by product is a "side show," that is, it is something that is obtained incidentally to the production of the thing that the concern is organized to produce. For example, a gas company is organized to produce gas, but in the making of the gas a considerable amount of coal tar is produced. The company is in business to make gas, not coal tar, but it gets the tar as a by product, and it is a by product of considerable value. In the same way a training department is in business to produce trained men, but, if it trains its men on real jobs, these jobs are a by product of the work of the department, and to that extent increase production.

The Value of the "Production by Product."—In the first place, production counts, and any work that can be turned out in connection with training is so much to the good, provided, of course, that the efficiency of the training is not impaired. In the second place experience has shown that the surest way to keep up the interest of a learner is to give him a real job. If a man knows that the work that he does is going to be subjected to the test of real use he is much more interested, if he knows that, no matter how good a job he does it will be scrapped. In the third place, instruction on real jobs gives the best instructional conditions because the man is trained to work under the same surroundings as he will work under later in the production department. If a man will have to work out of doors, or in heat, or with a lot of noise going on all around him, he should get used to these working conditions while he is in training, not after he gets into production. Training him to work under these conditions is an important part of his training.

Training Departments should Organize for Training on Production Material.—Any plan that may be put in operation for training should include in its organization, effective provision for training on production work, whenever such training is desirable. The degree to which this will be necessary will depend, to a considerable extent, on whether it is proposed to train trade extension men, conversion men or green men.

Production Work and Trade Extension Men.—As already pointed out, trade extension men are already well acquainted with a considerable portion of their trade; they usually need instruction either in some special operations or in technical jobs or need to be informed with regard to some particular sort of auxiliary knowledge.

Where special operations are called for such men can usually be trained on production work. Where the demand is for additional training in some special technical jobs production work can often be used to advantage, but, with such men, exercise work can also be safely used in many cases, as in blueprint reading for machinists. In some cases where there is need for passing out auxiliary information, training on production is not called for as a regular thing. In each case the training work should be organized to meet these special needs as they arise.

Organization for Certain Types of Trade Extension Work: Supplementary Job Training.—In many trades the need of the trade extension man is for an opportunity to learn how to do certain jobs that he cannot learn to do in connection with his regular work. A machinist who is familiar with the plain miller wants to learn how to operate a universal miller, or a man who can drive button head rivets wants to learn how to drive countersunk rivets. In such cases the man can, and should, be trained on production jobs, and, always without exception, must be handled by the method of individual instruction. In this case he differs from the green man in a number of ways. He has had considerable trade experience to fall back on and so will "catch on" quicker. His interest is usually strongly aroused, because learning to do the new job usually means getting a better job so the vocational motive is strong. As a rule, what he has to learn is a small extension of what he already knows. All of this makes the work of the instructor easier, but does not allow the substitution of exercises for real jobs.

Instructors often tend to plan to train this type of trade-extension man in classes and on non-productive work; this should not be attempted except in special cases that have been carefully considered, since training such men on non-productive work, means, in general, less efficient instruction.

Organization for Certain Types of Trade Extension Work: Auxiliary Material.—In certain cases the trade extension man only needs to be informed as to certain auxiliary material; for example, suppose that trade extension machinists only need to be informed as to a standard method of putting dimensions on the blueprint, or crane operators might need to have their attention drawn merely to the necessity of taking certain precautions in handling material. In such cases the class organization can be used to advantage under certain conditions, among the most important of which are that the men thoroughly know their jobs and already appreciate the necessity for securing and applying the information that is to be given them. Even under these circumstances the "first choice" would be to take up the matter with them on the job, if that were possible. With class organization when demonstration cannot be used, the discussion or the illustration should be used rather than the lecture.

As pointed out elsewhere, unless the handing out of information is strongly backed up by the discussion of problems in which that information comes into play, it is not likely to "stick" and only under such conditions with men of considerable experience in the trade.

Organization for Conversion Work.—In general, organization for conversion work will aim at giving auxiliary material or at training on jobs or at both. A house carpenter, for example, during conversion into a ship carpenter, may need to know certain terms (ship terms for example), and he may need to learn how to do certain jobs on the ways that he never has done as a house carpenter. His condition is therefore essentially the same as that of the trade extension man and the same general organization will meet the situation.

Organization for Training Green Men.—There is little doubt that under the ordinary working conditions the questions of effective organization for the training of green men will be of more importance than any other questions of organization for the training work. The problem of organizing for training green men is the one that will give the instructor the most trouble and will call for the most careful study to determine the best instructional conditions.

In general, it may be said that one instructor should carry

the group through the training course, both through the period of instruction proper and through the training period. One instructor should not instruct and another train. It is also true that under practical working conditions the conditions of elastic admission to the group, elastic progression through the group and elastic discharge from the group will have to be observed. Men will have to be admitted at any time, put through the training and instructional work as fast as they can individually progress, and be discharged as soon as they are trained.

In practice, therefore, the group organization will have to be such that the instructor can handle men in all stages of progression through his course of instruction, know where they are in the course at any given time and know when they are trained and ready to go out into production.

Organization for Training and for Instructing: The Order of Procedure.—As stated elsewhere there are two periods that a learner must be carried through: a period of instruction, in which he learns how to do the job and a training period during which he gets so that he can do the job rapidly and well.

In dealing with these two periods there are, of course, two possible methods of handling them: we could instruct the man in all the jobs in the instructional order and then train him, or we could instruct him on each job and then train him on that job before we instructed him on the next job. We can really take training and instructing as two independent blocks and use either the spiral or the block progression method.

The Proper Procedure to Organize to Train and Instruct Job by Job.—The most efficient method of procedure is undoubtedly to train and instruct job by job, and the organization should provide for this method of procedure. Some of the more important reasons for this are as follows: First, the man's interest will be much greater if he feels that he is getting "the whole of the job" at one time; second, if the training period is deferred until the end of the course, he will have forgotten a good deal of his instruction, and will have to be instructed all over again, which takes time; third, if, under the organization as outlined, the instructor has some men in his group who are under training as distinguished from being under instruction, these men will need but little attention except an inspection from time to time, and the instructor can give more of his time to instructional work with those men in his group who are under instruction as distinguished from being under training. This, of course, enables a large group to be handled which is an advantage.

The organization should therefore provide for:

1. Both instruction and training to be given by the same instructor and

2. Instruction and training to be given job by job.

The Instructor and the General Organization of the Plant.— The organization that an instructor sets up in handling his group is only a part of the organization of the plant, taken as a whole. It is very important that all instructors should "fit in" well with the general organization; should be careful not to "cross wires"; should carefully follow the methods of procedure laid down, especially in dealing with another department. In the push of the work the temptation is strong to "cut across lots" and save time, or to change some method of procedure in the immediate interests of getting the work done, but, in the long run such deviations from the established practice do more harm than good. The instructor who adapts his organization to that of the department or to that of the plant as a whole and who "plays fair" with the general organization, will, in the long run, do the most to promote speed in production.

CHAPTER XXXIII

THE ORGANIZATION OF THE INSTRUCTIONAL GANG

A. GENERAL PRELIMINARY

Preliminary.—Whenever work of any kind is to be done by a group of men under some sort of direction there must be some sort of *organization*. The character of the organization will vary with the particular sort of work that is to be done, with the conditions under which it is to be done, with the sort of men that the work is to be done with and with the particular purpose for which the work is to be done. Thus, we have the military organization for doing the military "job," the school organization for doing the "school" job, the special organization of the riveting gang for doing a riveting job, and so on, each organization being worked out with regard to the needs of the particular job that is to be done.

The Learner and the " Gang. "—Whenever a job is to be done by a group we always find that there must be the workmen who do the work and the leader; the "gang" and the "boss"; without the gang, the work would not be done; without the boss the work would not be well done; the different men in the gang would be working at cross purposes, there would be a lot of "crossed wires," nobody would know exactly where he "got off" and where the other fellow "got on."

The leader is responsible for the planning of the work, for the order in which the different operations are carried out, for the clearing up of difficulties, for keeping the work going. The members of the gang are responsible for doing the work, for doing it well and for intelligently carrying out the instructions of the leader. Without the leader the gang could not do their job, without the gang the job could not be done. The doing of a good job requires both a good boss and a good gang, and in order that both boss and gang can do their work there must be a good *organization*—the particular kind of organization being worked out to best meet the special requirements for doing a certain kind of a job.

The Purpose of Organization.—By organization is meant such arrangements as may be determined upon for enabling the boss and the gang to perform their respective functions, (do their jobs) with the greatest efficiency and with the least "lost motion" and friction. A good organization provides for good working conditions, for the right working relations between the leader and the different members of the gang, for the providing of the necessary working material, and, above all, it definitely fixes the responsibility of each man, that is, it determines his job.

Organization is therefore merely a means to an end, and that end is to secure and maintain good working conditions.

The Training Gang.—A training scheme is operated to train men, that is, to do a definite job, therefore there must be organization, as in the case of any other department that is organized to do a job. The general questions relating to the organization of a training plan mainly concern the general organization but since there must be a group of men to be trained by each instructor, that part of the problem of organization that directly affects the instructor is discussed in this chapter.

A training gang consists of an instructor, or "training boss," and a group of men to be trained, or the "training gang." The organization must be such that the instructor can instruct and the men can learn, and that the instructing process can be carried on as efficiently as possible, that is, the organization must provide for good instructional conditions and for the proper relations between the training department and any other department that may be concerned in the carrying on of the work.

Characteristics of the Training Gang.—In production work we find, in general, two sorts of gangs: the first sort of gang is a "team," that is, the gang as a whole are organized to do a job but each member of the gang only does a part of the job.

This would be true, for example, in the case of a riveting gang on structural steel work, or in machine box making. The other sort of a gang consists of a group of workmen, each of whom is doing a whole job; hence each man in the gang is doing an individual job for which he is responsible directly to the boss or foreman. This might be true, for example, in printing, or house carpentry or in the machine shop.

The training gang is of the latter type; each man in the gang is on his own job, that of getting training; he is responsible to the instructor for the whole "job"; that of being trained, and the instructor is responsible for putting each man through the entire training course that has been laid out for the particular training of each man.

This fact affects the character of the organization of the training gang in a number of ways, as will be discussed later. Another factor that affects the organization of the instructional gang is that it consists, not of men who know their jobs, but of men who are to be trained to do jobs later. They are not workmen but learners. A third factor affecting the organization is that the work of the gang is not production but instruction; the difficulties that must be met are not production difficulties but learning difficulties.

All the above factors and many others affect the organization of the instructional gang and must be taken into consideration. The chief fact to which attention is directed at this point is that there must be an effective organization but that it must be more or less different from the organization of a production gang.

Some Important Points in Organization.—In considering the problem of the organization of the instructional gang it will be found that it concerns itself mainly with ways and means for dealing with the following:

1. Bringing the instructor and the gang together.
2. Making up the gang. (Taking on men. Admission.)
3. Providing proper instructional conditions.
4. Providing efficient instruction.
5. Dropping men from the gang when trained. (Discharge.)

B. ORGANIZATION TO GET A PLACE TO WORK IN

Bringing the Gang and the Instructor Together.—This means that some place must be provided where the instructor and the men under instruction can get together. In order to meet this condition regular schools are housed in school houses, buildings especially constructed to afford such meeting places. In such buildings we find school rooms, assembly halls, gymnasium, laboratories, etc.

In the same way, for the work of the training department some place must be provided for the getting together of the instructor and the gang under instruction.

In considering this place problem the untrained instructor often thinks in terms of the general school; he thinks of school rooms, lecture rooms, etc., because he naturally thinks of his own school experience, and, if he is to be a "teacher" he thinks of his job as being the same as the job of the teacher that he went to school to in his younger days. He thinks of conducting "classes," in "school rooms," of using text books, of lecturing to his men, of giving "courses" of instruction; in general because students in the regular school are put in a special place to get their "schooling" he thinks of doing his work *away from the job and by regular school methods*, and tends to plan his organization accordingly, thus to a greater or less extent copying the organization of the regular school. In this he fails to take into account the totally different aim and the necessary working conditions that must be set up as between regular school work and trade training.

"Place Organization" in a Training Department.—With the possible exception of certain "trade extension work" as discussed elsewhere in these notes it is extremely improbable that any of the ordinary training will be carried on anywhere except *in the shops*. There will be no "school room"; all instruction will be given *on the job*, that is, each lesson that has been laid down in the order of instruction as determined by the instructor must be put over to a man in connection with the doing of a job that approximately meets the specifications of the type job for that particular stage of the learner's progression through the instructional order of jobs. The instructor will have no opportunity to sit in a chair behind a desk and talk to a group in front of him who are also in chairs; he and his men will be out in the yard, or in the shop, turning out jobs, but turning them out for purposes of *instruction*. If the instructor finds that it is necessary to give some instruction to his men and the noise is such that he cannot make himself heard, it is highly probable that he can only expect to be able to find some relatively quiet place somewhere in the shop where he can put over what he wishes to teach. The lee side of a building or the corner of the shop is about all the "place" facilities that he can expect.

Under these conditions it is evident that the organization of the regular school which is based on the carrying on of the instruction "inside," away from the actual production work (where such training is given, as in most school shops), will not work at all, and a totally different organization, much more like the organization of a working gang must be developed.

The effective organization for the sort of training conditions required by industrial training must therefore provide for the bringing together of instructor and instructional gang under practically the same conditions as for a production gang, so far as the place question goes, and the instructor must so organize his group with regard to this factor that good work in instruction can be done under these conditions. That is, the "school room" will be the yard or shop and the "school book" will be the job.

Exceptions to the Above Statement.—The above statements apply, of course, mainly to job training. Under some conditions, in trade extension work, a close approximation to inside conditions is possible.

C. ORGANIZATION FOR GETTING THE GANG TOGETHER

Organization for Making up the Gang (Admission.)— This part of the organization will deal mainly with provision for taking the man into the instructional gang. Under the conditions that will exist in job training it is extremely improbable that a gang can be given to an instructor so that all can start together. It is more probable that, as men are hired by the employment department they will be put into training and turned into a gang for that trade which happens to have a vacancy. This means that the organization of the gang, so far as admission goes, must be based on what is called *elastic admission;* that is, the instructor must be able to take on a man at any time and start him on the training course without regard to where any of the rest of the group are on their progression through the same course. This means that the instructor will have in his group men in all stages of progression, that he will be discharging men any time on the completion of their training and that he will organize so that he can take in new men whenever he has a vacancy.

Of course the organization of the regular school which is intended to deal with exactly the reverse situation (admissions at stated times only) will not work at all, and the instructor who has the regular school organization in mind will find himself unable to organize for effective work under industrial conditions unless he breaks entirely away from such notions.

Organization for Elastic Admission.—So far as organization for admission goes it must be based upon the principle of elastic admission and not on the principle of admission at fixed intervals.

It is, of course, possible that in large plants it might be possible to organize for admission say three times a week, but this would only be true in cases where the number of instructing groups was so large that a man could be taken into some group on any day. An organization as to admission that assumes that a man will stand around for several days or a week waiting to get into a training section will not work, nor is it proper that that amount of the man's time should be lost; time is too valuable; every day of time that is lost, even with one man, slows up production.

D. ORGANIZATION TO SECURE PROPER INSTRUCTIONAL CONDITIONS

Proper Instructional Conditions: Organization.—In order that effective instruction can be carried on the group must be organized in some way. In general it may be said that there are three well known methods of organizing a group for instructional work: (a) Class Instruction; (b) Group Instruction; (c) Individual Instruction. Class Instruction is the condition usually found in general schools (High Schools, Grammar Schools, Colleges) and, in general, is the least efficient condition under which teaching may be carried on in industrial training. Group instruction is seldom found in general schools, but is often found in some forms of industrial training, and has some value in shop training. Individual instruction is rarely found in general schools, but is often the only effective device in practical instruction (as in instruction on production work). An instructor should be familiar with all of these three methods, although he is likely to work mostly with the last two.

Class Organization: The Class as Distinguished from the Teaching Group.—In the strictly school sense the term "class" means a group of pupils assigned to an instructor. Its use does not imply any special method of organization for instruction. From the standpoint of organization for *instruction*, the term class is also often used to mean a group which are to be simultaneously taught the same lesson. This double use of the term leads to so much confusion that it is better to use the term "instruction group" when referring to the group of learners assigned to an instructor and confine the use of the term class to its meaning in connection with organization from the standpoint of instruction.

Conditions under which Instruction may be Given: Class Organization.—In class teaching all pupils are assumed to be taught the same thing at the same time. In theory they are all assumed to know the same things, to have the same knowledge, or to be able to do the same thing at the time of the particular lesson. Thus a class of fifteen men, all of whom knew how to run a miller and none of whom knew how to set an index head, might be simultaneously taught how to perform this operation. Or a group of girls, all of whom knew how to sew, might be simultaneously taught how to make a button hole. In all cases of class instruction the characteristic is that, as illustrated above, every pupil is assumed to be taught *the same thing at the same time*. Efficient class organization must therefore meet the following theoretical conditions, and will be effective in proportion as it meets them in practice:

(1) All pupils must know the same things when they come into the class.
(2) All pupils must be taught the same new things during that lesson (same teaching unit).
(3) All pupils must leave the class with the same additional amount of knowledge or training.

Organization for Instruction: Group Organization.—Group organization differs from class organization in that it is not assumed that all learners are to be taught the same thing at the same time, but that the whole gang consists of sub groups, and that the members of each sub group can be instructed in the same thing at the same time. Thus an instructional group of fifteen men might consist of three sub groups of 7, 5, and 3 men and it would be assumed that the instructor would teach one lesson to sub group 1, another lesson to sub group 2, and a third to sub group 3, and that he can carry on the work with all three groups at the same time.

It is not assumed that the membership of these sub groups will remain the same from day to day, or that the same number of groups, or the same number of men in the different sub groups will remain constant. That is, the instructor forms groups as he happens to find men in the same stage of progression, and simply takes advantage of such a situation when it happens to occur.

Efficient organization for group instruction must therefore meet the following conditions and will be efficient as it does deal effectively with them in practice.

1. Sub groups must be found wherein all members have reached the same stage of progression in the instruction program.
2. All members of the group must be ready for the next lesson at the same time.
3. All learners leave the lesson for that particular sub group with the same additional amount of knowledge or training.

Whenever use can be made of temporary groups time and energy are, of course, saved, since it does not take as much time to instruct a group of men as it would to instruct each individually, and the total expenditure of energy by the instructor will not be so great. Instructors should therefore be on the lookout for chances to work in the group organization and the organization should permit of this being done whenever it appears that it can be done to advantage.

In order that effective use may be made of the method of group organization it is evident that an instructor must keep a very careful record of the progress of each of his men on the course of instruction that he has prepared, and when he finds that certain men happen to have reached the same stage of progression, bring them into a group for the next piece of instrumental work. Unless this is done of course the organization fails entirely; groups are not properly made up and the work suffers accordingly.

Conditions under which Instruction may be Given: Organization for Individual Instruction.—Organization for individual instruction differs from organization for class or group instruction in that it is assumed that no two men are instructed in the same lesson at the same time, so that the instruction group merely consists of a number of learners assigned to that particular instructor for instruction, each individual to be instructed as a unit, without regard to any other individual. This means that a different instruction unit must be simultaneously put over to each individual learner, and that the instructor occupies essentially the position of a foreman who is bossing a gang of men each of which is on a different job, or is at a different stage on the same job.

Under this organization the instructor must evidently carry on as many lessons as there are men in his group, and, if new men are continually coming in and instructed men going out, these individual lessons may cover any stage from the most elementary to the most advanced teaching units that are laid out in the instructional order.

Evidently for efficient individual instruction the instructor must know where each man is on the course of instruction, so that he can assign the next job in the proper relation to what the man has already had. It is also evident that under these conditions there is no assumption that the work of any one man is in any way connected with the work of any other man, so that the instructor is in no way concerned with the progress of his men as regards each other. Under these conditions problems of admission and of progression are reduced to a minimum.

Efficient teaching conditions for individual instruction exist (1) where the teaching group is small enough to enable individual attention to be given to each learner. (2) Where the subjects of the lessons can best be taught individually (as in production work). (3) Where the instructor is skillful enough to successfully handle a reasonably large group by this method.

Organization for Progression: The Time Factor.—So far as organization is concerned, the question of the different speeds with which men progress can be met in two ways. By one method the organization can be based on the notion that the man will be given a fixed amount of time, in which he can either go as far as he can, or can "get what he can" as it is often put. This is essentially the method of the regular school; classes are carried for a given period. The difficulty with this organization so far as trade training is concerned is that, if a man is to be taught to do a job he must be entirely taught, so that he can do that job, not half taught, or two-thirds taught, but entirely taught. If the fixed time interval is used, a slow man can be thoroughly taught fewer jobs than a fast man, but he must be thoroughly taught what he is taught. The quantity of instruction can be reduced, but the *quality* cannot be cut down and still do the training job.

The method of organizing to deal with the matter of unequal progression that will best meet the needs of emergency training is undoubtedly that that provides for keeping the learner in the course until he is completely trained according to the "requisition for training" in his case, rather than in only partially filling the requisition in order to make time even.

Organization for Efficient Progression.—No matter what the organization for getting the gang together, it will be composed of men who will progress through the instructional order at different rates. Even if they all started together, they will soon be strung out all along the line.

Evidently there must be included in the organization for working conditions some provision for dealing with the matter of unequal progression. Under the class organization, no provision is made to meet this condition; the fundamental assumption is that all learners will progress at the same rate, and no class organization can be worked out in practice on any other assumption. That is, the class organization is based on an assumption that everybody knows is not correct. It is true that, given a carefully selected group to start with, and more or less special help by the instructor, so that the "advance guard" can be held back a little and the "rear guard" jacked up, some approximation to equal progress can be maintained, but it is even then extremely difficult, and, under the conditions existing in shop training practically impossible to secure effective "progression control" with a class organization. The group organization offers but little more prospect of success. The only practical organization that will enable the instructor to maintain good "progression control" is to organize for individual instruction. Under this organization the differences of the men in their progression due to entrance at different times, with different powers of taking in the instruction, with different degrees of education, are easily taken care of. The organization for individual instruction is therefore the only one that offers hopes of success in the ordinary work of training and is the only one that should be used under ordinary circumstances to meet the problems caused by the certain unequal progression of the different men in the instruction gang.

Where the Class Organization will Work the Best.—Under industrial training conditions the only place where the class organization will be of service is possibly in some forms of trade extension work for advanced men. Thus, for example, if it were desired to give all the shipfitters in a yard the standard method of marking templets, and that was all that it was desired to give them, this work might be effectively done under the class organization. It is not probable, however, that the class organization will find much place in the work of training in industrial plants. It will certainly find no place in the training of green men; it may have some value in certain cases in the giving of conversion training, but, as stated above, it is most likely to be of service in trade extension work on technical jobs, or in passing out technical information to advanced men on a trade extension basis.

Where the Group Organization will Work the Best.—The group organization will work the best where the work happens to be of such a character that a number of men can be simultaneously instructed on a given teaching unit. This is most likely to happen in instruction on relatively simple jobs, and possibly in handling technical rather than production jobs. It is not probable however that, as a form of organization it will find much place in organization for industrial training. It is, of course, an attempt to combine the good points of both the method of class and of individual instructional organization. Conditions seldom arise in practice where it can be successfully worked out, and it is not a type of organization that the average instructor will find of much service except for the special cases noted above. It is probably more difficult to work effectively in practice than either of the two other organizations discussed in this section.

Individual Instruction.—Individual instruction always seems the most difficult to the untrained instructor but in reality, lends itself the best to efficient training. Under the conditions that usually exist in shop training it is the only method of organization that promises efficient results. If the group is organized for individual instruction no difficulties as to admission or relative speed of progress come up, each man is dealing with the instructor and has no concern as to the work of any other man, nor has the instructor, in instructing any one man any need to consider the work of any other man. The greatest problem for the instructor in working under this type of organization is to so dovetail in the different lessons that he has to teach, and to so arrange the work, that while he is putting over say, step 1 with one man, the other men in the group are on steps 3 or 4 in their respective lessons. Unless the gang is too large, this can be done however with a careful progression control and with good distribution.

So far as efficiency goes there is no question; if each man can be instructed individually, the time required for training will be greatly reduced, the man will be much better trained, the work will be much better done. This is the organization that should be adopted for the general run of instructional work.

The Rotating Gang.—Undoubtedly the best organization for meeting the requirements of a training department is one that provides for what may be called the rotating gang, that is, the organization is such that an instructor always has a group of the same size; as soon as a man is discharged from the group another man comes in, so that the group consists of men in all stages of progression, but is always full.

This organization evidently provides the best conditions so far as expense for instruction goes; of course it can only be carried out when the group is organized for individual instruction.

E. ORGANIZATION FOR DISCHARGING FROM THE GANG

Organization for Discharging Men from the Gang.—The organization should make possible the discharge of a man from the gang as soon as he has completed his training and the instructor is ready to O. K. him out of the training work. If the work is organized for individual instruction this is easy, and no question will come up. Under class organization however, the man must be held until the class is through, or the instructor will find himself with a gradually diminishing group until he is left with only one man to work with, which, is, of course, an unduly expensive situation.

The General Conditions that Affect the Size of a Training Gang.—The more an instructor distributes himself the thinner he must spread out his instruction, the less attention he can give to any one man, the more chance there is for waiting around and for the development of conditions that will reduce interest. The less men an instructor has in his gang, the more he can concentrate, the more intense can he make his instruction and the less chance will there be of lost motion and general drop in interest. Below a certain point however the instructor will not be entirely occupied. If he were training one man alone there would be a good many times when he would be standing around waiting for the learner to do something before he could go on with the instruction. Evidently an instructor who only has one man in his gang could handle more men and not lower the efficiency of his work. It is equally evident that if an instructor undertook to instruct a thousand men in one gang he could do no instructional work at all. This is, there is a maximum and a minimum size to the group that can be effectively handled by an instructor at one time. Among the more important factors that affect the size of a class for good instructional conditions are the character of the trade, the working conditions, the class of the work and the sort of men that are to be instructed.

This problem corresponds in a general way to what is called the "economical steaming speed" of a ship. If she goes too slow and so takes too much time to make her voyage, too much coal will be burned per mile; if she is driven too fast, she will get there sooner, but the coal consumption will be so greatly increased that, in spite of the decreased time required for the voyage, the coal bill will also be too much per mile.

It is always possible to find a speed at which these two factors, time and coal consumption per mile balance up so that the cost of coal per mile is reduced to the minimum. This is the economical speed.

In the same way the general tendency of increasing the size of a class above the effective minimum is to slow down the speed of instruction, that is, the larger the group the longer it will take to put a given man in the group through the course of training. In the same general way it can be said that the smaller the gang down to the effective minimum the more rapid will be the instructional speed. The problem is to find the "economical size" for a given course of instruction.

Some details of these points are discussed in the following paragraphs:

Size of the Gang as Affected by the Sort of Men that are to be Instructed.—A training plan may have to deal with any or all of three classes of men; trade extension men, conversion men and green men, and the detailed meaning of these terms have already been given. It is sufficient here to point out that a trade extension man is a man who already knows considerable about his trade and a conversion man knows all about his own trade but little or nothing about the trade to which he is to be converted, while the green man knows nothing of any trade. Under these conditions it is evident that trade extension men can be handled in larger gangs than conversion men, and conversion men in larger gangs than green men, always, of course, with regard to the other factors that have been discussed.

It is also true that in trade extension work it is often possible to handle relatively large groups when the men are well advanced and the character of the instruction is largely technical, as in the case of work with second class steam engineers working for a first class license. Probably in such a case from twenty to twenty-five men could be successfully handled, but this is an extreme case.

Effective Size of Gangs as Affected by the Working Conditions.—Even in the same trade the working conditions will affect the size of the effective gang. During some portions of the instructional course it may be necessary to distribute the men so widely that the instructor could not exercise proper supervision over a gang of a certain size, possibly of a smaller size than in other parts of the course. For example, this might be true in training in house carpentry, where, in order to get work for different men that fitted to the type job specifications for their individual checking levels, it might be necessary to put one man on the roof, another in the attic, another on the cellar stairs, or in a machine shop where men might have to be put on widely distributed jobs on account of the way in which the machines were grouped. The possibility of such situations coming up in connection with the working conditions that go with that particular trade must be taken into consideration in determining the effective working size of the gang for that trade.

Effective Size of Gangs as Affected by the Character of the Trade.—Experience has shown that the character of the trade that is to be taught affects the "economical group size." Where jobs are simple and the men in the gang can be concentrated more men can be economically handled than where the reverse conditions prevail. For example, more men could probably be efficiently handled in training machinists or printers than in training sheet metal workers. So far as available experience up to date bears on the problem it is pretty well established that, in no case, can an instructor handle a gang of more than ten men efficiently, and in many cases the actual training output will be increased if the number is held down to not over five or six; much larger groups can often be handled in trade extension work.

The Instructor and the Size of Gangs.—In general an inexperienced instructor does not sufficiently study his problem in order to know how large a gang he can handle for economical instructional work, but he almost always thinks that he can handle a larger gang than he really can, or he thinks that he cannot handle as large a gang as he can. He is either ready to take on more men than he has or he wants men taken out of his gang so that it will be smaller. He does not take into account the factors just discussed and so fails to see why he cannot handle twenty men just as well as ten, or he thinks that he can only handle two men when, with the proper organization and management he could handle seven or eight.

The trained instructor will study his problem intelligently, will take into consideration all the factors that apply, and will base such recommendations as he may make on a scientific study of the conditions.

CHAPTER XXXIV

INSTRUCTIONAL CONDITIONS AS THEY ARE AFFECTED BY SURROUNDINGS AND MATERIAL

Preliminary.—This chapter discusses some of the considerations to which an instructor must give attention in planning his work, first with regard to the surroundings in which the work is to be done and second, with respect to the special material that he proposes to use.

POSSIBLE INSTRUCTING CONDITIONS

"**Inside Work**" **and** "**Outside Work.**"—According to the trade for which training is to be given instructional work may be carried on either under cover or out of doors, that is, it may be "inside work" or "outside work." Inside work may be carried on either in some place especially provided for that purpose (a "school room") or on the floor of the shop. We may therefore have:

(1) Inside Work.
    (a) Shop work.
    (b) "Class room" work.
(2) Outside Work.

General Characteristics of "Inside Work."—In general in inside work the instructor has relatively few conditions that are entirely out of his control. For example, weather conditions do not appreciably affect the work, in the shop such equipment as may be available for instruction "stays put," the instructor can depend upon its being there when it is wanted.

As between the shop and the class room however, the control of instructional conditions as to surroundings and material is much better in the class room than in the shop. The shop

THE INSTRUCTOR

(unless it is operated especially for training, as in trade schools) is operated for production, not instruction, while a class room can be fitted up for instructional purposes only. In general it may be said that a class room and, in a less degree a shop, offer the following general characteristics:

(1) Instruction can be carried on independently of weather conditions.
(2) Relatively quiet conditions can be obtained. (Some shops and all class rooms.)
(3) Learners are physically comfortable. (Not cold or wet, under ordinary circumstances.)
(4) The group can be concentrated around the instructor. (Some shops, all class rooms.)
(5) Special demonstration and illustrative material can be set up and kept in place as long as desired. (All rooms, some shops.)

General Characteristics of "Outside Work."—As contrasted with inside work, outside work offers the following general characteristics:

(1) It is affected by weather conditions.
(2) In many cases there is much noise.
(3) Learners may be physically uncomfortable (may be cold, wet, or in uncomfortable or cramped positions).
(4) The group may be more or less distributed.
(5) Special demonstration and illustrative material can rarely be permanently set up and kept in place as long as desired.

As will be more fully discussed later, these conditions affect the selection of methods and the determination of the best surroundings for a given type of instructional work, and must be taken into consideration by the instructor in planning his training management. This may even be true in some cases, for some one lesson or even for certain steps in a given lesson.

The Two Kinds of Work Compared.—As an example consider training in printing and in house carpentry. In the printing shop there is an almost unobstructed view so that supervision is easy, the instructional material is largely presses, type cases, paper, etc., and the men are under cover. Weather does not interrupt the work. The instructor can be sure of being able to carry out his plans from day to day. He can handle a relatively large group effectively.

In house carpentry the men may be concealed even from each other, may be scattered, material is more complicated (timbers, planks, stagings, etc.). An instructor in printing has a very different problem to handle from that of an instructor in house carpentry. His work may be interrupted any time by bad weather, his instruction may be given in all parts of the house, according to the distribution of his men. He can only handle a small group effectively. Supervision is difficult.

Or against either of these examples take the case of a trade extension group under instruction on blueprint reading as it might be conducted in a class room. Material is simple (largely blueprints and diagrams) and can be kept on the wall as long as is necessary, the room is quiet, the men can sit in chairs or at tables in perfect comfort. The instructor can bunch the group as much as he desires. Here again we have a very different problem for the instructor than that of the instructor in printing or in house carpentry.

Relative Advantages and Disadvantages of Shop or Outside Conditions vs. Class Room Conditions.—Evidently, under "inside" conditions, so far as surroundings go, the instructor has an easier job than under "outside" conditions. The "inside" man can group his class; hence his supervision is easier, he can depend on keeping his work going regardless of weather conditions. In the class room he can use models and demonstration material, if their use seems desirable. As against this, the outside or shop instructor must instruct under working conditions, he must instruct on production materials on outside work; he and his men are exposed to the weather as much as are the regular working force. Sometimes he must "fight" against noise or other factors that distract attention. He unquestionably has the harder instructing job, in the sense that his surroundings are more likely to make his work difficult unless he plans in advance to take care of them.

The Effect of this on the Attitude of the Instructor.—The greater difficulties that must be surmounted in outside work make many untrained instructors tend to look for the "easiest way" and so tend to steadily shift from outside conditions to inside conditions. For example, an instructor in house carpentry or brick laying finds that his men cannot be "bunched," that hammering on construction work going on near his job makes talking difficult. Often the only solution of the difficulty that he will suggest is to get his group off the real jobs and either give them fake jobs (exercise), or even get them into a class room and lecture to them. He sees that it would be easier for *him* but forgets or does not know that his instruction will be either much less efficient or that it will have no value at all. A man of the right type is always thinking how he can minimize these difficulties and instruct his men on the job where the instruction can be most efficiently given. In the end, a man of the first type usually fails as an instructor and a man of the second type usually succeeds.

When the Good Instructor Will Use Inside Work.—The efficient instructor will only substitute inside instruction for instruction that should be given outside when it is clearly evident that, in view of all the circumstances, it is the way to get the most effective instructional surroundings. In general, any departure from actual working surroundings in the shop or on outside work results in a loss of instructional efficiency. Special cases may, of course, arise, where part of a lesson on "outside" work can best be given under "inside" conditions, but this should only be assumed to be true after careful study of the problem, and a determination that inside conditions are, under the special circumstances, clearly the best for the sort of instruction that it is planned to give.

The good instructor on work that is regularly carried on in the shop or on "the outside" will therefore always start with the theory that his instructional job is to be done in the shop, or on the outside, as the case may be, and will only be "driven" into the class room as a "last resort," while the poor instructor, working on exactly the reverse theory, is "driven" to the class room from the shop, at the first difficulty. The first insists on "going out" or "staying out," if he is out; the second insists on "coming in."

Need of Ingenuity and "Pep" to Stay out.—The instructor will need both ingenuity and "pep" if he "stays out" as long as he can. He must keep thinking in advance about getting suitable surroundings, and make every effort to secure them for his group. He faces the necessary surroundings that go with his teaching job when it is done right, and uses forethought and ingenuity in dealing with those surroundings so that he can do his instructing job effectively. There are very few cases where it is necessary to take "outside" work "inside" if sufficient forethought and careful planning are used in arranging for the work, though, of course, under some conditions, cases might occur where, as a temporary measure some lesson or part of a lesson (most probably steps 1 and 2) might be taken away from the place where the rest of the lesson was to be carried out (probably steps 3 and 4).

The Type of Work as Affecting the Surroundings.—It is pointed out elsewhere that training in any plant may have to deal with any or all of three classes of work, training green men, training men on a conversion basis and giving trade extension work, though in many cases this latter form of instruction will probably be of minor importance. Each of these three types of instruction offers certain possibilities as to the best instructional surroundings, and these are discussed in the following paragraphs.

Surroundings in the Training Department: Trade Extension Work.—Trade extension work consists largely either in giving auxiliary knowledge, instructing in technical jobs, or instructing in special operations on an individual basis. This third case will apply almost entirely to shop trades and can, of course, be given only in the shop. The giving of auxiliary information can, however, often be given effectively in the class room. This is particularly true of relatively well advanced men, in fact work of this sort is sometimes given with a very considerable degree of effectiveness in evening classes entirely outside of the plant.

Instruction in technical jobs can, to a less degree be effectively handled in the same way, because such jobs are often carried on under cover in surroundings that can be practically duplicated in a class room, and because, with well advanced men, methods of illustration will sometimes work fairly well.

Surroundings in the Training Department: Conversion Work.—Conversion work offers two distinct training problems: such men nearly always need a considerable amount of auxiliary knowledge of the trade into which they are going, and, in some cases, a portion of this can be given in the class room. On the other hand such men also need more or less experience on jobs, and these can only be given under actual working conditions, on the job. On the whole the general tendency is to use the class room too much in conversion work, and consequently to use less efficient methods of instruction. In order to handle these men under "inside" conditions they are told when they should find out for themselves, they are shown diagrams or models when the real things are available and could be used if the work were carried on outside of the class room.

Methods of doing jobs are described to them when they should learn by doing the jobs themselves. This tendency to handle conversion work too much in the class room should be carefully guarded against and the class room only used when it is evident that it furnishes the best surroundings for the particular form of instructional work in hand.

Surroundings in the Training Department: Green Men.—In the case of the training of green men there is but little opportunity for the use of the class room. They must be trained under the same conditions that they will work under in production work; if the training is in shop trades, they must be trained in the shop; if in outside trades, they must be trained outside. This is for two reasons: first, the instruction should be given on jobs and the auxiliary material tied up with the different jobs, as described in Part VI, Chapter II, and second, because, the green man, having behind him no experience in the trade, as has the trade extension man, or an experience in a trade, as has the conversion man, must be trained to work under real working conditions from the start, if instructional bases are to be established.

The surroundings for the training of the green man will therefore be those of his prospective jobs, and there will be no use for the class room in this case. The only exception to this statement might be in the case of the passing out of some of the general information not connected with the direct trade training.

The General Question of Instructional Material.—Instructional material means anything that is used in the instructional process. Books, tools, machines, stock, models, diagrams, demonstration apparatus and even in some cases, other men are all instructional material. If a man is under instruction in lathe work, the lathe, the tools, the blueprint, the stock are all a part of the instructional material for that particular instructing job. If a man is to be instructed on some one man's work on a gang job (say riveting) and the other men in the gang know their jobs (say in riveting, the heater, the passer and the holder-on) these other men may be considered as a part of the instructional material. If a boy in a regular school is studying his Latin lesson, his book, his dictionary, his paper and pencil are all a part of the instructional material that is put into use in connection with the teaching of that lesson.

The matter of the character of the instructional material that is required for the effective putting over of different types of lessons, and for different types of learners is discussed in the following paragraphs.

INSTRUCTIONAL MATERIAL

Possible Kinds of Instructional Material.—Instructional material may be of several kinds. These may be designated as:

1. Demonstration material.
2. Illustrative material.
3. Working material.
4. General material.

Demonstration and illustrative material is material that would be used in connection with the putting over of a lesson by the use of either demonstration or illustration. It includes such articles as pictures, charts, diagrams, models, etc., for use in illustration, and any real working materials, such as machines, tools, etc., that might be used in connection with the method of demonstration. Working material is any material that is used in doing a productive instructional job; where a man is trained on a production job, the working equipment, etc., constitute working material. Where a man is trained in a machine shop, the machine on which he works, the stock that he works up, the special tools that he uses, all form a part of the working material.

General material is material that is of general use in instructional work but that does not especially apply to the requirements of any particular teaching job. Blackboards, reference books, etc., would belong to this class of instructional material.

For convenience we will characterize all material except working material as *non-productive instructional material*.

The following paragraphs discuss some of the questions that may come up in connection with the choice and the use of the different sorts of material in connection with the work of an instructor in a training department.

Some Characteristics of Non-Productive Instructional Material.—Non-productive instructional material is not usually found in connection with the equipment of a production plant. So far as it is used it must be purchased or made, either by the instructor, or according to his specifications.

But little of this material can be purchased to advantage: the sort of instructional material that is on the market has been mostly prepared for general school or technical school work and will not serve the needs of this sort of training. With the exception of some of the more common general equipment, such as blackboards, a few good reference books, note books, etc., there is little that will be of value on the market in the general run of instructional material of this class. This point is emphasized because, especially in trade extension work, instructors often wish to buy instruction material of the standard type that is used in schools or colleges. Such material is usually of very little value because it is generally made to meet the needs of courses in general education, general science, etc., and does not meet the requirements of specialized trade training. Where demonstration material is to be used the most effective sort will be that made by the instructor or designed by him to meet the needs of the particular lesson for which it is to be used.

Written or Printed Instructional Material.—In many cases written or printed material can be used to advantage, but nearly all such material must be prepared especially for the special conditions, and hence is only of value when prepared by the instructor who uses it. Such material is chiefly of value with advanced men in steps 2 and 3 in the lesson. If it can be used it saves a portion of the time of the instructor and so has value, but the over use of material of this kind should be carefully guarded against, and it should only be used when it is very certain that it can actually be used to advantage.

The Right Kind of Non-Productive Instructional Material.—Where models, diagrams, or special pieces of demonstration apparatus are used, they will be effective in proportion as they are simple and employ articles or are based upon ideas with which the men are already familiar. The less the appearance or complication of the demonstration or illustrative material distracts the attention of the man from what is being put over, the better. Two pieces of joist, hinged together at the top with their bottoms on two pieces of gas pipe can be used to illustrate the use of a tie rod better than it can be put over with a small, elaborately constructed piece of apparatus.

The Wrong Kind of Non-Productive Instructional Material.—Complicated pieces of apparatus, text books unsuited to the work, over elaborate charts or diagrams are examples of the sort of instructional materials that should be avoided. Some instructors seem to feel that the use of such material indicates that they are very efficient; as a matter of fact, it generally indicates the contrary.

Instructional Material for Different Types of Learners.—As in other cases, the type of learner, whether trade extension, conversion or green man, affects the relative use of the different classes of instructional material and the following paragraphs discuss some of the more important points in this connection.

Instructional Material in Trade Extension Work.—There is probably a considerable use for non-productive instructional material in this class of work. As already pointed out, men of this type often require more auxiliary knowledge than "job" knowledge. They have a large amount of experience behind them, and so can be more effectively instructed by methods of illustration or demonstration than any other type of learner. It is in this work that the instructor will find the greatest field for the development and use of non-productive special instructional material, especially for illustrative material of special kinds or of charts and diagrams.

Non-Productive Instructional Material in the Training Department: Conversion Work.—Conversion work may also offer opportunities for the use of non-productive instructional material but to a less extent than in trade extension work. The conversion man is, up to a certain point learning a new trade and, to that extent, is in the same situation as the green man. He needs training on actual jobs and instruction under production conditions. In giving auxiliary information about the new trade special non-productive instructional material may find a place under some conditions as when the different kinds of shipyard rivets are charted out in "converting" structural steel men or certain diagrams are used in giving out information as to location terms or when lists of terms used in the new trade are prepared.

Non-Productive Instructional Material in the Training Department: Green Men.—There is but little field for the use of non-productive instructional material in the training of green men under ordinary conditions. These men must be practically trained entirely on the job, must get their auxiliary information on the job, hence in the general run of such work all instructional material will be productive.

CHAPTER XXXV

HOW SURROUNDINGS AFFECT INSTRUCTION

The Instructor must take Material and Surroundings into Account.—Evidently the instructor in planning a lesson must take both material and surroundings into consideration. If he were going to put over a lesson on a shop job (say, in a machine shop) he would know, that under these conditions, he could work under cover, that there would be relatively little noise to interfere; that his men could be easily supervised on the shop floor, etc., so that he would take these facts into consideration. On the other hand, suppose he were going to put over a lesson in drop forging, he would know that supervision would be more difficult; that disturbing factors might be more prominent (noise, etc.), and would not, for example, plan to use methods that would require much talking. Again, in forging, the question of available equipment might affect the situation; for example, he might undertake to put over his lesson in a forge shop where only a few drop forges were available and so fall down on his application, whereas he might have planned to put over steps 1 and 2 in some quiet part of the plant where one special machine might be installed for that part of the lesson, and then, for steps 3 and 4 (where noise, etc., would not make so much difference) shift to some other part of the plant where enough machines could be used to admit of all the men on that particular lesson being given steps 3 and 4 with sufficient equipment. All such things would affect the speed and efficiency with which he was able to put over the lesson, and so should be taken into consideration in advance.

How Material and Surroundings Affect Choice of Method in Putting Over a Lesson.—While it is true in general that the demonstration is the best method for step 2, it may be that other methods can be used in certain cases. Sometimes available material will affect choice of method. An instructor may be forced to adopt a less effective method owing to there being no material for the more effective method available. As where he is obliged to use pictures or diagrams in instructing in the control of a machine, or in the methods of its operation. Of course this is bad practice and would only be followed in case of necessity.

How "Inside Work" Affects Instructional Methods.—Inside work gives a better chance for the carrying on of work by what may be called "standardized" methods. The instructor on this type of work will have to exercise less ingenuity in meeting unexpected situations than will the man on outside work. In class-room work with trade extension men and to some extent with conversion men he can make considerable use of non-productive instructional material. If he deems it wise, or has to meet a temporary situation he can, with relatively less loss of efficiency use methods other than demonstration and testing on the job.

How Outside Work Affects Teaching Methods.—Outside work affords but little choice of method. Demonstration, application and testing on the job are practically the only teaching methods that are available for steps 2, 3 and 4 in the majority of cases. There will seldom be an opportunity to use illustrative material, nor should it be necessary in this class of work.

How Surroundings Affect Organization for Putting Over a Lesson.—As already pointed out the organization may be affected by the conditions. Thus the number of men that one instructor can handle in a class room, a shop and in outside work, such as bricklaying or shipyard work would vary, and this would also be affected by the character of the trade taught (drop forging vs. machine shop). Surroundings that require the scattering of the group or enable the group to be bunched would also affect the efficient size of the instructional gang.

The Need for Adequate Equipment.—Whatever may be the nature of the instructional material it should be adequate. Many people have the idea that "any old thing" is good enough for instructional work. In the shop some foremen will think that a man can be instructed on a machine that has died of old age, or a worn out air gun is set aside for instruction in riveting. Good instruction can not be given with junk.

In the class room, if one is used, the general instructional material should be good.

Men should not be put into seats designed for six-year-old children; the equipment should not be a collection of odds and ends. "Good work requires good tools" and this is as true of the instructing trade as it is of any other trade.

Special Training Equipment.—Where it can be arranged the effectiveness of the instruction will be increased if certain equipment units are used exclusively for the training work, and this should be done whenever possible. It is obviously an advantage if this training equipment can be grouped, since better supervision can be secured under these conditions. Of course such grouping can be much more readily secured in training in shop trades than in training for outside occupations.

Summary and Conclusion.—Surroundings and material have to be considered by the instructor in connection with the type of learner, the working conditions, the gang organization and the selection of suitable methods of instruction. The selection is affected largely by the character of the trade as shop trade, yard trade, and as between "inside" and "outside" instructing conditions. Instructional material should always be in good condition and suitable to the use to which it is to be put. It is an advantage for the Training Work to use its own training equipment.

CHAPTER XXXVI

HANDLING THE GANG FOR EFFECTIVE INSTRUCTIONAL CONDITIONS

A. GENERAL PROBLEMS

Preliminary.—Whenever a number of men are working under the supervision of one man the effectiveness of the work is greatly affected by what may be called the "working relations" between the leader or "boss" and the group, or the "gang." However good the organization, however effective the equipment, the efficiency of the work for which the gang is organized and directed will be largely affected by what may be called the way in which the gang is "handled."

While this is true in general for any gang on any job, a rowing crew, a base ball team, a production gang, it is especially true in the case of an "instructional gang," and the manner in which the instructor "handles" his instructional gang, or group, will largely determine the success or failure of his instruction.

The Instructional Gang vs. the Production Gang.—While in many respects the problems of the instructor in charge of an instructional gang and those of a foreman in charge of a production gang are similar, there are certain vital differences owing to the fact that the production foreman is on the job to turn out *work* and the instructor is on the job to turn out *trained men who can do work*. This difference in the aim of the two kinds of groups, the instructional group and the production group, must never be lost sight of. As an illustration it may be said that the job of a production foreman is to keep his men *working* and the job of an instructor is to keep his men *learning*, or, to put it another way, the job of the production foreman is to keep his men thinking about *getting the job done* and the function of the instructor is to keep his men thinking about *learning how to do the job*.

EFFECTIVE INSTRUCTIONAL CONDITIONS

Special Conditions Affecting the Work of the Instructor.—The differences in the problem of handling men under instructional conditions and under production conditions are largely determined by the fact that, for effective instruction, the relation that exists between the instructor and the men affects the effectiveness of the instructional work more than does the relation between the foreman and the production gang. Unless the relations are too bad the production foreman can get a fair job out of his gang even if the relations are not of the best, but if the relations of the instructor and the instructional gang are not just right, the instructional work suffers severely. This is because up to a certain point, men can be made to work but they cannot be made to think or learn. "You can lead the horse to water but you can't make him drink." Unless the desire to learn is there, and the learner is in a state of mind so that he can learn, the work of the instructor will not be effective. For example, a man may want to learn, but he may be so confused or scared that he cannot learn; or a man may be in such a state of mind that he will not learn. If the former condition exists, it is up to the instructor to recognize that state of confusion and know how to help the man out of it; if the latter to so handle the case that the cause of the man's negative attitude is removed, he does want to learn and goes at it effectively.

Some Special Conditions that Affect the Handling of the Instructional Gang.—Among the more important factors that affect the handling of the instructional gang are, the relation of the instructor to the learner, in that the instructor understands clearly what the best relations are and how to maintain them, the command of what is called the interest factors by the instructor and his ability to use them intelligently, the ability of the instructor to recognize and deal with the state of mind of the learner at different stages of his progress, and his general capacity to deal with unexpected situations in such a way that the work is not slowed up and the interest of the men reduced. Some of the more important factors affecting this work are discussed in the following paragraphs.

The Relation of the Instructor to the Learner.—An important difference between the trained instructor and the untrained instructor is that, in many cases, the latter takes a wrong point of view as to whether he is to drive his men or to direct his men. Is he the engine of the automobile or is he the driver? Does he furnish the power or does he direct the power? Since the answer to this question affects the whole problem of handling the group effectively it should be answered in the beginning. The instructor will succeed in proportion as he gets his men so that they furnish the "power" and he directs it. If he undertakes to furnish the "power" he will fall down on his job. This is because, as already pointed out, the learner *must teach himself;* nobody can teach him, the instructor can only get the learner into a state of mind where he *wants* to learn, and then see that the learning conditions are made as efficient as possible. That is why a well planned progressive course of instruction will work better than a poorly planned course, or a course that has not been planned at all. The well planned course will make the getting of the instruction easier for the learner, but if the learner did not want to learn, the best planned course in the world would not help the situation, although it is true that a well planned scientifically progressive course will make some learners want to learn who would not want to learn if the course were poorly planned, the reason for this being brought out in the discussion on interest.

The poor instructor, not appreciating this fact, tries to be the power himself; he "does the work of his men" as is often said: he works hard and then is greatly disappointed because his men fail to profit by the instruction. He does the work instead of his men doing it. The trained instructor, knowing this principle, so handles his group that *they* do the work, "they furnish their own power" so to speak, and the instructor directs it. This situation is often expressed by the statement that so and so "wants to learn," but the other fellow "don't seem to want to learn," or that one instructor "gets the work out of his men" and another instructor "doesn't seem to be able to get the work out of his men."

As has been mentioned in another part of these notes, it sometimes happens that an untrained instructor has the "knack" of getting his men so that they want to learn, but such a man is rarely aware of the principles that he is applying in his handling of his men and so even then does not do as good an instructing job as he might do. Some foremen have learned by experience something of the same thing, but in both cases it is generally "rule of thumb work" at the best.

It may therefore be stated in general that the instructor will succeed in proportion as he stimulates his men to want to learn and then directs their activities in learning. He must direct the way in which the "power" works, but must not furnish the "power" himself.

For stimulating his learners he uses an appeal to what is called *interest* and then directs the activities of his men towards the accomplishment of the special ends for which they are placed in his charge. His first problem, therefore, is to thoroughly understand what things will arouse and sustain interest, that is, he must be familiar with *interest factors*, must know their relative values, and be able to use them effectively in the different situations that may come up in connection with his work with his gang.

The Typical Attitude of Mind of the Learner.—In general, any learner goes through three periods: when he first comes into the instructional group he is often scared or over anxious to please the instructor. Under these conditions he will often say that he understands when he does not understand at all. He is afraid to ask questions for fear that he will be considered stupid. He is often antagonistic; is ready to "fight" at the least provocation. Sometimes he thinks that the whole training proposition is a joke; often he is confused; sometimes he does not know why he has been put under an instructor; he thinks that it is some new way of doing a regular job, and that the instructor is some new kind of a foreman, whose only business is to push him in some new way. Under these conditions his only thought is to do the job and he has no notion that his real job is to learn to do the work correctly.

The Three Periods.—The learner coming into a training department in any or all of the states of mind just described will, in general, go through three periods as he progresses through the training course. First, a period of *adjustment;*

second, a period of *waking up;* third, a period of *getting down to business.* For each of these periods the instructor, if he knows his business, will be prepared to deal with the learner effectively, using different methods of handling for each period, and even using different methods for different men in the same stage, doing all this with judgment, patience and tact.

The First Period.—This is the critical period; it is during this period that the man generally decides to stay or quit, and his decision will be determined largely by the way that he is handled by the instructor. If he can be got safely over this first period he is likely to wake up and make good.

In dealing with a man during this first period the instructor will have to exercise all his tact: in general it may be said that his problem is to convince the man (and he cannot be convinced just by telling him) that the instructor is there to help him, that he will get a square deal, that the instructor knows that he feels, "like a cat in a strange garret" and is allowing for it.

In proportion as the instructor succeeds in doing this he will succeed in holding the man, in getting his interest aroused and, as is sometimes said, in getting him over the "hump." While each instructor must work according to his own personality and according to the special case the following suggestions may be of value, though, of course, nothing can take the place of experience.

The Relation Between the Instructor and the Green Man during the First Period.—During this first period it may be said that the instructor "pulls" the man, that is, the instructor takes the initiative, he "keeps ahead of the game," he foresees what is coming and plans to meet it. He anticipates what the man will do that is wrong and heads him off in advance. He studies the man, notes his state of mind; if he finds that he is scared, he plans to deal with him so that he will get over his scare; if he finds that the man does not know why he is in training, he plans some way of casually enlightening him as to what the training work is and what it is for; if the man is antagonistic, he plans some way of getting the man "into line."

In general, during this period the instructor is, so to speak, "ahead of the man all the time," anticipating, planning, studying the situation. It is during this first stage more than in any other that the tact, patience, and leadership of the instructor comes into play, and the difference between a good instructor and a poor instructor shows up so far as gang management goes.

It is hardly necessary to point out that, no matter how technically good an instructor may be, no matter how well he may be able to put over what he knows, no matter how well he knows his trade, no matter how well he plans his work and lays out his instructional order of jobs, if he fails to "get his man" during this first period, "the game is up" and the instructor will never be able to do a good instructional job so far as that man is concerned.

Length of the First Period.—The length of this first period will vary greatly with the man. One man will "catch on" in a few minutes, others will require several days, depending largely on the general make up of the man himself, his experiences before he came into the training work, what has been done for him by the employment department by way of giving him suitable information before he was put into training, in the way of informing him as to what he was hired for and what the training work can do for him.

No general rules can be given for this stage of the instructor's work; he must be on the alert, watch his man, and the more experience he has had in handling men, either as an instructor or as foreman, or both, the more likely will he be to handle the different men in this first stage successfully, provided he clearly understands the difference between the job of an instructor and the job of a production foreman.

Some instructors who are otherwise well equipped for their work never succeed in dealing effectively with their men during this first stage, and in consequence their "group mortality" is large; they lose too many men.

Under these conditions they usually blame the quality of the men that are assigned to them and do not realize that the trouble is with them.

When an instructor finds that he is not "holding" his men it is up to him to carefully consider the way in which he is handling them, and make sure that the trouble does not lie there.

Where there is a definitely organized Training Department a consultation with the Director will often help matters very much, since the "slant" that an outside man who knows the game will get on a situation will often help the man on the job to see where he is falling down.

The Question of Work during the First Period.—Since the chief point to be attained during the first period is to help the man to become adjusted, the instructor will not push him either on quality or quantity of the work that he gives him. That is, he will not worry about the grade of work that the man does or the amount of work that he turns out. Of course, he will keep the man at work, give him all that he can do, get as good work out of him as can be reasonably expected, but, at this stage of the game will regard that as secondary to getting the man adjusted. He uses the work mainly as a means of helping him to help the man to wake up and get into line.

An instructor who is impatient for results will often spoil the game by "speeding up" the work too soon for the man to stand it; by "pushing a man too hard." As in other cases tact and patience together with experience is the only guide and the only means of handling this situation.

"Do's and Don'ts" for Handling a Green Man during the First Period:
Don't "bawl him out."
Don't scare him.
Don't discourage him.
Don't expose him to ridicule if he makes a mistake.
Do encourage him.
Do help him to think that he is getting somewhere.
Do see that he knows why he is in the department.
Do "give him a show."
Do make him feel that the instructor wants him to make good.

While the above suggestions are applicable to the work at any stage of the learner's progress they apply with particular force during the critical first period.

The Second Period.—Having got over his original state of mind the learner sooner or later "wakes up," finds out what he is in the training department for, and gets an understanding of what it all means. Under normal conditions, if he has been properly handled in the first stage his interest begins to be aroused, he begins to want to take hold, that is he "wakes up."

At this stage of his progress it may be said that the learner will "go as far as the instructor"; he will attempt to do what the instructor gives him to do, but will not go much further on his own account. He is still "green" however and still needs careful handling.

Usually in this stage he will learn well but will learn slowly. He will make a number of "shots" at an idea before he gets it. He will make several tries at an operation before he can do it right. He is still more or less "clumsy" in his thinking and in his doing.

The instructor can now establish a business basis with the learner; he can be held up to standards of quality, but it is not, in general, good management to also attempt to push for quantity. Get him to thinking about doing a *good* learning job, but not necessarily a *quick* learning job.

The general relation between the instructor and the learner can now be placed on the basis that the man is there to be taught and the instructor is there to instruct him. This relation will be largely affected at this point by the degree to which the learner feels that the instructor thoroughly knows his job, both as a tradesman and as an instructor because at this stage it is very essential that the man should have confidence in the ability of his instructor to *do* the various jobs himself and that he should be thoroughly convinced that his instructor can train him so that he can do those same jobs. If the man does not believe that the instructor is "onto" his job as a mechanic he loses confidence in the ability of the training department to train him correctly; if he does not believe in the teaching ability of the instructor, he feels that he can not learn because the instructor "don't seem to be able to put it over."

The chief problem of the instructor at this stage is to make the transition from the "adjustment" basis to the "business" basis at just the right time, when the man is ready for it. This point is usually indicated by the fact that the man "begins to take hold," begins to ask intelligent questions, shows signs of individual thinking on the learning job.

It is easy at this stage to discourage a man; his first questions may be pretty absurd from the standpoint of a competent workman, some of his notions may be pretty crude, but if they show that he is beginning to wake up he should be encouraged to keep on thinking and trying and helped by tactful suggestions rather than by too much criticism.

Do's and Don'ts for the Second Period:
Do encourage him to ask questions.
Do give him a chance to think things out.
Do make him think more of doing a good job than of doing a fast job.
Don't show him too much.
Don't let poor work get by.
Don't push him too hard.

The Third Period.—As stated, this is the period when the man really gets down to business. He can now be pushed for quality and for quantity; criticisms can be direct and on a "brass tacks" basis.

In this stage the man will begin to draw ahead of the instructor; he will do considerable thinking on his own account; his suggestions will be direct and good. He will begin to "put the suction pump onto the instructor," and will often push the instructor with his questions.

It is in this stage that the relations of the instructor and the learner approximate the most closely to those of the foreman and the workman. As a learner the man is now beginning to feel that he is onto his job, that he knows how to go at the learning game, and that the instructor is a sort of "learning foreman."

Relations at this stage will therefore be mainly those of the man who knows and the man who wants to learn; the instructor will be able to concentrate most of his handling problems on keeping the instructional work going in good shape and in keeping up with the learner.

Do's and Don'ts in the Third Period.
Do hold up to good work.
Don't push too hard for speed.
Don't do his work for him.
Don't help him too much.

CHAPTER XXXVII

INTEREST AND INTEREST FACTORS

A

Preliminary.—The preceding paragraphs discussed in a general way some of the special conditions that confront an instructor in connection with the handling of the gang under instruction during the different stages of the learner's progression through the training department. The following paragraphs deal with some of the factors that an instructor be familiar with and must use in the handling of the instructional gang if the best instructional conditions are to be secured.

Among the most important of these is what is commonly called *interest*, and in the following discussion there is given a statement of what interest is, what some of the so-called interest factors are, and some description of the more common devices for bringing these interest factors into play, under conditions of emergency training.

What is Interest?—In general, the term *interest* means whatever makes the learner *want* to learn. A learner who has, in some way, been brought into a state of mind where he wants to learn is said to be interested. Anything that will make him interested is called an *interest factor*. This term is used in the same sense in which it is used in everyday life: we know what we mean when we say that we were "interested" in what somebody said to us; we simply mean that we wanted to understand what he was telling us; if we were not "interested" we merely mean that we did not care whether we understood what he was telling us or not. We have all had experience with some things that "interested us" and some things that did not "interest us," but, unless our attention had been drawn to the fact, we have never thought of *why* some things did appeal to us, or *aroused our interest*, and *why* some other things did not appeal to us, that is, *did not arouse our interest.* That is, we have never thought of the *interest factors* that came into play and determined our state of mind in the case.

Attention vs. Interest.—Many instructors fail to distinguish between *attention* and *interest.* Attention is sort of "instantaneous" interest. Attention is usually *attracted* by something uncommon or unexpected or startling. The public speaker of a certain type bangs on the table or the instructor suddenly "calls down" a man, or a foreman yells at a man to "get onto his job," the notion being to attract attention by the suddenness of the thing. Attention is a transitory state of mind on the part of the learner that does not last long enough to serve any really useful purpose. Interest is relatively permanent. To illustrate the difference one might say "My attention was roused by the barking of a dog but I was not interested enough to get up and see what the matter was." Attention only serves a useful purpose when the instructor sees to it that it is immediately followed by interest; taken alone, it has little or no value in instructional management in connection with handling the gang under instruction.

Instructors often mistake attention for interest and undertake to base their gang management on the attracting of attention rather than on the development of interest. The results are, of course, unsatisfactory, for reasons that will appear in the following discussion.

It seems sufficient merely to draw attention here to the fact that management that is based on attention is not likely to give effective results but that if the handling of the gang is based on interest, satisfactory results will be obtained, if the instructor knows how to handle his men through the skillful use of suitable interest factors.

The Instructor and Interest Factors.—A good instructor knows how to use interest factors to get his men into the "learning" state of mind, that is, to get them interested. He is the director of their learning activities; he cannot supply motive power. The men under instruction must in some way be brought into a state of mind where they want to learn the lesson and will keep wanting to learn it until they have got it.

That is, interest must not only be *aroused* but must be *sustained*. So every instructor must in some way secure the interest of his men and then keep that interest up or he can teach them nothing. As will be pointed out in the following paragraphs, interest may be developed in various ways and by various devices; that is, there are various interest factors and they can be "worked" through various "managing" schemes.

The best instructor is the one who uses the best interest factors and puts them over through the use of the most effective methods.

Just as in the teaching of a lesson there are different steps and various methods can be used in putting over each step, the instructor selecting the best method for the particular instructional situation with which he wishes to deal, so, an instructor will use the different interest factors according to the situation and will get those factors to working by the use of the most suitable factors.

The following paragraphs describe some of the more important interest factors, discuss their relative values and describe some of the more common devices through which these different factors can be brought into play.

Interest Factors.—As already stated, in its instructional sense, interest means the cause of a desire on the part of the learner to comprehend or to do; to understand how to do a job or to do it, or both. Among the more important factors which have been recognized as producing interest, or assumed to produce interest are:

(1) Realization by the learner that the thing that he is learning is going to aid him in accomplishing something that he desires to accomplish, as when a man realizes that, when he is trained he will get a job at more pay than he has been getting, or when a man who has gone into a shipyard from purely patriotic motives "for the war" realizes that what he is getting will enable him to be of more service than he could be without the training.

(2) Feeling on the part of the learner that he can grasp what is being given him; that he can "get it." A learner who feels sure that he is "getting there" is much more interested

than one who feels that he "can't get it." Confidence means interest; discouragement means loss of interest.

(3) Curiosity, as when a green man wants to learn the names of tools and processes when he first comes into the training department, or when a child takes the clock apart "to see the wheels go round."

(4) Desire for approbation or praise; recognition of good work. The learner who knows that he has done a good job and has been told so, is more interested in tackling the next job than if he had not felt that his good work had been recognized. This is human nature.

(5) Fear: of ridicule, of punishment, of loss of self-respect. As when a pupil in a regular school is kept after school or the teacher uses sarcasm, or ridicule in reprimanding him before his class.

B. COMPARATIVE VALUES OF THESE FACTORS

The Learner Feels that a Desired Aim is being Achieved.— When the learner feels that something that he wishes to attain is being attained, that he is on the road and is progressing in the right direction, we unquestionably have the strongest factor that can be appealed to in arousing and maintaining interest. In proportion as a learner definitely wishes to satisfy an ambition that he has clearly defined in his own mind and he understands the conditions under which he can achieve success in realizing that ambition, his interest is aroused in mastering the problem, or learning how to perform the operation whose mastery or comprehension means one more step towards the desired goal, and that interest will be sustained and permanent. This ambition to gratify a definite aim is the strongest interest factor known to instructors and the one on which the most effective instructional management can be based. It may be regarded as the one condition that must be met in effective group management. Given a learner with a known aim, or one in which a definite aim has been aroused by the instructor, the problem of effective management is largely solved if all the work of the learner is so arranged that it "lines up" to that aim, and the learner knows that all his work does so "function."

Confidence in Ability to do the Job.—This is undoubtedly one of the most valuable factors that can be used in developing and sustaining interest. A discouraged learner, one who expects to fail, has not the interest of one who believes he can master the operation or "get" the lesson. Hence to secure and maintain interest great care must be taken to see that at each step of his progress the learner is given only work that the instructor is sure that he can learn to do. Every success means greater confidence in attacking the next step. Each partial failure means a loss of confidence in going at the next problem. Each total failure means loss of time, energy and interest, each success means useful expenditure of energy, and increased interest. In this lies a arge portion of the value of progressive courses of instruction where each new task is carefully chosen so that it is within the learner's capacity. A failure to recognize this principle lies at the bottom of much poor instruction. Thus learners are required to attempt too big a learning job at once, an apprentice who can give a good description of how to grind a certain tool may fail entirely if asked to describe the entire job of making a tool post. The girl who cannot describe how to make an entire dress can deal effectively with the question of telling how to thread a needle. The man who cannot make an instrumental drawing with regard to all fine points of instrumental work, at a certain stage of his instructional progress may nevertheless be able to make a good usable sketch with pencil and paper, or perhaps can work out a detail when he cannot at that stage of his progress make an assembly drawing.

The learner who feels that he is succeeding, that he can "catch onto the job," can be trained more rapidly and more effectively than one who is not confident that he can make good. This is a very important factor in effective training. The efficient instructor will make considerable use of this confidence factor.

Curiosity.—Curiosity has value as an interest factor particularly when the learner first comes into the yard. He runs across a lot of things that are new to him and strongly attracts his attention and which he is very anxious to learn. As a rule, however, curiosity is of more value in attracting attention than in securing interest and is confined largely to a desire to acquire auxiliary information.

On the other hand the kind of interest which will carry a man through a difficult lesson or teaching unit, which will make him drive himself is not based on curiosity to any great degree.

Desire for Approbation.—In trade training desire for approbation can be used as an interest factor. The recognition of accomplishment provides an effective means for developing interest. A foreman or an instructor can stimulate considerable interest in a learner by using personal approbation when satisfactory progress is made, or a job is particularly well done. When properly used this interest factor can be utilized to very great advantage in training, especially with green men during the first period of their work.

Fear.—It is often assumed in connection with industrial training that fear is effective in arousing interest on the part of the learner. A foreman will threaten to have a learner "fired" if he does not learn to do a job correctly. The foreman will "bawl out" a man for not knowing how to do a piece of work the first time he is put on that job, or for not following instructions correctly.

The use of fear as a means for developing interest is based on the assumption that a man who is scared can think more clearly than a man who is not, this of course cannot be true. A scared man will probably run faster or jump higher than a man who is not scared, but under the influence of fear a man will not comprehend or think clearly. His mental engine is "stalled."

The appeal to fear is most commonly used by the untrained instructor, it is the only method he knows for developing interest, hence his instructional conditions are often very bad. The efficient instructor will not attempt to use fear, but will use other interest factors and will do a much better teaching job in consequence.

The Learner and Interest Factors.—In common with any organization established to render a service, any industrial plant gets learners whose special characteristics can be set forth in a general way. Among the chief characteristics of the men with which a training scheme in an average plant will have to deal are:

a. The learner has a more or less definitely developed trade aim. That is, it can be fairly assumed that the man who comes into training is there because he wants to learn a trade or, at least, that he wants to be trained so that he can do a job, "he knows what he is there for." In this respect the training scheme is in the same class with a law school or a medical school; that is, the existence of a determined aim is a characteristic of the learner.

b. The learners in training will be, at least, relatively mature; where training is scientifically carried on it is not likely that many very young persons and certainly no children will be included in its teaching groups.

c. He is under pay and usually knows that as soon as he is trained, he can get additional pay.

d. In at least many cases he may be not any too well equipped along general educational lines.

e. His motives may be varied; he may be merely after better pay than he has been getting or under war conditions he may be in the work for patriotic motives. He may be working for promotion, or his motives may be mixed; this, of course, is only human nature.

Interest Factors will Have Different Values for Different Types of Men.—Evidently different types of men will respond in different degrees to different interest factors, and allowances must be made for such differences in considering the relative values of the interest factors just discussed. For example a man who is extremely anxious to learn the trade will respond more quickly, "catch on" more rapidly, and progress faster than a man whose aim is not so well determined; the former man will be more interested than the latter.

More mature men will respond more to the interest factor of accomplishment of aim while more immature learners will be more strongly affected by curiosity and desire for the recognition of good work. A man who is under pay and is looking forward to more pay or a better job later is more likely to keep up his interest than a man who is giving his time to get his training, but the value of the financial incentive as an interest factor is, in many cases considerably overrated. Ambition, desire to make good, interest in the trade itself and desire to master it, are all in some cases, stronger interest factors than the immediate financial returns. A man taking the training for purely patriotic motives is likely to respond to the "war" appeal much more than a man who is in it only for what he can get for himself. A man who has relatively little general education is likely to have his interest roused and sustained more by spoken than by printed instruction and discussion, and by homely and direct illustrations based on the experiences and incidents of everyday life.

All such factors must be taken into consideration by the instructor in working interest factors with the different men that come into his gang, and each man must be handled according to his special characteristics, but the general principles laid down in these notes for the guidance of the instructors will hold, though, of course, nothing will take the place of good sense, experience and judgment in using the different interest factors in managing the gang under instruction. This is probably particularly true as between the trade extension man, the conversion man, the green man and the apprentice.

The Kind of Learner and Interest Factors: The Trade Extension Man.—From the standpoint of interest the trade extension man offers the simplest problem. He knows what he wants, he is usually well advanced in his trade, he is usually relatively mature. Under these conditions the only interest factor that applies to any great extent is accomplishment of aim. If the man knows what he wants and knows that he is getting it, the problems of the instructor in the handling of the group are reduced to the minimum. All of his men are practically in the third stage as described in previous paragraphs, and the same general relations that obtain there would obtain in a trade extension class.

Of the other factors, fear is, of course, practically nonexistent, curiosity practically at zero, and desire for approbation, while of some value, of much less account than in the case of less mature men with less trade experience behind them.

The Learner and Interest Factors: The Conversion Man.—A man coming into training from an allied trade who desires to secure such additional information and training as will enable him to "convert" his trade into the new trade, offers little difference from the trade extension man. Usually at first, his curiosity is more acute, and can be used to a somewhat greater extent as an interest factor. Other factors rate about as in the case of the trade extension man.

The Learner and Interest Factors: The Green Man.—This case offers of course, the greatest opportunity for the skillful use of all the desirable factors and the abuse of the undesirable ones. (Fear, for example.) As already pointed out, the relative values of the different factors vary with the stage of the learner's progress. In stage one, curiosity has some value, desire for praise a considerable value, if worked through the proper devices, the development of confidence has great value, and the accomplishment of aim can be worked to good effect, but probably not as effectively as in the later stages of the man's progression.

In stage two, curiosity drops considerably, accomplishment of aim goes up and the other factors remain about the same. In stage three, accomplishment of aim becomes the strong interest factor, the others dropping to relatively low values.

The young man or apprentice is less likely to have clearly seen the bearing of his training on his future work than is the mature man, hence the appeal to vocational aim is not likely to have so great a value in the earlier stages of his training. Desire for approbation will run stronger than in the ordinary green man. In general it may be said that the apprentice offers about the same situation, so far as interest factors go, as the green man, with the value of the different interest factors rather more strongly developed, that is, the apprentice comes back on a given interest factor rather more rapidly and intensively than does the green man.

C. THE APPLICATION OF INTEREST FACTORS IN THE MANAGEMENT OF THE GANG UNDER INSTRUCTION

Preliminary.—The foregoing paragraphs have discussed the general principles affecting the use of interest and its value in handling a gang under instructional conditions. The following paragraphs suggest some specific ways in which the instructor can apply these principles in his working practice.

Some General Suggestions.—As a preliminary the following general rule for good teaching may be suggestive. Probably the advertising field shows as expert use of the factors of interest as any line of work in which people have to be handled and the following rule given for the principles of good advertising by an advertising expert will apply equally well to the work of the instructor.

1. Attract attention.
2. Maintain attention until it becomes interest.
3. Keep up interest until it results in action.
4. Guide the action in the direction of efficient results.

The working out of this principle can be seen in any advertising device. Pictures, striking sentences, are used to attract attention, snappy reading matter to develop interest, follow up work to get the interest to result in action. Salesmen to direct the interest to the desired end, the sale of the product.

In a sense the instructor is a salesman and in order to sell his goods he must also be a good advertiser, so the general principles of good advertisement and salesmanship apply to him as well as to the man with a manufactured product that he puts on the market.

Some Things that Affect the Development and the Maintenance of Interest.—In connection with effective group management there are a number of things that affect the development of interest and its maintenance after it is developed. In proportion as these things are handled well by the instructor the interest will keep up, to the extent that they are not handled well the interest will fall off. Among the more important of these conditions are, good teaching, the avoidance of overfatigue (especially mental) on the part of the learner or the group, the instructor's manner and voice, too much interference by the instructor, rattling the learner through trying to give him too much at one "bite," failure to clear up a given point in the instruction about which the learner is confused at the time that he first knows that he is confused, "lost motion" in carrying on the instruction, standing around owing to poor planning on the part of the instructor and "playing favorites."

Good Teaching the Most Effective Agent to Develop Interest.—Undoubtedly the most effective method of maintaining interest is good instruction. Under good teaching methods the learner develops confidence in his ability to do, because he finds that the learning "comes easy," if, as a result of efficiently planned and presented instruction, he progresses rapidly, he feels that his desire to "learn his job" is being attained. On the other hand, no condition will make gang management more difficult than poor instruction: men that feel that they cannot do the work lose their interest, if they feel they are not progressing rapidly, the interest falls off. Too much emphasis cannot be laid on the value of well planned and carried out instruction work in arousing and maintaining interest, and so making the handling of the instructional gang easy for the instructor. Failure on the part of the instructor to carefully plan his lessons, to lay out his work progressively, to select the best methods of instructing for the different jobs that are to be put over, probably accounts for more difficulty in handling the group under instruction than any one factor, because of the questions of lack of interest that inevitably result from such a condition.

The Question of Fatigue.—After a group of men have been learning for a certain period they become fatigued and the interest falls off. This condition is likely to come sooner with a group on work that requires much thinking, as in the case of instructing on a technical job, but it will come at some time in all cases. The instructor must be on the alert to recognize this condition and be ready to deal with it.

There are two common methods of dealing with fatigue; the first is to "knock off" for a little while, the second is to change the character of the work, or to take the minds of the group off the work for a moment. Public speakers often use this latter device when they inject a funny story or an anecdote into a serious argument. In "class room" work where the learner works almost entirely "with his head" interest can sometimes be revived by getting the learner to do something that requires some physical exertion; expert instructors will sometimes in such a case, even contrive some errand for the man to do so that he does a totally different sort of work for a few moments. The main point to always bear in mind is that it is no use to attempt to drive a fatigued learner; the problem is to get him "rested" so that his interest will revive again. A skillful instructor is always on the lookout for signs of fatigue in his learners, and is always ready to deal with the situation.

The unskilled instructor hammers away and goes from bad to worse. Usually he finally winds up by declaring that his learners are no good, never were any good and never will be any good, all of which means that he is not onto his job, and that probably there is nothing the matter except that the men were fatigued and the instructor did not know it. Of course the learners did not know it; they know that they had lost interest in the work, but they did not know why, and it was not their business to know why; it was the business of the instructor, part of his job, to see that they did not get into that condition, or if they did, see that they were got out of it at once.

The Instructor's Manner and Interest.—An instructor can affect interest very largely by his manner in dealing with the men under his instruction. In this respect it may almost be said that the class reflect the instructor. If he is brisk, businesslike and energetic, he will arouse the interest of the men and they will be brisk, businesslike and energetic. If he is negative, slow, "logy" he will seriously impair the interest of his men and they will be "logy" too. If he is not quite onto his job his men will lose interest and not be onto their jobs. If his manner is "snappy" and his "put over" is neat, the interest will go up; if the reverse, interest will go down. If the instructor is "full of pep" the interest will go up and the men be full of "pep."

One of the most common causes of diminished interest is an inaudible voice: if a man under instruction cannot hear all that is said he quickly loses interest; this is a very common failing on the part of many instructors. One large transit company in its suggestions to conductors says "Always speak to the passenger who is farthest from you when you call out streets." This is a good rule: always if you are talking to more than one member of the gang, be sure that every man who should hear you does hear you.

Interference by the Instructor.—Too much interference by the instructor is often the cause of loss of interest by the learner. The instructor becomes impatient, shows or corrects the learner when he does not need it. Some instructors will take the work out of the learner's hands at the first mistake. "Here, I'll show you, you get off the job." This kills interest, especially if the learner is getting along all right and merely needs more time or a bare suggestion.

Instructors habitually fail to distinguish between the fact that while they thoroughly understand the teaching unit, the learner has still to be made to understand it. As a result they forget that what they can easily do, the *learner has yet to be taught to do*. The instructor has got it, the learner has yet to get it, consequently the instructor undertakes to present in one teaching unit more than the learner can take in one learning operation. Of course the learner gets "rattled," he "goes to pieces," he "lays down on the job," consequently he loses his confidence, hence his interest. Had the instructor been "on to his job" and had used a smaller teaching unit, the man would not have gone to pieces, would not have lost his confidence, and would have kept up his interest. For instance, if a learner is given a series of lessons on the different parts of a long job, he will get them one by one, and will keep up his interest; whereas if he is given a whole job in one teaching unit, he is liable to "lose his nerve," and so make a bad job of it.

Another cause of loss of interest occurs not from rattling the man by throwing too much at him at one time, but by causing confusion with regard to a certain point, through the learner not being immediately straightened out as soon as he becomes conscious of the fact that he is confused and wants to be straightened out. Under these conditions, if the instructor does not immediately remove this confusion, a great loss of interest will result because he will not keep his understanding of what he is confused about and his desire to get straightened out in "cold storage" very long.

The necessity of the instructor's planning his work ahead appears plainly in this connection. If this is not done there will be a lot of "lost motion" with corresponding loss of interest.

Probably nothing reduces interest more than "standing around." If a learner finds that he must wait while materials are got ready, or because he does not know what his job is, or he does not know what to do next, his interest will be rapidly reduced.

It is very necessary to prevent loss of interest from this cause by seeing that where material should be ready it is ready. That when a man has completed a job, or been instructed in a lesson, that he knows what his next job is to be.

Playing Favorites: The "One Man Instructor."—One of the most difficult situations that an instructor can get into comes about through playing favorites. This is a very easy thing to do, especially in the case of a particularly good man; the temptation is always strong to give him more than his fair share of attention and help. Another type of man will happen to be a good talker and will follow up the instructor with calls for assistance or questions, the instructor will unconsciously give him more than his fair share of attention. Whatever may be the cause such an unequal division of the instructor's time will always cause an undesirable situation in the group. It is even worse when the instructor allows personal bias to affect his work with different men; the temptation is always to work with the man that he likes and neglect the man that he does not like, and this tendency must be carefully guarded against. As soon as the men in the group get the idea that the instructor is playing favorites, the proper relation of instructor and group is disturbed.

Under the conditions just described all the men lose interest: the neglected men because they think that the instructor does not care how they come out and the other men because they think they have a "pull" with the instructor. In either case interest is reduced and discipline suffers.

An excellent way to keep clear of such a situation is for the instructor to keep some sort of a check list and keep track of the time and attention that he gives to each man, so that he has some sort of a check.

Of course the above statements do not mean that an instructor might not properly give more time to a backward man than to a bright one, but when this is done the reason for doing it should be so obvious that no one can complain.

Distribution.—In putting over a lesson or a set of lessons to a group it is very easy to do all the work with one or two men. In the case of group instruction, especially off the job, as in trade extension work, and especially with rather large groups, improper distribution is especially likely to occur if the instructor is not on his guard against it. A properly distributed lesson will make approximately equal demands on all members of the group or the class. In "inside work" (where the use of this device is possible), a check list, on which the instructor can check off the names of different learners as he works with them, is one of the best devices for avoiding improper distribution.

In "outside work" the use of the list of names is not so easy: the instructor will generally have to rely on knowing his men and, with the small groups that he will probably work with, there should be no special difficulty in securing reasonably good distribution.

Evidently questions of distribution in group or class work will come up mainly in connection with trade extension work or possibly instruction to groups on technical jobs, rather than on production jobs in the yard. In the case of "outside work" where the instruction will be, of necessity, mainly individual, the question of proper distribution will be even more difficult to deal with. Under the teaching conditions unavoidably set up in this case (more or less wide distribution of the men, noise, men on different jobs, or on different stages of the same job, or both), it is extremely difficult for the instructor to avoid doing most of his instructing with a few of his men, and leaving others to get along as well as they can. The instructor should take every means that he can to avoid such improper distribution. Some sort of a memorandum card that he can carry in his pocket and on which he can check up his work with the different men will be helpful, even if it is only used as a temporary record and thrown away at the close of the day's work or transcribed onto some permanent record form. The following form might be suggestive:

Group, No. 2.	Job	Step	Times
Jones	Flush rivets	3	4
Robinson	Flush rivets	2	3
Smith	Snap rivets	1	1
Deane	Countersunk	4	1

This means that Jones was on the third step of the lesson, (Application) and so the instructor put in time with him four times during the morning. Robinson, on step 2, got three intervals of the instructor's time. Smith, only got time from the instructor once, and Deane, on Testing (presumably driving right along and only requiring an inspection), got inspected once.

Distribution According to the Stage of the Lesson that the Man Is in.—As already stated when working with a group on production work in the yard, the instructor will get men who are on different lessons and who also may be in different stages of the same lesson, as in the checking record shown above. The way that an instructor should distribute his time among the different men is affected by the stage of the lesson on which the man is under instruction. In general, a man in steps 2 and 3 will require more of the instructor's time than a man in step 1, and step 4 will, in general, require the least of the instructor's time. In distributing his time the instructor should bear these facts in mind.

Of course the above statement does not mean that the individual men will not require instruction and help in various degrees, according to his special characteristics, and the demands of the special situation, but is intended to draw attention to the fact that an instructor can set up a few general standards for time distribution that may serve him as something of a check and help him to keep away from ineffective distribution.

Concentration.—In its general sense this means sticking to the lesson in hand and not getting diverted onto other subjects during the progress of the lesson. This will, of course, be most likely to occur in group or class work but the same principles will apply to instruction of production work. If a man has a group of say six men under instruction, he has six definite lessons to put over, and in all probability he has to put them over at different times, unless the men happen to "bunch." The question of concentration therefore applies as much to the individual lesson as to the group lesson, except that with one man the chance of keeping the work concentrated is much better.

With an interested man or group poor concentration may easily come about unless the instructor has, at all times, the aim of the lesson and the particular teaching unit clearly in mind. The problem of holding a group of men or one man to the particular learning job in hand and still not destroying interest is one calling for much skill, tact, and practice on the part of the instructor. A great aid in doing this is the use of a lesson plan or sufficient memoranda to form an "operation sheet," even when the instructor is experienced enough to put over the lesson without such fully worked out memoranda as would be required by a man who was relatively "green" on the teaching job.

Distribution and Concentration as Affecting Interest.—Both poor distribution and lack of concentration seriously affect interest. Poor concentration, whether in a group or in instructing an individual man will rapidly reduce interest. This is particularly serious in step 2 of the lesson because in this case it tends to nullify the effects of good preparation.

Poor distribution also affects interest: if the man feels that he is not getting the attention that he should have, or help when he needs it, it is easy for him to get into an "I should worry" state of mind which, of course, kills interest.

In either case the results are bad and the efficient instructor will be on the alert to avoid reducing the interest of his man through distribution or lack of concentration.

Indications of Lost Interest.—An interested man is "onto his job" and an uninterested man is not "onto his job." Generally when a man gets "off his job" it means that in some way, the interest is gone. It is then up to the instructor to get busy, find out what the matter is and get the man to going again as soon as possible. He must be an expert in determining the cause of lost interest, and he cannot take too much time to study each individual case as it comes up; in fact, an experienced instructor will often be able to tell that the interest of a given man is going to "let go" before the man himself is aware of what is going to happen. Of course the longer a man's interest is allowed to lapse without being started up again, the more of a job the instructor will have to get things moving, so the more nearly the instructor can be "Johnny on the spot" when the interest of a given man begins to "let go," the less of a "repair" job the instructor will be making for himself and the more efficient will be his work with his gang.

The General Value of Interest in the Instructional Management of the Gang.—Considerable space has been devoted in these notes to the question of interest and to the factors that affect it. This is because, after all is said, the success or failure of an instructor so far as the management of his gang goes will be largely determined by the degree to which he can work interest for "all that it's worth." An interested man will work, he can be easily instructed, he will not loaf on his job, he will ask intelligent questions, he will want to learn. Under these conditions the problems of management become easy, and the instructor can put in all his time and energy on his real job, instruction. Under reverse conditions the problems of management become more difficult, require more of the time of the instructor, thus drawing him to that extent away from his real job; the instruction is not so effective and the whole training program suffers accordingly.

Instructors cannot give too much attention to the study of interest and interest factors, and to the methods by which interest can be developed and maintained in their men. Time and energy spent in this work will be well repaid.

D. THE INSTRUCTIONAL TURNOVER AS IT AFFECTS THE INSTRUCTOR

Preliminary.—In any training department, as in any production department, a certain number of men who enter will not complete the training work. Some will prove to be misfits, some will quit for one reason or another, some will show that they should be transferred to another line of training. In the ordinary use of the term we can say that there will be an *instructional turn over*. In any department a large turn over is an indication of something wrong and it is generally considered that the most expensive thing that can be done with a man is to discharge him when he has once been employed and set to work.

The same general problems that apply to the production turn over apply to the instructional turn over; many of these problems lie outside of the instructor's job, but, to the extent that they affect the turn over of a given group under a given instructor, they are problems that affect that instructor, and to that extent he should give them consideration. Some discussion of the factors that affect turn over in the group, and the effect of turn over on the problems of training, are therefore included in this section.

It is a well known fact that different instructors will show very different results as to turn over in their groups: one instructor will show a large turn over and another instructor a small turn over, when both men have the same general class of learners and are instructing in the same line of work. One man will "hold" his men, the other man will fail to "hold" his men. Both men are earnest and doing all that they can; what causes the difference? Such questions as these may well be given careful attention by the instructor whose problem is to turn out as many effectively trained men as he can from all the men who come to him for training. The following paragraphs discuss some of the more important points that come up in this connection.

Firing a Man is not Training Him.—It is evident that, whenever a man who has been put into a group is dropped before the end of the training course, he has not been trained. For some reason, and it may be a satisfactory reason at that, the training work has failed to deliver the goods. Whatever time, energy, and money have been expended in carrying the man up to the time that he was dropped constitute a dead loss. Firing a man from a training group costs money just as much as firing a man from a production department costs money. This is a cold fact.

A Good Man is Worth Saving.—It may be said in general, that a man who is "good stock" is worth saving at the expense of additional time and effort. The cost of the extra time will usually be more than offset by the loss in investment if he is dropped. If an instructor thinks that the man is "good stock" he should exhaust all means for getting him trained before he recommends his discharge.

A Really Poor Man is a Useless Drag and Expense.—It is also a cold fact that retaining a man who really cannot be trained costs money, time, and energy. He is taking the place of a man who could be trained. He is a drag on the work and is putting in his time to no advantage.

An instructor is therefore between two fires in considering the desirability of retaining or dropping a man.

Some suggestions in this connection may be of assistance to the instructor in coming to a decision in this matter.

Questions that an Instructor Must Face when he Decides that he Cannot Train a Man.—As pointed out the instructor must face a decision based on a balancing of two factors: the chance that the man is "good stock" or that he is "poor stock." The average untrained instructor will usually decide too quickly that the man is "poor stock"—he will not wait long enough to be sure. Any decision that he makes is largely a guess at best. He does not know which of the three periods the man is in, he does not know that all reasonable efforts to arouse and maintain interest have failed. The trained instructor, knowing more, makes his decision much more on all the facts of the case, and so deals with the case much more effectively.

Where Some Instructors Fail on the Matters of Turn Over.—Many instructors always assume that failure on the learner's part is the fault of the man. They never think that it may be their fault. They instinctively take the position that, of course, they are all right and so it must be the fault of the man. Such an attitude is not unnatural in an untrained instructor, but an experienced man will look first at his end of the problem to see where he has fallen down, because, as a matter of fact, it is not improbable that he is partially or wholly to blame.

The Case of the Failure: Who is to Blame?—When we have failure the cause may be due to any or all of several causes. It may be due to poor instruction, poor management, poor teaching conditions, or may be due to the fact that the learner was "unteachable." The first three causes are within the control and field of responsibility of the instructor, the last is not. In a case of *approaching failure* the instructor should carefully study the situation in order to determine whether the cause does or does not lie within those causes that he can control, if that seems probable, see what he can do to improve conditions. Before he puts it up to the man alone he must be sure that poor instruction, poor management, or poor teaching conditions are not responsible.

Poor Instruction.—By this is meant that the work of the instructor has been badly planned, or not planned at all, or he has used unsuitable methods for putting over his instruction, or he has failed to use a good instructional order. Poor work in this respect has often been the real cause of a large "turnover" in an instructional group.

Poor Management.—Failure to meet any or all of the conditions of good management, especially with regard to the instructor's relations to his men, his handling of interest factors, etc., may be the cause of an apparently approaching failure, or of one that has actually come about.

Poor Teaching Conditions.—In many cases the instructor's turn over has been unduly increased because he undertook to instruct under improper instructional conditions. He takes too large a group, he tries to work with defective material, he tries to demonstrate without proper demonstration material. In these cases and in all cases of this character, while poor teaching conditions may or may not be due to causes beyond the instructor's control, he should carefully consider them as possible cause for an approaching failure.

Poor Learner.—By a poor learner is meant a man who, if all the other causes of failure were removed, would still fail to make good. While such men are much more rare than is usually assumed, especially where the employment department has exercised due care in selecting men for given lines of training, such cases do occur. A man may prove physically unfitted for the work, he may not seem to possess the sense of accuracy required for a given trade, he may not possess enough power of forming mind pictures to successfully master a trade composed largely of technical jobs. When the instructor is satisfied that he has a man of this type, after careful study of the situation, then, of course, it becomes his duty to bring about his removal from the instruction group.

E. SOME SPECIAL POINTS IN GANG MANAGEMENT

Preliminary.—The following paragraphs present some special points that concern the instructor in the problems of the management of his gang. These problems concern themselves largely with the matter of getting the gang to work, keeping it at work, and some general questions that seem to be worth drawing attention to in these notes.

Problems Connected with Getting the Group to Work.—It is essential to the maintenance of interest and of discipline that the group under instruction should be started promptly when work is supposed to begin. Any delay in this matter is a serious failure in handling the gang. There are several reasons for this: in the first place the training organization that has the job of training men to do their jobs *right* should do, in a way, a model job. If the men are allowed to loaf in the training department why won't they loaf on their jobs after they are trained? In the second place men are being trained in correct habits in the training work. In the third place the training work is the place of all places where speed and snap should prevail.

Among the more important points to be looked out for by the instructor in this connection is planning so that there will be no delay in securing materials, in each man knowing just where he knocked off and where he starts in again, and being prepared for a "quick shift," as in the case where the weather changes over night and makes the continuation of out of door work impossible. So far as the instructor can foresee and provide for "starting contingencies" he will be able to start his gang promptly when the whistle blows, and it is a part of his job to do just this thing.

In this connection one or two suggestions may be of service. It will pay the instructor to be on the job a few minutes before the work starts, so that he can make a preliminary inspection of conditions before his men come onto the job. He may have left things all right but something may have happened in the interval that will need attention, and which if not attended to will seriously interfere with the work of some man or of all the group.

Again the instructor will find it highly desirable to keep his work planned out in advance so that he knows what sort of equipment will be needed and can provide it in advance of the need for its use. In selecting and laying out suitable jobs for his men this must be planned for well in advance; such planning cannot be carefully worked out under pressure. An hour spent on this sort of work each day, even in the instructor's own time, will be well repaid in increased efficiency and the satisfaction of doing a good job. In this connection it is probably needless to remark that the instructor who "works by the clock" is generally an inefficient instructor and should get some other kind of a job. The real instructor has a job to do and does it without regard to hours.

Problems Connected with Keeping the Group at Work.— Having started the group to work promptly there is still the problem of keeping the work up continuously during the working period. Many considerations, some of which have been touched upon in these notes, make this imperative. The instructor has several men who probably are none of them at the same stage of progress, they each may be requiring a different lesson or may be in different parts of the same lesson, or there may be any other possible combination. They may be bunched in a room or, what is more likely in emergency training, scattered over a greater or less space under instruction on production work. The effective handling of this situation is a considerable problem for the instructor.

The Double Function of the Instructor.—It may be said in general that the instructor on the job has all the problems of a foreman and then some of his own. As an instructor, his job is to instruct, to teach effectively, efficiently, and rapidly. This is his primary job. In order to carry on his instructional work efficiently the instructor has also many of the problems of the supervisor, that is, he must keep the instructional work going, just as a production foreman must keep the production work going. Of course, it must be clearly understood that the instructor is up against problems of instructional supervision and not production supervision, even if his men are being instructed on production work, which of course they are under any good training plan. The instructor must be sure and not get his responsibility for instruction confused with responsibility for production; in his case production is a by-product of instruction, although, of course, considerable production will come out of the instructional work.

The Instructor as an Instructor.—The instructor's job is, of course, to "put it over," that is what he is hired to do. He must carry out the instructional process effectively under the working conditions. He must put each of his learners through the series of teaching lessons as they are laid out in the course of progressive instruction that he has prepared. He must put over the different teaching steps in their order, put over each step effectively, in short, do a good instructing job. He will have to do this generally under conditions of individual instruction, rarely under ordinary conditions will he get group and probably never class instruction. The final test of his efficiency is the effectiveness of his teaching.

In order that the instructional work may go on effectively however, the instructor must also keep track of the teaching conditions, and in this sense he becomes also a supervisor.

The Instructor as a Supervisor.—One important part of the work of the instructor consists in keeping track of just where each man is in his work and to do this he needs some sort of a record; he should not attempt to rely on his memory for this information. He needs to know what job each man is on, when he is likely to be through, what sort of a job he should have next, etc. He must know how each man is getting along, when he is stuck and needs a little help, when he is ready for a new lesson, when he needs a little supplementary instruction and so on. The work of the instructor so far as he may be called a supervisor consists in keeping the whole group under his eye and knowing just what is needed at any given time by any given man, seeing that conditions are right, that nothing has happened to interfere with the effective carrying on of the instructional process. This is supervisory work, and does not, in its essentials, differ from that of a good foreman.

The Proper Attitude of the Men towards the Instructor.—Effective or ineffective gang management will show more in the attitude of the men towards the instructor than in any other way. Under good management the men and the instructor will evidently be all on the job together, on a straight man to man basis: the men will not be afraid to ask questions and the questions will be to the point; there will be much discussion but there will be little argument; the men will be on the job whether they are under the eye of the instructor or whether they are not; all conditions will be business-like and "natural." The men will evidently think of the instructor as a "coach" rather than as a production foreman; the instructional work will proceed rapidly and effectively, with no confusion; work will start promptly and will go on until the end of the instructional period.

Under conditions of poor management the reverse conditions will prevail; men will loaf on the job when they can; the instructor will become involved in arguments with the men or the men will get into arguments that lead nowhere; the instructor will be working with one man with the rest of the gang standing around waiting; the instructor and the men will be "rowing" more or less; the work will be "slack."

The Man who Works the Instructor.—In any instructional gang there will be from time to time a sample of the man who tries to "work" the instructor; he puts up a bluff that he is greatly interested, that he is very anxious to get ahead as fast as possible and so on. The instructor may have some difficulty at first in distinguishing this type of man from the man who really wants to know, but in the long run he will show himself for what he is because he will fail to "deliver the goods" in his work. Of course the method of dealing with such a man is to stick to straight business with him, give him his fair share of attention but no more, and give him a chance to find out that he is not getting anywhere. Of course the last resort, when the instructor is "sure of his man," is a straight talk and a "call down." The great danger here is that the instructor may make a mistake and seriously depreciate the interest of a really interested man if he takes action before he is sure of his facts.

The Man who Stops Working.—When a learner stops working it may be due to any one of several causes and the instructor should determine the cause before he undertakes to deal with the matter. First, the man may not know what to do next; in this case he needs additional instruction; the instructor must find out just what point he is stuck on and set him right. This can often be best done by the use of suggestive questions. Second, the man may be tired, mentally or physically; in that case the instructor cannot give further instruction and generally that is not what he needs, but he must be given a change of thinking or a rest, as the requirements of the case may call for. Third, he may have reached a point where he is confused; he thinks that he knows what to do next but is afraid that if he goes on he may spoil the job; he hesitates; in that case a little suggestion from the instructor will generally get him to going again because it is more a question of a choice between possible things that can be done rather than not knowing what to do. In the fourth place the man may have struck some combination of circumstances that was not contemplated when the lesson was taught; in that case he needs additional instruction from the instructor.

Cases of this kind will most often occur in the progress of the lesson in steps 2 and 3, rather than in steps 1 or 4.

Since the method of dealing with the case will be different according to the cause of the "slacking up," the instructor must be an expert in determining the cause of the particular difficulty before he undertakes to straighten it out. If he attempts to deal with a confused man as if he were a tired man, he will only make a bad matter worse, and so with other possible cases.

The Man who Loafs on the Job.—Another type that will come along from time to time is the loafer; he means to get by with as little work as possible. Such a man needs, of course, to have his interest aroused, and, if this can be done, the situation will remedy itself. If he is really a loafer he is a dangerous member of the group; he will interfere with the work of others, set them a bad example, and should be summarily dealt with.

Great care should be used not to mistake a man who has slowed down because he is fatigued, or because he is stuck and needs help, with the sort of a man just described. Mistaking the latter for the former type may spoil a good man.

The General Question of Discipline.—In general there are two ways in which instructors approach the question of establishing and maintaining good working conditions; that is, discipline, as it is called. The first method is based on what may be called "school discipline," that is, the instructor who undertakes to enforce this sort of discipline is thinking of the sort of discipline that is found in a regular school. The instructor who uses the other sort of discipline has in mind the discipline of the yard or the shop. The second method is right, the first is wrong. "School discipline" has no place in shop training, even with apprentices.

Many men on becoming instructors feel that they must take on all the conditions and attributes of the "regular school teacher" as they suppose the regular school teacher to be. They are generally wrong in their notions as to the make up of the good modern teacher, but that is not important. In doing this they feel that they must "sustain their dignity," must have "discipline," etc. Of course the only result of such notions is that the work of such an instructor is poor, his turn over is large, and he generally ends by giving up the instructional game either because he wants to or because he has to. Usually he never knows what the matter is.

Why Regular School Discipline Will not Work in Industrial Training.—In the first place the conditions are entirely different in a regular school and in trade training, and the sort of discipline that has to be enforced in a school is not required in training work. In a school large numbers of comparatively immature students must be handled, moved about, and controlled in very limited space. Teachers often have classes as large as twenty-five or thirty; working periods are short, rarely exceeding an hour, except in special cases. Under these conditions a certain amount of "military" organization is often required. Again it is still largely assumed in regular schools that students must be forced to work; that they cannot be trusted to take care of themselves in a proper way and attend to their jobs as intelligent human beings. The best general school teachers have got away from this notion, and the discipline of a good modern school is much more like that of the production department in a good concern than it was a number of years ago.

The conditions in shop training are entirely different; the learners are relatively mature, they know what they are there for; the groups are small, much of the instruction is carried out on the job in the shop or the yard; in general, none of the special conditions that were assumed to require "school discipline" exist in a training department.

The Sort of Discipline that should Exist in a Training Department.—The discipline should not be essentially different from that of a good production department. The fact that the training organization is on the job of turning out training does not noticeably affect the question. The instructor has no need to feel that he must look out for his dignity; if he knows his job and knows how to teach it, the dignity question will take care of itself, because the men will respect him; if he does not know his trade and does not know how to instruct, his men will not respect him. In a good training scheme, where the organization and the management is good, and the instructor knows his job, the question of discipline will become a very minor one.

Conclusion.—In conclusion it may be said that no amount of effective management will give good results unless it is handled by a man of sympathy, tact, and patience. Without these the best planned instruction will fail, the best organization will fail to work, the best management will fall down, and, above all, the instructor must be resourceful and able to make a "quick shift." The final suggestion on handling the gang can be summarized as follows: when you have planned as well as you can always figure that something is going to happen to interfere; that is, *always be prepared for the unexpected*, have an alternative plan and be ready to put it over—always keep things moving.

PART VIII

ORGANIZATION FOR TRAINING IN AN INDUSTRIAL PLANT

CHAPTER XXXVIII

THE ORGANIZATION FOR TRAINING

Preliminary.—In organizing training there are a number of questions that must be answered through the application of certain general principles. In general these questions are of two kinds. (1) Those relating to administrative organization and (2) those relating to educational or training organization. Good administrative conditions permit good training work to be done: make it possible. Training work organized according to sound educational principles gives effective results. Both kinds of organization are needed if training is to be efficient.

The following chapters present certain forms of administrative organization and certain educational principles which if taken into consideration in organizing training will make for training efficiency.

A. ADMINISTRATIVE ORGANIZATION

In the past the tendency has been to organize with training as subsidiary to some other activity of the plant. Naturally, in the majority of cases it has been included in the organization for production. In other cases it has been organized on the theory that it was a part of the labor problem and has been made a part of the responsibility of the employment organization. Sometimes it has been thought of as an educational problem and on the theory that education was a part of the welfare work has been headed up into the welfare department. As a matter of fact training should be given in *an independent department*.

The Training Department an Independent Department.—Like any other department the training department has a job; it renders definite service by turning out a definite product. It is, of course, a service department, its service consisting in taking in men with less skill and trade knowledge and turning them out with more skill and trade knowledge.

In order that the training department should be able to do its job it should be organized as a distinct department. There is no more reason for combining the training department with, say, the employment department, than there would be in combining the maintenance and the hull construction departments. If the different production departments of the plant must each have their own staff, their own head, their own organization suited to the particular job that they have to do, it is equally true that the training department should have its own staff, its own head, its own organization suited to the particular job that it has to do: any other organization will only result in inefficiency.

Why Training should be Given in an Independent Department.—First, training to be really effective *should cover the plant*. It should not be confined to a selected few. There should be *quantity* training as well as *quality* training. A large number of men trained to do their various jobs in the best way is as important an efficiency asset as a few men trained on a few special jobs. Where this is done it makes enough of a job to warrant a distinct organization.

Second, effective training is a job for *specialists*. To be carried on effectively it requires trained men who give all their time and attention to the training job.

Third, the conditions for effective training are so different from the conditions under which the other activities of the plant are carried on, that it cannot be effectively carried on under the conditions required for good work in other departments.

Fourth, the training force must be under the direction of an expert head: a Director or Superintendent of Training. Such a Superintendent must be in a position to work coöperatively with the heads of the departments with which the training department must maintain working relations, hence *he should be responsible to the same executive that other department heads are responsible to*.

Assuming the existence of a training department organized in accordance with the principles given above, the question of its relation to other departments is of importance especially to the employment and production departments.

B. THE RELATION OF THE TRAINING DEPARTMENT TO THE PRODUCTION DEPARTMENTS

Preliminary.—Under ordinary conditions, a very great proportion of the training that is given must be given in connection with jobs. Since job training must be carried on on production work and this work must come from the regular work of the plant, the relation set up is not merely a coöperative one, but calls for the setting up of definite *working relations* between the departments furnishing the work and the training department that uses it, since a condition of mutual responsibility is set up.

The Character of the Relation.—The Training Department, a Customer.—The general relation of the training department to any given production department is similar to that of a man who wants something that another fellow has got (a customer), but who also knows that the particular thing that he wants is mixed in with a lot of other things that he does not want. He knows that what he wants is there somewhere, but he doesn't know *where* (strictly speaking, in some cases, he only guesses that it is there, and sometimes he guesses wrong). The general relation is therefore that of a customer and a dealer, with the training department as the customer and the production department as the dealer. It is therefore necessary that some effective working plan or *method of procedure* should be established to enable the "customer" and the "dealer" to work together in such a way that the "goods" can be delivered.

Two Ways of Going at the Job.—Two possible methods of going at the job may be illustrated by the different methods followed in a city store and in a country store. In the former the customer tells the salesman what he wants, the salesman finds it and brings it to the customer. If the customer knows exactly what he wants he may never see the article until it is delivered, as in the case of mail orders.

In the country store the customer often "looks around"

through the stock to see if what he wants is there and, if he finds it, tells the clerk, or even sometimes brings it to the clerk, pays for it, and carries it off.

The first method consists essentially in the customer's telling the dealer exactly what he wants and leaving the dealer, who presumably knows his own stock, to fill the order. That is, the customer *draws a requisition* on the dealer, for the particular thing that he wants, and the dealer fills the requisition.

In the second case the customer draws no requisition, but undertakes to find what he wants himself and then tells the dealer that it is there and that he wants it.

Evidently the "country store" method may work under country conditions; small stock, few customers, etc., but would not work with a large stock and many customers, since it would evidently cause too much confusion and misunderstandings.

In the same way the method of procedure for securing work for instructional purposes might be based on either the "city store" idea or the "country store" idea. Under efficient training conditions, the "country store" idea will not work, the *working plan* for securing work must be based upon the "city store" idea, that is, on the use of requisitions and these requisitions must be handled according to a regular method of procedure, so as to avoid any confusion or crossed wires.

The General Characteristics of a Proper Working Relation.— The general plan of organization on which any detailed method of procedure should be based may be illustrated as follows: At the request of the training department, a production department assigns suitable jobs or classes of work to the training department. The production department indicates so far as may be necessary, how the work is to be done, but has no responsibility for the men under training or for the supervision of the training work, that being entirely the responsibility of the training department. Such work when completed is, of course, turned back to the production department, inspected, and if good, accepted.

During the use of this work for instructional purposes the men under training are under the authority of the instructor, not under that of the production foreman though, of course, coöperative relations must be maintained between them.

This puts the training department essentially in the position of a sub-contractor, taking on certain work, doing it with his own men, who are responsible to him, and turning in the finished work.

As an illustration of how such a procedure could be worked out in practice, the different steps in such a method are given below.

A Working Plan.—A practical working procedure for carrying out this general plan would involve the following steps:

(1) An instructor draws requisitions on the office of the Director for work that meets his instructional needs—this may, of course, be more than one kind of a job, but a job that fits the type job specifications.

(2) The Director draws a requisition on the proper department for the sort of work that will meet the specifications.

(3) The department on which the work requisition is drawn either finds work that will serve, that is, fills the requisition, returns it to the Director's office with all necessary information as to where the work can be found, or, as might happen, finds that it cannot "deliver the goods," in which case the requisition would come back with that information.

(4) The Director's office notifies the instructor that his requisition can, or cannot be filled, and if it can be filled furnishes him with all necessary information as to place, quantity, etc., so that the instructor can make the necessary assignments.

(5) The instructor puts his man onto the work as indicated and instructs him on the job. When the instruction value of the job is exhausted he takes his man off and notifies the Director's office that he is finished with that job.

(6) The Director's office then notifies the production department to take over the work.

Of course the plan of procedure just outlined is only one of a number that could be developed, it is presented here as an illustration of how the relations between the two departments could be worked out on a proper basis, so that responsibility is fixed at all steps of the procedure, and the danger of misunderstandings and "lost motion" is reduced to a minimum.

The Coördinator.—In connection with the effective operation of such a plan as that just described, it has been found that the work can be carried on much more efficiently if a certain man in each department (or, in a small plant, possibly one man for all departments) is designated as the representative of that department, and if a man from the staff of the training department performs a corresponding function for that department. Such men are often called *coördinators* and may be designated as *Training Coördinators* and *Production Coördinators* respectively.

The Job of the Production Coördinator.—The production coördinator must be acquainted with all the work that is going on and which will be coming on in the department or the departments that he represents, where it will be located, who will be the foreman in charge, and, in general, be in possession of all information necessary for the filling of requisitions for work from the training department. He is, for the purposes of this work, the representative of his department acting under authority delegated to him for this purpose by the head of his department.

The Job of the Training Coördinator.—In the practical working out of such a working plan as described there are always many adjustments to be made. The training coördinator must know the training department and also the yard, so that he can, in conference with the production coördinator, attend to necessary adjustments and details. In practice, the production coördinator will not be familiar with instructional requirements (proper instructional conditions, etc.), and most of this knowledge will have to be supplied by the training coördinator. Again, there will often be cases where work of the exact type called for cannot be found but where the training coördinator, if he knows the instructional use to which it is to be put, can suggest modification that will permit the requisition to be filled fairly well.

As a matter of fact, it will generally be found that the training coördinator will have to do most of the adjusting, since it will frequently happen that the production coördinator will have other duties and responsibilities.

Just as the production coördinator represents his department head, so the training coördinator represents the Director, and acts under delegated authority for the special purposes implied in his function.

The Limitation of the Field of the Coördinator.—An effective coördinator will carefully confine himself to his function, that of arranging for the filling of requisitions for work as they come to him from the instructor through the Director's office. He is not himself an instructor, it is not his function to undertake to determine what work should be given, but only to see that the work that is given fits the specifications. A coördinator that confuses his function with that of an instructor can cause endless confusion.

Advantages of the Plan.—A properly worked out plan which includes the use of requisitions that originate with the instructor, and includes the use of coördinators has several advantages. In the first place it *fixes responsibility*, in the second place it provides a *uniform method of procedure*, in the third place it provides for the designating of *definite individuals* whose job it is to see that the details of the plan are regularly carried out and to make any necessary adjustments in practice, in the fourth place it permits the work to be carried out rapidly and effectively with the minimum opportunity for misunderstandings and crossed wires. Lastly these results are secured with the minimum amount of "red tape" compatible with the efficient doing of the job.

A plan including these characteristics should therefore be adopted for carrying out the relations between the training and the production departments so far as securing instructional work goes.

The Necessity for Informal Conference.—As in any other case, whatever the plan adopted, it will work efficiently or inefficiently in proportion to the tact and patience of those affected by it. Informal conferences between the training coördinator and the instructors, in which the coördinator finds out just what the instructor wants to do, conferences of a similar nature between the production coördinator and the training coördinator, as well as between both coördinators and the production foremen, are, of course, essential. Any attempt to carry on the work on a purely official basis *alone*, will, of course, only lead to inefficiency and failure.

C. THE RELATION OF THE TRAINING DEPARTMENT TO THE EMPLOYMENT DEPARTMENT

Preliminary.—The employment department bears much the same relation to the training department that the training department bears to the production department. If the employment department has a man who needs training it calls on the training department to furnish that training; it is the "customer," the training department is the "seller." This relation has been often lost sight of because the functions of the two departments have been confused, and, because an employment department places men in production because of their skill, it has been assumed that where a man lacked skill it was the business of the employment department to furnish it. That is, such training schemes as have been established heretofore have frequently been thought of as part of the job of the employment department.

The question of the proper relation of the training department to the employment department is therefore discussed in these notes, especially from the standpoint of its effect on the work of the instructor.

The Job of the Employment Department.—The job of the employment department consists essentially in knowing where there is a job without a man to do it and in finding a man that can do that job. It can get two kinds of men: somebody that has already learned how to do the job, in which case all that is necessary is to bring the man and the job together, or men that can be taught how to do the job by turning them over to somebody whose business is training. In this case, after the men have been trained, they are on a level with the first kind of men and the employment department can then place them.

The training department must therefore come in as an intermediary between the employment department and the production department whenever a man has to be equipped with additional skill or knowledge *before* he can be put on the job.

The Proper Working Relation of the Training and the Employment Departments.—The proper working relations of the two departments should therefore be through some system of requisitions similar to that discussed in connection with the relations of the training department and the production departments. That is, the man should be employed by the employment department and then, if he needs training, he should be turned over to the training department with a "requisition" calling for the sort of training that he needs. This training department should "fill" this requisition and then return the man to the employment department. The employment department would then proceed as it would have done had the man known how to do the job when he was first employed. The principle on which such a working method should be based should be that *employing and placing men* and *furnishing training* are two distinct jobs, each of which can best be done by an organization especially established to do that job.

The Proper Method of Procedure.—According to a proper method of procedure the following steps would be taken:

1. The man would be employed by the employment department.

2. The employment department would determine whether he could be placed at once on some needed work, because he knew how to do it, or that he required some sort of training before he could do the job.

3. In case the man needed some sort of training the employment department, from a study of his past work and his

other qualifications would determine what sort of training he needed and would send him with a requisition calling for that particular training to the training department.

4. The training department would fill the requisition by training the man as rapidly and efficiently as possible.

5. The training department would send the trained man to the employment department.

6. The employment department would then place him as if he had been competent when he was first employed.

What Department Does the "Sorting"?—It will be noticed that under the above suggested procedure the determination of the sort of training required by any given man is made by the employment department and not by the training department, which confines itself strictly to its job of giving training. This draws a clean cut line between the functions of the two departments and tends to prevent much confusion and difficulty. The two departments must, of course, work in the closest coöperation: the Director of the training department and the Head of the employment department must "sit in together" all the time, but the "sorting out" of men to be trained and of men that do not need training, and the determination of the character of training required in the case of any given man should be *officially* the responsibility of the employment department. This is true for a number of reasons, among the more important of which are:

1. The employment department is the only one that is in a position to know the needs of all the departments in the yard.

2. It is the department that has the job of meeting those needs as they arise.

3. It is in the best position to ascertain just what the requirements of any given job are.

4. It is in a position to obtain records of the past trade experiences of the men and to size them up at time that they apply for employment, which is the best time to secure such information.

A method of procedure similar to that suggested above is therefore to be recommended in the establishment of a working plan to effectively carry out the relations of the two departments.

How such a Plan Affects the Instructor.—Under the operation of such a plan as that just outlined, the instructor will not "pick out his men at the gate" but will get his men and the "training requisitions" that go with them from the Director of the department. Should a man prove "unteachable" the instructor will report the fact to the Director, not to the employment manager. Should a man be O. K.'d as properly trained or dropped from the group, he will be returned to the office of the Director, not to that of the employment department.

Such a plan relieves the instructor of all work except that of instructing, and, to that extent, makes for efficient instructional conditions.

D. THE RELATION OF THE TRAINING DEPARTMENT TO THE WELFARE DEPARTMENT

Preliminary.—It has already been briefly pointed out that there is a tendency to confuse the jobs of the welfare department and of the training department, that is, to think of training as a species of welfare work. It has therefore seemed worth while to include in these notes some discussion of the relation of these two departments.

The Jobs of the Two Departments.—The training department is organized to instruct and train: the welfare department is organized to promote the general welfare of the men. It may concern itself with the working conditions, with questions of general health and sanitation, with the promotion of those things that will aid the men "to get more out of life," it might even concern itself with matters of *general education*, as when it encourages men to learn to speak English, or encourage the formation of classes in citizenship. All these things and many others are extremely valuable services, but they have nothing to do with *training a given man so that he can do a given kind of work*. That is the job and the only job of the training department.

As a matter of fact, if we clearly see what a training department is for, what its job is, we see that except as any department would coöperate with any other department, there is no relation between the Training Department and the Welfare Department. Each has its own job and the less the two jobs are mixed the better work will both departments do.

Where a clear distinction has not been drawn between the functions of the two departments the staff of a training department often feel that they are on a welfare job as well as on an instructing job and the instruction suffers accordingly.

E. ORGANIZATION FOR TAKING ON AND DISCHARGING MEN

Preliminary.—Since any training department must take in men who lack certain training and discharge them after they have secured such training, some effective organization is called for to handle this problem. Some "machinery" must be set up that will get men into the instruction groups, take care of them while they are under instruction and discharge them from the group and from the department when their training is completed.

Organization for Taking Men into Training.—The most efficient type of organization for this purpose will be one that keeps the function of the training department clearly in mind and does not bring in the function of any other department. As an illustration it may be said that it is not uncommon to find training departments that have included in their organization provision for sorting out the men in addition to training them, or to find departments so organized that more or less provision is made for "welfare work" as well as for training work. Such organizations are not efficient; the more closely a training department sticks to its job, that of training, and only training, in its organization, leaving work that should be done by other departments to those departments, the more efficient will be the training work that is put over. On the other hand the more a training department organizes for doing any work that is not strictly its *job*, the less efficient will be its work.

The best organization for taking men into the department will be one that provides for the men being sent to the office of the director from the employment department with something corresponding to a requisition for training. The employment department should, in effect, say to the training department, "Here is a man that lacks certain training; give it to him, and when you have done so, send him back to us."

The organization should further provide that the man should be assigned to a proper instructional group and that the instructor in charge of that group should be properly informed as to the requirements of that particular case.

In this way the instructor would be left free to attend to the business of instruction, which is his business.

The organization should not be such that the instructor is expected to pick out his men at the gate, or to spend much time in determining what training the man should have; this work should be done by the office of the employment department.

Organization for Getting Men out of the Department.—In the same way, in order that the training department shall be left free to attend to its job without any other responsibilities, the best organization would provide that a man, on the completion of his training, as certified to by his instructor, should be sent back to the employment department, not to the production department for which he has been trained, leaving it to the employment department to place him as it would a man who knew his job when he was employed first. The situation with the trained man is that he has now the same status as the competent workman who was hired by the employment department and sent directly to a production department, only the training experience has intervened between his hiring and his being put to work on production.

F. THE SPECIAL JOB OF THE DIRECTOR OF A TRAINING DEPARTMENT

Preliminary.—Under the most efficient organization the Director is the head of the Training Department. He has full charge of all matters pertaining to the training or "breaking in" of workers and has general supervision of the department. He has full charge of all workers under training in the plant. He directs the work of the instructors, organizes special schemes for training, inspects the efficiency of the instruction and renders every assistance possible to enable the instructors to do effective work. The Director should have the standing of a department head. The Director of training and the instructors should devote their entire time and attention to the work of training and should not be charged with the usual duties of production foremen.

The following paragraphs discuss some of the more important duties of the Director as distinguished from those of the other members of the instructing staff of the training department.

The Job of the Director as Distinguished from that of the Instructor.— The Director is, in general, the Superintendent of Training; the instructing staff constitutes the working force. He is the man who is ultimately responsible for the efficiency of the training, for the development of the organization that makes efficient training possible, and for the smooth running of that organization. It may be said in general, that a large portion of the work of the director is to bring about and maintain such conditions that the work of the instructors can be carried out effectively and under the best working (instructional) conditions.

The instructor, on the other hand, has the responsibility, under the Director, of "delivering the goods," of putting over the instruction. He deals directly with the instructional groups, he comes directly in contact with the men. The problems of "gang management" are largely his problems. Under good conditions he is responsible for the quality of the instruction, for the way in which the men are taught to do the jobs, for the proper passing out of the auxiliary information, for the selection of proper methods. That is, the conditions are much the same as they would be in a good production gang where each man knew his job and the foreman or superintendent knew how the job should be done and exercised a general supervision of the work of the department.

Neither the director nor the instructors can do the work alone; each must do his part, and it is important that each should know his part in the work of the department as a whole. Confusion on the part of either the instructors or the Director

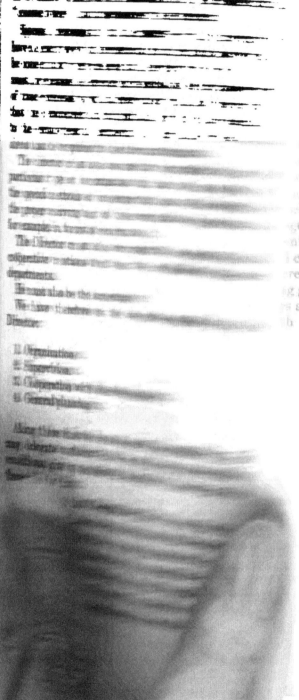

One of the problems of the Director is to secure and maintain such coöperation. He must act as a leader, and as a part of his "leadership" must confer frequently with his staff, both at stated staff meetings and through individual and even group conferences.

The Director as a Training Leader.—A very important part of the work of the Director is that of acting as a "leader" for the instructing staff. The instructors are, by virtue of their work, pretty closely tied down and the Director must furnish the helpful suggestions and the general view that can come from the supervisor and from no one else. There is great danger that a Director may neglect this side of his work, especially under the pressure of routine administrative work, but he should insist on sufficient help to enable him to carry out this side of his work effectively. Among the most effective means of doing this work are the staff conference and the individual conference.

The Value of the Staff Conference.—The efficient Director will make a great deal of use of the staff conference. In order that these conferences shall be effective he must see to it that they are really worth while; that there is a program and that it is carried out. Nothing will do more to weaken the value of the staff conference than to bring the staff together for aimless discussion. An excellent method is to send out a memorandum in advance covering the points that are to be discussed and to hold the discussion strictly to those points. It is in staff meetings that the Director can get the concensus of opinion as to the desirability of a certain contemplated plan of procedure, or of the way in which a certain proposition is working out.

The Value of the Individual Conference.—The staff conference is greatly reduced in value unless it is supplemented by many individual conferences with members of the staff. Staff conferences serve to bring out general opinions and allows an opportunity for general discussion, but the individual conference will give opportunity for the taking up of individual points and receiving individual points of view that, in many cases, would not come out in the general conference.

The value of the individual conference with regard to the work of the individual instructor is obvious.

The Director as an Instructor.—The director must himself be a competent instructor in the sense that he must be familiar with the principles of good teaching. Unless he has this familiarity he cannot properly supervise the instructing work of the staff.

The General Relation of the Director and the Staff.—Just as the effectiveness of the work of an instructor depends on the establishment of the right relations between the instructor and the members of the group, so the effectiveness of the work of the Training Department depends largely on the setting up of the right relations between the Director and the members of the instructing staff, and much that has been said in these notes in connection with instructional management will apply with equal force to the problems of departmental management. The general value of tact, patience, helpful criticism, realization that men must gradually develop increased power and ability, hold here as well as in the instructing group, especially as in many training departments instructors after only a brief training, are dealing for the first time with the problems of "how to put it over."

CHAPTER XXXIX

INSTRUCTIONAL BOOKKEEPING

Preliminary.—Whenever a product is turned out there is a necessity for the keeping of certain records: cost records, time records, production records and so on. In the same way a Training Department, turning out a product, training, must provide for some form of "instructional bookkeeping."

This section discusses some of the more important features of such "bookkeeping" for a training department especially as the demands of such a system affect the instructor.

Why Records are Necessary.—Any particular business requires records that will give the information that will answer certain questions. The answers to these questions tell those engaged in the business whether they are succeeding or not, whether it is possible to do the work any better, or any cheaper, whether methods can or can not be improved and so on. The particular questions asked in each case depend upon the nature of the business and upon just what those in charge wish to know.

Collecting and Recording.—Where such records are kept it has to be made somebody's business to get the data and to record it, but often one set of people furnish the information and another set of people record it, so we have what is often called the *recording department* of a business, which very often depends upon other people to collect what it records.

A considerable part of the information required by a recording department can only be given by people who got it at first hand—it must be noted down by the people who are doing the job. Other information can be collected by other people, but, in all cases it must be brought together, studied, and the desired questions answered according to the data as obtained and recorded.

A discussion of records must therefore include answers to the following questions:

(1) Why records must be kept.
(2) What sort of records must be kept.
(3) How the records should be kept and who is to
   (a) Collect the information and report it.
   (b) Record or compile it.

A. WHY RECORDS MUST BE KEPT IN A TRAINING DEPARTMENT

Preliminary.—In general, records must be kept by a training department for the same reasons that they would be kept by any other department, but in addition, the special conditions under which emergency training is carried on require the keeping of certain additional records.

Among the more important reasons for which records must be kept are:

(1) As a check on the work, as when an instructor consults his progression chart in order that he may determine what sort of a job a man should be given next, or when the Director wants to know in what group there is a vacancy for a man who is to be given a certain training. (Checking records.)
(2) To secure data for improving the efficiency of the work, as when the time required to train for the same job by different instructors is compared in order to find out the best methods. (Efficiency records.)
(3) To determine whether or not any given piece of training work is worth doing, as when it is desired to determine for example, whether rivet sorters can be trained to any advantage. (Justification records.)
(4) As a basis for administrative action, as when a man is discharged on the basis of his progression record, his production record, etc. (Administrative records.)

In all these cases and in similar ones not mentioned in these notes, the records are made for definite reasons in order to answer definite questions, or to give a basis for definite action.

Why Checking Records are Needed.—The general purpose for which checking records are kept is to enable those in charge of the work to know "where they are at" at any given time. The instructor must know what stage a given man has reached in the instructional order before he can determine what sort of a job the man should have next, he must know whether his men are all present, and if not, who is absent, the Director's office must know what men are working under each instructor and where they can be found. If an instructor O. K.'s a man as properly trained there must be a record of that fact before the man is turned over to the employment department or sent into production work.

Unless all such facts, and many others, are made matters of record, the department is in the condition of a ship at sea with no means of determining where she is, and everybody on her simply guessing as to her whereabouts.

Checking records are almost invariably records of facts; these facts are known to somebody, but if they are not recorded, if that particular individual cannot be reached or if he has forgotten, the information is not available or is lost forever. A business that is conducted on a memory basis is not in good shape, sooner or later there will be trouble. Some questions that need to be answered cannot be answered because the man who knew has forgotten, or cannot be found, or has gone somewhere else.

In a training department well organized as to checking records it ought to be possible to answer all questions of this sort without depending in any way on the personal knowledge of anybody, in fact, if the entire staff were to be "wiped out" it ought to be possible for perfect strangers to step in, determine just what the situation was and go on with the work from that point.

The department without an efficient system of checking records is in the condition of a little country store where the proprietor "keeps his accounts in his head." Such a store usually eventually goes out of business and a department trying to do its checking in the same "backwoods" way, cannot do efficient work.

Why Efficiency Records are Needed.—Distinct and apart from the question of checking records is the matter of efficiency records. The purpose of such records is to enable those in charge of the work (instructors, the director, the Industrial Training Department) to study their work in order to see how it can be improved. For this purpose it must be possible to compare the efficiency of the training work as given under one set of conditions (instructor, methods, yard, etc.) with that obtained under other conditions. Emergency training calls for training to be given as rapidly and as efficiently as possible. Unless we keep track of our work in this respect we have no means of knowing if we can do the job any better than we are doing it.

Much of the training work is in the nature of an experiment. Up to the present time but little attention has been paid to problems relating to the *best* methods of training men efficiently and rapidly. The only way to secure such knowledge is by the keeping of such records as will show the speed of training under different instructional conditions, both in a given training department and in different departments. For example, suppose that one concern is operating a number of plants with training departments and that a department in one plant succeeds in training men for a certain job in a certain time, say two weeks, while another training department trains men for the same job in a longer time, say six weeks. If these facts are a matter of record, and the "time training" records of the two departments can be compared this fact will come out and the method used for the more rapid training can be studied and the information as to how it was done can be given to all training departments so that that particular training can be speeded up all along the line. Thus the information as to the more rapid method of training becomes of value to all engaged in the work instead of only being known to the instructor who developed it, or even not known to him because he might not know that he had done a better job than the instructors in some other yards, unless he had records, the other men had records, and these records could be compared by somebody whose business it was to look out for just such things.

The question of the establishment of "improvement records" that can be effectively used is therefore of great importance in emergency training where speed and efficiency are such important factors.

Why "Justification" Records are Needed.—A training department is only of value when it can be shown that it is doing its job better than the job has been done before. For example, men have entered the different trades and have learned their jobs somehow. They have acquired a certain degree of skill in a certain time. This is true even when they "stole" their trades. Every man working in a shop to-day has secured his training somehow. A training department, to justify its maintenance, must therefore be able to show that it is doing the training job better than it has been done before. It is not really doing a new job but only doing an old job, and is established and maintained to do that old job in a better way; to do it more quickly and more efficiently. If it cannot show this, it has no reason for existence. It must be possible therefore for the training department to secure such facts as will enable it to answer the question "Are you doing a better training job than was done before" in the affirmative, *and prove it*. This can only be done if suitable records are kept.

It should not be forgotten that, especially for certain trades, definitely planned training is still on trial; many foremen still believe that the best way to train a man is to set him to work in the production department and let him learn as he can from observation and from what he can get from other workmen and from the foreman himself. In many cases these men are honestly "from Missouri" as to the value of training in a distinct department with trained instructors; the right sort of records are necessary in order that they may be "shown."

Questions of this sort may even come up with respect to the value of planned training in certain trades; for example, it is sometimes said that the only shipyard trades that require training are mould loft work and shipfitting. The others can all be picked up on the job. A training department would not take this view, but, in order to show that it was right and the other fellow wrong, there must be definite information obtained and recorded as to the facts in the case, as, for example, the time required to train men to the same degree of skill inside and outside of the department, etc.

An effective system of "justification" records is therefore a very necessary part of the instructional bookkeeping of a training department.

Why Administrative Records are Necessary.—In many cases the Director, in discharging his responsibility, must act on the reports or opinions of his staff, or, in certain cases, with reference to standards that have been established and which must have been met if certain action (discharging a man to the employment department as trained, for example) is or is not to be taken. In case of criticism his only defense is the data on which he acted. This is just as true of an instructor; if he recommends that a man be dropped, as unteachable, he must have his records to show as the basis for his action, and if he has not done this he may find himself unable to justify his action at some future time, or even immediately in case of protest. Instructors often only come to an appreciation of the value of records of this sort after a number of very disagreeable experiences, as for example, when he has made a recommendation based on facts that he had in his head, but had not recorded, and later, when he had forgotten the facts on which he acted, a question came up as to why he acted as he did, and he could not answer it.

B. WHAT SORT OF RECORDS SHOULD BE KEPT BY A TRAINING DEPARTMENT

Preliminary.—This section suggests the general character of the records that should be kept by a training department. No attempt has been made to do more than suggest the main points that should be covered and to present reasons why covering such points is worth the expenditure of time and money involved. The purpose of presenting them is merely to indicate the general character of such records, and to give the prospective instructor and others a general understanding of what they are rather than to enter into any special details.

"**Checking Records.**"—Records of this character will, in general, include, among others:

(1) Records dealing with men.
(2) Records dealing with material.
(3) Records dealing with instructional work.
(4) Records dealing with costs.

For each of these classes recording systems must be operated. The following paragraphs discuss briefly some of the more important points to be taken into consideration in this connection.

Records Dealing with Men.—The department must know where each man should be and that he is there. Hence, as in any school or factory there must be *attendance records*. Records of this kind are not difficult to keep up and, in whatever form they may be called for, usually offer no special difficulties.

The department must also know when a man began his training and when he completed it. The reasons for this are obvious. "Man" records will therefore consist at least of:

(a) Records of Admission and Discharge.
(b) Records of Attendance.

Records Dealing with Materials.—In order that these men may be trained, material must be used. When instructional material is used, somebody must be responsible for it, whenever a job is turned over to the training department for instructional work, records must be made as to where it came from, what instructor is using it and when he got through with it. In all such cases the records would deal with material, when it came, where it came from, who used it and when it was returned or finished. This calls for a suitable system of requisitions and receipts, as in any business.

Records dealing with materials would therefore include at least:

(1) Records of requisitions for instructional material.
(2) Records of the delivery of completed work.
(3) Records as to the filling of requisitions by the department on which it was drawn.
(4) Records fixing responsibility for all material in the custody of the department.

Records Dealing with Instructional Work.—Men under training must be put through a definite instructional order. Records should show the stage that each man has reached at all times, in order that the instructor may properly plan his work; they should show whether the man was put through the whole instructional course or only through some portion of it (as in the case of trade extension men), and, in so far as may be necessary, data with regard to the size of the group at any given time, or other teaching conditions that may be of importance.

Such records would therefore at least include:

(1) The stage that each man had reached in his progression at any given time.
(2) The particular training that was to be given him.
(3) The amount of training that he was to be given as measured against the complete instructional course for that trade.
(4) The teaching conditions.
(5) The instructor's estimate at any time as to the man's attitude, intelligence, capacity, etc., and on which he finally bases his recommendation for discharge from the group.

Records Dealing with Costs.—In common with any department in a production plant the operation of a training department involves expenditures of money, which is charged to the department and product whose value is credited to the department. In an ordinary production department the product is work whose value can be easily determined. In the case of the training department, its product is of two kinds, production material as a "by-product" of training, and its direct product, training itself. Cost records must therefore show not only operating costs, and material credits, but also the value of the training. In addition to the ordinary financial accounts the training department must therefore work out and operate a system of records showing the value of its training to the yard.

Up to the present time but little attention has been paid to this side of the cost records in training departments, and the problem of working out a satisfactory system is, admittedly difficult. The following suggestions may be of value. The "credit" value of training would appear in such items as increased productive power in its trained men as compared with that of men who had "picked up" or "stolen" the trade. It might appear in reduced junking due to lack of skill or carelessness, or in increased earning power.

With the greater trade intelligence and skill that should come from definitely planned and effective training, men who have been trained to do their work well from the start are more likely to be satisfied with their jobs, so, that all other conditions being equal, the results of the work of a training department should show in a reduction of turn over, and in a longer period of employment. Men trained to do their work under competent instructors should work faster and more skillfully so that results of training should show in increased speed of production and a smaller junk pile.

While data relating to such information as that suggested above might be difficult to obtain, it will probably be necessary to attempt to work some recording system to obtain at least a part of it. If no more can be done in the present state of our knowledge it would seem to be highly desirable that at least a record should be kept for each man after he leaves the department and that, so far as possible, all information bearing on the questions discussed above be secured, since a part of the justification data for the maintenance of a training department may lie outside of the field of direct costs and credits.

It is suggested therefore that some system of "following up" men after they leave the training department, that would include production, reduction of waste, and earning power should be maintained. Of course such information would only be of value if checked against corresponding data for men who had not been trained in the department.

Summary.—A training department should therefore in some way, provide for records covering men, material, instructional work and costs, and should also provide for such additional "justification" records as may be necessary. Records for men should, *at least*, include attendance, admission and discharge. Records for material should show at least, what it was, who was responsible for it, what it was used for and what became of it. Instructional records should show *at least*, the position of each man in the instructional order, and the data on which the instructor forms his opinion as to new work and the man's being ready for discharge. Cost records should show both expenditures and credits, including values due to increased production or to better work due training. "Justification records," in addition to the information that is contained in the records noted above, should be used so far as necessary. Probably the most valuable record in this connection is an individual follow up record for each man after he leaves the department and goes to work.

C. HOW RECORDS SHOULD BE KEPT IN A TRAINING DEPARTMENT

Preliminary.—The form in which records are kept is almost as important as the keeping of the records themselves. Records are only of value if they can be used, and the form in which they are kept determines, to a large extent, their availability.

In these notes no attempt has been made to indicate the exact form in which records should be kept, since that is a matter of the special organization of each department, but some general suggestions may be of value.

The Value of Clear Records.—Whatever records may be kept, their value is increased in proportion to their simplicity and clearness. It is a great advantage to keep information that is to be used for one purpose separate from that used for another purpose. A common mistake is to attempt to consolidate too many different kinds of information in one form. For example, it is much better to keep attendance records distinct from production records, or from time training records.

The Value of Using a Good Form in which to Keep Records.—A great deal of thought and attention has been given to working out devices for recording different sorts of information in the best way. Of these the two most important are either adaptations of the *graph* or "curve," or of the so-called "loose leaf" or "card" system.

The Value of Graphed or Diagramed Records.—Whenever the required information can be secured by checking on a list of items or by drawing a line, or curve, or by using a diagram much time is saved for the recorder. Thus for example, if an instructor will lay out his instructional order of jobs on paper he can draw an instruction line (as in Pamphlet 1), that will show the position of each learner correctly and easily. Many uses of the graph principle will suggest themselves. Where it can be applied it is the most time saving device for the recording of information that can be used.

The use of the instruction line as described in Pamphlet 1, in connection with the unit and spiral methods of progression is an illustration of how the diagram can be used to advantage in instructional recording. Time required for training different men, or training the same man on different jobs can be easily shown by this method. It finds many applications in the practice of many recording departments.

The Value of the "Card Method."—Fully as valuable in certain cases is the use of the "card system." It is finding a greater and greater use in recording methods. It can be adapted to nearly all requirements, but is especially valuable where new information may have to be added from time to time or where the information may have to be brought together in more than one way; or rearranged from time to time.

Probably almost any records required in a training department can be efficiently recorded and used if use is made of either the graph method or the card method as the requirements of that special case may require. A good illustration of the value of the card method is its adaptation to the getting out of an effective instructional order as described in Pamphlet 1, where continued changes and readjustments are easily made that would be very difficult were the different teaching units listed out on sheets of paper.

The Untrained Instructor and the Form of Records.—The untrained instructor is very likely not to be informed as to the existence of labor saving devices for records, or is not inclined to study their possible value in record systems. Sometimes he will keep his records on scraps of paper, or in a little blank book without realizing that scraps of paper are easily lost and that, in the use of the blank book, he often has to copy lists of names, or rearrange them, all of which takes time that a card system would save him. In general an instructor, so far as he keeps records as a part of the instructional bookkeeping of the department, cannot afford to use any but the most up to date and efficient recording devices, this is, of course, equally true of the department as a whole.

It will pay the instructor to acquaint himself with the various devices for easy recording that are now on the market and consider their availability for the work of the training department, especially in the line of saving time and energy.

D. WHO SHOULD KEEP THE DIFFERENT SORTS OF RECORDS IN A TRAINING DEPARTMENT

Preliminary.—The preceding paragraphs have discussed the need for records, the general kinds of records called for and the desirability of keeping these records in proper form. These records must be kept by somebody, and the following paragraphs discuss this phase of instructional bookkeeping.

The Two Sides of the Securing of Records.—In general there are two steps in the securing of records, the facts, or *data* as they are commonly called, are first secured and then these facts are recorded. The bookkeeper records facts with regard to sales that the selling force has secured, or certain purchases that the buying force has made. Certain articles have been sold at such and such prices, or certain articles have been bought and certain amounts paid for them, and so on.

In many cases the *recorder* is not the same individual who gets the facts; the bookkeeping department does not sell or buy, it only records.

In the same way a training department "sells" training. The instructors are salesmen, they "make the sales" (put over the instruction), and, in certain cases, are the only people who know the facts, and so must report them. In other cases the facts can be secured by other people, even from the records of other departments, so that it is important that the system of "instructional bookkeeping" of the training department should provide for the securing of all necessary data by the individuals who can best furnish it, according to the particular case under consideration.

As just pointed out there are certain data that only the instructor can furnish. As these are of more particular interest to the prospective instructor they are discussed somewhat more in detail than are those that are of only indirect interest to him.

Data that must be Collected by the Instructor.—Among the different kinds of data that have been discussed there are some that must be furnished by the instructor because no one else can furnish them. As is pointed out elsewhere, an instructor should be asked to do no work of this sort that any one else can do, but when he has been as fully protected as possible there still remains certain data which he alone can furnish. These data can, and should be *compiled* by others (the staff of the Director's office), but they must originally come from the instructor. Among the most important of these are (for his group):

(1) Attendance reports.
(2) Admission and Discharge reports.
(3) Reports on use of material—(Requisitions for Instructor's Material, etc.).
(4) Reports of his estimate of the capacity of the men that go out of his group.

Copies of all reports of this character should, of course, be retained by the instructor for his own use.

In addition the instructor in connection with his own group should keep at least:

(1) Progression records for each man.
(2) Personal records for each man on which he bases his estimate of the capacity of men discharged from his group, and his reasons for discharging them at that time.

The special form in which the above data would be reported or recorded would depend upon the special way in which that particular department provided for it.

The Importance of Uniformity.—Whatever may be the special form provided it is essential that the data from all instructors should be kept, or turned in, as the case may be, in the same form. If this is not done the work of compilation will be greatly increased, errors will be much more likely to occur, and it will be much more difficult to compare the records of different instructors for efficiency and justification data.

Data that can be Secured Directly by the Director.—A considerable portion of the necessary data can be secured directly by the Director's office. While this sort of information does not directly affect the instructor it is mentioned here as a matter of general information. Among the most important records that can be handled entirely in the Director's office are:

(1) Admissions and discharges from the Department.
(2) Assignments to instructing groups and transfers.
(3) Records of requisitions drawn on other departments.

In addition the Director's office should deal with all general compilation work such as:

(1) Complete attendance records, and enrollment records.
(2) Lengths of instructional periods.
(3) Comparative production records.
(4) Reports required in connection with the bonus (where the yard is working under these conditions).

Data that can be Secured from Other Departments.—Considerable information of value can be secured from other departments. Some of this information might be:

(1) Production records during and after training.
(2) Records of pay secured by men after leaving the training department.
(3) Previous training of men taken into the department.
(4) Promotions of trained men (especially trade extension).
(5) Cost figures.

And a great many other kinds of information. Information of this kind must, of course, be compiled in the office of the training department if it is to serve a useful purpose, since it must be usually selected from a mass of other data that has no bearing on the special use that is to be made of it in the training department.

Conclusion.—This section has drawn attention to the need for "instructional bookkeeping," why it is necessary, and by whom it should be done. The purpose of doing this has not been to describe in detail methods, or even to fully cover the ground, but to draw the attention of the prospective instructor to the fact that a system of records, in which he takes an important part, is necessary, so that he would appreciate the value of such work and the necessity of its being thoroughly well done in order to be of value.

The Untrained Instructor and the Keeping of Records.— Untrained instructors usually fail to appreciate the necessity of the keeping of records; they often feel that record keeping is merely a "spotting" device or implies a doubt on the part of the superiors as to the efficiency of their work. They often object to being asked to keep such records as they may be asked to keep on the ground that it is a waste of time, or, if the matter is pressed, do that part of the work in a perfunctory way, so that the results are often of but little value.

The trained instructor knows that there is as much use for the keeping of records in his business as there is in any other business and will do his part of this work intelligently and willingly. What records he keeps will be well kept, and he will intelligently meet any special demands that come in from time to time because he knows, that, outside of his own particular part of the work the Department, as a whole, has many problems to solve whose correct solution depends largely on the securing and compiling of information that is accurate.

CHAPTER XL

TRAINING PRINCIPLES AND POLICIES

KINDS OF TRAINING THAT A TRAINING DEPARTMENT MAY HAVE TO FURNISH

These may be:

(1) Training for supervision.
(2) Training for higher skill in a given trade.
(3) Training men already skilled in another trade.
(4) Training green men.

Under any given set of conditions training for any or all of these four kinds of training might be included in the field of a training department, according to the special conditions that might exist at any given time in any given concern, and it is equally true that the *relative* demand for the different type might vary owing to similar causes.

Training Supervisors.—Any production force includes supervisors (leading hands, inspectors, foremen, etc.), and the number of these supervisors bears a certain relation to the total size of the working force.

While there is always a certain turnover in the supervising group (promotion, resignation, death, etc.), and a limited amount of training can always be offered for this special purpose, it is, under normal conditions relatively small and forms a very minor part of the training work department. Under emergency conditions, as where the amount of production called for is suddenly greatly increased there may be a correspondingly sudden demand for a corresponding increase in the supervisory force, and a corresponding demand for a considerable amount of training for this special purpose. The natural source from which additions to the supervisory force would come would be the working force of the plant.

In general, the sort of men who can become supervisors are the best and most intelligent workmen in the force. Such men often lack certain training to fit them for such supervisory positions and it may become a part of the work of the training department to provide the opportunity for the securing of such training.

General Character of Supervisory Training.—Training for supervision, is in general, along technical rather than production lines, and is likely to consist of various unrelated lines of work rather than to constitute a definite "course of instruction" as the term is commonly used. It might, for example, deal with certain forms of applied mathematics, or practical mechanics, or the particular procedure for routing and checking work in that particular plant, or with methods for keeping the work going or of handling men. Such courses would evidently be disconnected so far as what was taught in one course was likely to help a man in another course, and the order in which he took the different lines of work would be of little importance.

Instruction of this Kind must be Specialized.—Instruction for prospective supervisors will be of little value unless it is *specialized*, that is, unless it deals with the particular problems that come up in the particular plant in which the training department is located; with the particular methods followed in that plant, with the methods of handling the particular sort of men employed, etc. Only in rare cases, and with very advanced men will "general" courses be effective.

Thus, in mathematics, general school or college courses in algebra or geometry are not likely to find much place in the ordinary run of this work, but work in solving equations of certain kinds, or certain kinds of applied geometry (descriptive geometry, as used in sheet metal work, for example) might be of value. All such work must be of direct value in the supervisor's work if it is to serve any real purpose.

General Instructional Conditions for Supervisory Training.— Work of this sort can generally be given on a basis of *voluntary attendance*. Speaking broadly, the green man, the conversion man and the apprentice must be trained, to get the job done, but the supervisory work need only be given to men who want it because they want supervisory work when the chance comes, and incidentally, it is only men of that sort of push, ambition and foresight that are likely to "have the makings" of good supervisors. It is therefore often possible to give such work outside of working hours, in evening classes or sometimes on Saturday afternoons.

Probably work of this sort affords more field for the use of printed instructional material, text books (where books of the right sort are available, which is not often the case) illustrative methods of presentation and use of "home study" than any other line of work given in a training department. The men should be a highly selected group, of a high degree of intelligence, ambitious, thoroughly familiar with the practical aspects of their trade, and so much more likely to do effective work under the instructional conditions just described.

Conditions of Admission in Supervisory Training.—Working under such conditions it is evident that desire to enter the class is not, alone, sufficient reason for admitting,—the man must be qualified. Work of this character therefore calls for the setting up of *conditions of admission*, so that the instructional group will be, so far as possible, confined to those who can "profit by the instruction." This is, of course, equally true with regard to retention in the group.

Conditions of Admission and Retention in Supervisory Training.—It may be stated that, as a general principle, no man should be admitted to work of this character until he has set up a clear presumption of his ability to do the work effectively and that he promises to become an effective supervisor. While this general principle is easy to state it is exceedingly difficult to work out in practice. The following suggestions may be of value:

There are three general sets of evidence that can be used in connection with admission requirements, they are: (1) Credentials, (2) Personal Interviews, (3) Examinations.

By *credentials* is meant any evidence that may be submitted as to past experiences—in the trade, in different sorts of work, in schools of different kinds, the written opinion of others as to his ability, etc.

By *personal interview* is meant any sort of a "talk" with the instructor or director that serves a purpose in getting a line upon the man's qualifications.

An *examination*, of course, is intended to test a man's knowledge or skill by the method of "sampling" as described in Pamphlet 2.

It has been generally considered that admission conditions for work of this character should not be based, to any great extent, if at all, on examinations, as that term is defined in these notes, but that considerable use should be made of the interview and credentials.

Since the demand for supervisors will always be relatively small, attendance on such groups can be safely limited so that selections may often be made from a group of applicants that is larger than the size of the proposed instructional group. In such cases it is not uncommon to attach numerical values ("points") to various elements that enter into credentials, age, length of experience, general education, etc., and do the same with different aspects of the personal interview.

Anyone desiring to look further into methods of admission will find many suggestions in the methods used by employment departments and by school departments in examining applicants for teaching positions.

The chief point to bear in mind is that admission requirements and selective admission should be based, largely, if not entirely on the personal interview and credentials, and that the examination, if used at all, should be made a decidedly minor factor. This is because *personality*, as it is commonly called, is such a large factor in the "stock in trade" of the good supervisor. He must, of course, know his job but that alone will not "get him by."

The examination is therefore of relatively minor importance since it gives little information as to personality. It can, of course, be used to indicate a man's skill through a shop examination, but, for applicants for training work for supervision, especially if they come from the force of the plant itself, such a test is seldom necessary. In the general run, credentials give sufficient information as to experience, and the interview not only covers personality, but if well handled, can be made to serve as an "examination" as well.

The examination therefore is of relatively minor importance.

Instructional Organization.—Of the different possible forms of instructional organization work of this sort is most likely to be organized on the class basis by the untrained instructor or director. It is probably true that the defects of this organization do less harm in this class of work than in any other, just as it is true that poor instructional methods do less damage with work of this character than in any other. Ambitious, intelligent men can get what they want in spite of poor methods and poor instructional management, but they will get it *better* and *quicker* under good conditions nevertheless.

Probably one of the best organizations for this class of work is what is known as the seminar, which is really a combination of individual and class work. Under such an organization the different men in the group, while each working on specified problems come together with the instructor at frequent stated intervals for discussion and reports. At these same meetings the instructor may, as he may deem it desirable, present certain phases of the work, assign new work, etc.

This special form of instructional organization is used to a considerable extent in the graduate schools of universities and would seem to offer distinct advantages for many forms of supervisory training.

The Abuse of the Lecture in Supervisory Training.—There is probably no class of work in which the lecture method is more misused than in work of this kind. It has a limited use, but the general tendency to depend upon "talking" in training men for supervisors is unfortunate. An instructor should be very sure that it will be effective in a given case before he uses it. The very fact that men in work of this kind are commonly especially intelligent makes it all the more important that they should be made to work out their own problems and trained to think for themselves. In general, the lecture method will not do this, and, where it is used is likely to greatly decrease the possible efficiency of the work.

It is, of course, an easy method for both the men and the instructor, but easy methods are not, in training advanced men, usually the most effective ones.

The Supervisory Instructor.—Effective training for supervision depends largely on the qualifications of the instructor. It is absolutely necessary that he should have the proper trade standing with the regular production force that they should admit that he knows more about the work than they do; he must have a thorough working familiarity with his subject, preferably through experience in the plant itself, and he should be old enough to assure respect. He should, of course, be a good instructor and, if possible, a trained instructor, but under many conditions it will be fortunate if a man otherwise qualified turns out to be a "natural" teacher.

Men competent to give this sort of work are very difficult to obtain. If found, they will usually have to be drawn from some department of the plant and used as "special" instructors, each man dealing with the particular field in which his expert knowledge lies.

Characteristics of Learners: Supervisory Training.—As already stated, work of this sort can only be effectively given to a selected group of men. Such men are ambitious, alert and enter the work with a strong vocational aim that is well defined. Their trade experience gives them a large foundation on which the instruction can be built up. They are usually relatively mature and are likely to be men who have already availed themselves of such trade extension work as may have been available. They are "farsighted." They are able to work out problems with but little suggestion and aid from the instructor. With such men there is, of course, no question of discipline, but, on the other hand, in such work very careful organization of the instructional material is necessary. Unless such men know that they are getting what they want, and getting it quickly and effectively, they will not continue in the work.

Training for Increased Skill: Trade Extension Training.— The aim of trade extension work is to enable a man already somewhat advanced in his particular work to *extend* his trade knowledge or his trade skill, or both, as the case may be. Its aim differs from that of supervisory training in that it is a form of true trade training in that it does not aim to train a man "out of his trade" but to make him a better man in his trade.

General Character of Trade Extension Training.—Trade extension training is, in general, characterized by the facts that groups of men will seldom be found who all want the same thing at the same time. In at least many cases each man will want some distinct thing, although it is true in some cases (as in training first class firemen for third class engineers) a group having a common need will be found.

In the shipyard trades extension work is more likely to meet the needs of the shop and loft trades than of the yard trades.

The Two General Types of Trade Extension Work.—There are two general types of trade extension work. In shop work each man usually wants special training on some particular operation or on some special machine, and each man must therefore be taken care of according to his individual needs. In technical work this may or may not be the case. In the passing out of auxiliary knowledge there is the greatest chance that a group will be found that have a common need.

Conditions of Admission to Trade Extension Work.—It was pointed out in discussing admission requirements for supervisory training that such training would, in general, have to be given to a highly selected group, partly owing to the limited demand and largely on account of the special personal qualifications and trade experience that would admit of profitable instruction.

In general these conditions do not apply in trade extension work. It is to the interest of all that every man should be as good a man in his trade as he can be—hence the only ground for limiting *numbers* is that the number of men that can be effectively handled with the available facilities, has been reached. For another reason it is, however, essential that certain precautions should be taken in admitting men to trade extension classes. These precautions consist essentially in making sure, first, that the man knows what he wants and second, that he knows enough about his trade to get it. A man will often want something so far ahead of what he already knows that it would be only a waste of his time and the time of the Department to undertake to give it to him.

Unquestionably the best procedure in admitting to trade extension work is the personal interview with the instructor. In this way a good instructor who knows the trade and knows men can ascertain if the man means business, if he knows what he wants or that what he thinks he wants is not what he really wants (which is often the case), and if the man knows enough about his trade to "get" what he wants at that particular stage of his trade progress.

General Instructional Conditions for Trade Extension Training.—Organization for individual instruction will be generally found to be best adapted to this particular line of training. Class organization will, as already stated sometimes serve under special conditions, where certain definitely defined technical instruction is called for. Shop work almost invariably requires individual work and must be organized to provide that type of instructional conditions. Technical work will generally call for the same conditions as shop work. Auxiliary knowledge is most likely to lend itself to class organization.

Under no circumstances should men of more than one trade be placed in the same group and the efficiency of the work will be increased in proportion as men of about the same degree of trade advancement are handled together. A group made up partly of apprentices, partly of journeymen and partly of "master workmen" will offer exceedingly difficult teaching conditions and should be avoided.

The Trade Extension Instructor.—Probably nothing has caused more failures in trade extension work than the attempt to employ unqualified instructors, especially men having a technical or a "school" knowledge but without sufficient practical experience. Above all a trade extension instructor must command the "trade respect" of the men that he instructs. They must admit that he is a better man on the job than they are. In addition, he should be a good instructor, many competent men have failed as trade extension instructors because they did not know how to put over what they knew. The trade extension instructor should always be at least one "notch" ahead of his men. For apprentices he should be at least a good journeyman, for journeymen he should be a "master workman" and so on.

Characteristics of Learners: Trade Extension Training.— Men who apply for trade extension work are of two kinds. The first kind know exactly what they want, know why they want it, and, if they cannot get what they want will not attend. The second kind do not know what they want— they have an idea that they want "something that will help them along."

The first type is easy to deal with; the second will often require much patent questioning before what they really need can be determined. The aim is usually immediate advantage—a chance to "get a better job" if he can get additional information or command of another process or operation.

The trade extension man is not generally as "farsighted" as the man who seeks training for supervision, as a rule, "deferred values" do not attract him; he wants a "quick return" on his investment of time and energy. Under these circumstances the "Short Unit Course" as described later in these notes is often the best form in which to organize trade extension work.

Training Men Already Skilled in Another Trade—Conversion Training.—It was pointed out in Pamphlet 1, that, under certain emergency conditions, there is a demand for a redistribution of skill, so that men skilled in one trade may need to secure certain training in order to enable them to "convert" their trade into one that will meet the new conditions.

The Function of Conversion Training.—The function of conversion training is therefore to give a competent workman in a trade *that is not a shipyard trade* such additional knowledge, skill and training as will enable him to work effectively in a shipyard. Such a man is in no sense a green man—he brings to this training a large "capital" of trade experience, nor is he a trade extension man, since he requires training in a trade that is not the trade that he has been following. "Conversion work" therefore offers certain difficult problems some of the more important of which are discussed in the following paragraphs.

The Problem of Conversion Training.—In order to do effective conversion work and to do it as rapidly as possible, it is evident that the more "assets" the man brings to the training department the better. If a man, out of his trade knowledge and skill already possesses, seventy-five per cent. of what he needs in order to do a given job, he can evidently be more rapidly trained than a man who has only thirty per cent. asset for the new trade. Trades that furnish the greatest asset for a given trade are often called *allied trades*.

What is Meant by Allied Trades.—An allied trade is therefore one which contains a large proportion of the trade knowledge and skill required for a given shipyard trade. For example, a good house carpenter already knows a great deal about a number of jobs that are required in constructing a wooden ship; a structural steel riveter, especially if he has worked on tanks as well as buildings, is already, to a considerable extent, familiar with the sort of jobs that are carried on in steel ship construction, and only needs additional training to enable him to rivet on ship work.

The Determination of what Additional Training is Needed.— As already stated a conversion man has a thorough command of his old trade, but all that he knows will not necessarily form a part of his equipment for the new trade. Out of all his trade knowledge there must be picked out what he can use in the new trade and, in addition, what he needs for the new trade must be determined. The laying out of an instructional course for trade conversion requires therefore that answers should be secured to the following questions:

(1) What can be used out of a man's old trade.
(2) What more does the man need to know to fit him for the new trade.

Probably the best way to secure this information is to compare the trade analysis of the old trade with the trade analysis of the new trade, check up what appears in the analysis of the old trade that has a value in the new trade, and then check off what appears in the new trade analysis that does not appear in the analysis of the old trade. In this way an effective training course can be laid out, which only provides for such actual conversion training as may be necessary.

Speed in Conversion Training.—The same requirements for speed in training apply in conversion work as in training of other types—conversion training must be carried on as rapidly as possible so that the man can be got to work as soon as possible. The more the matter of determining conversion requirements is handled in a scientific way, and the less it is guessed at, the more effective will be the results obtained.

General Character of Conversion Training.—In general conversion training will call for at least any or all of the following:

(1) Actual training on new jobs.
(2) Knowledge of new working conditions and training in working under these conditions:
(3) Additional auxiliary knowledge relating to the new trade.

An illustration of the first case would be the case of a structural steel riveter on Pullman cars who had never driven certain kinds of rivets that are driven on ship work, (say, for illustration, countersunk or flush rivets). The second case would be illustrated by the same man if he had driven all kinds of ship rivets in the open air, but had never worked in different places where space was small in the hull, and uncomfortable attitudes must go with the work. The third case would be, for example, where many new terms must be acquired—ship location terms, for example.

Evidently all or any of these two kinds of training and giving of auxiliary material might occur in any given case and must be provided for.

Instructional Conditions for Conversion Training.—The trade experiences of men vary so much that, for cases one and two, as just discussed, individual instruction will be required. It is possible that the auxiliary knowledge can be, to some extent, passed out to groups or as to classes. For example, if none of the men know ship terms a class organization might serve for this particular part of the work.

The Conversion Instructor.—The requirements for a conversion instructor vary from those for a trade extension, or trade instructor, in that he should, for the best working conditions, know both the "new" trade and something of the "old" trade. Probably a man who knows the "new" trade but who is generally familiar with the "old" (allied) trade is likely to do well, although a "converted" man from the allied trade might be as good.

Other requirements would essentially be those of the good trade extension instructor.

Characteristics of Learners: Conversion Training.—In his general characteristics the "conversion" man resembles the trade extension man and the general problems of instructional management will be about the same as for that type of learner.

Trade Training.—As the term is used in these notes, trade training proper, as distinguished from trade extension or conversion training, means training a man with no knowledge of a given trade so that he can do work in that trade. So far as the term is used here it is immaterial whether he is trained completely for a given trade, (all around trade training) or for some part of a trade, (specialized trade training) or for certain jobs, or whether the jobs would be rated as skilled, semi-skilled or "unskilled," if he is not a trade extension man or a conversion man, any training that is given him is trade training as the term is used in these notes.

The Function of Trade Training.—The function of trade training is therefore to take a man who does not know or who cannot do anything in a given trade, and give him what he needs so that he does know or can do. Theoretically, so far as trade ability goes it starts with a man at zero, and carries him up the scale to whatever point may serve the purpose for which the training is given, (as in the case of apprentices) or helpers, so far as their experience is a training experience.

The Problem of Trade Training.—Of the three types of training discussed, trade training offers, in many ways, the simplest problems. It really offers but two:

(1) Find out what the man must have to make good in the trade or on the job.
(2) Give it to him.

Finding correct answers to these questions in the case of any given trade require, of course, the effective carrying out of certain steps such as:

(1) Analyzing the trade.
(2) Setting up an effective instructional order.
(3) Determining suitable methods of instruction.
(4) Setting up proper conditions as to instructing conditions, management, etc., as discussed in the different parts of these notes.

Trade Training, Trade Extension Training, and Conversion Training in a Training Department.—The relative importance of these three types of training *under* any given set of conditions is an important consideration especially as to relative demand and value in raising and maintaining the general level of efficiency. The following discussion is suggestive only.

Trade Extension Training and Size of Operating Force.—Trade extension training does not, strictly speaking, increase the working force of a plant. It does increase the skill of the force already at work. As an agency for increasing skill *of the same kind* it is important, as an agency to bring in more skill from "outside" or from allied trades it has no value. So far as trade extension work goes it will therefore only increase the efficiency of men already employed in certain lines *in those* lines. It can only produce more skill, intelligence, and promotional capacity in the working force already employed. It can increase *quality* of skill but not *quantity* of workers.

Conversion Training and Size of Operating Force.—Conversion training serves to bring into the operating force more men who can do by "capitalizing" the skill and mechanical experience already existing in other trades.

Much of this skill, knowledge, and experience they can apply to the trade that they go into. Conversion training therefore adds *both men and skill* to the operating force.

In the case of conversion it is also true that in case of a reduction of force they can readily go back to their old trade.

Trade Training and Size of Working Force.—Trade training proper, also serves to increase both man power and skill in the shipyard trades, differing from a conversion training only in that the men that are trained start practically at zero.

Comparative Values of the Three Kinds of Training.—We have:

(1) To increase skill in a given working force.
    (a) Trade Extension Work.
(2) To add man power and skill to the working force.
    (a) Conversion Work (men from allied trades).
    (b) Trade training proper (green men).

Evidently if a higher degree of skill with given working force is all that is required, trade extension work is the agency to turn to, but if *both* man power and skill are insufficient trade extension work will not help the situation and conversion work and trade training must be used.

The Relative Value of Conversion Training and Trade Training.—As pointed out the relative values of these two forms of training, the degree to which each form can best be used, and the particular sorts of trades or jobs for which the two types are best fitted consitute a problem in training efficiency that seriously affects the character of the work that a training department may be called upon to do. The following suggestions bear upon this question.

The Trade Conversion Man a "Quick Asset" for Skilled Trades.—The trade conversion man may be said to already possess a considerable proportion of the new trade. He is already 50%, 75%, or 80% trained. Moreover he has behind him the trade experience in his old trade which enables him to "catch on" rapidly, he can therefore be trained *quickly*. If he comes from a closely allied trade, but little conversion training will enable him to work on similar jobs in the "new" trade. He is therefore a "quick asset."

As contrasted with the conversion man the "green" man has neither trade experience in an allied trade or trade knowledge or skill. To train him for a skilled trade would take much more time than would be required for a conversion man. The green man can therefore, in general, be more economically trained for relatively simple or specialized work.

The Green Man a " Quick Asset " for Semi-Skilled Work.—The green man can therefore be most effectively trained for semi-skilled work. He can be trained for this sort of work more rapidly than for the more highly skilled work, and moreover, can do this sort of work, after training, effectively and rapidly. If a man from a skilled trade is trained for semi-skilled jobs it practically means throwing away an extremely valuable asset, and is neither efficiency or economy. In general, therefore, conversion work would train for the more skilled work and trade training with green men would deal with the less skilled occupations. This would, in general, be the most efficient training condition, *provided that a sufficient number of both kinds of men could be secured.*

The Situation where Labor Supply is Limited.—Where the supply of men available is limited, it may be necessary, if an insufficient number of conversion men are available, to train green men for the simpler work of the more skilled trades, in order not to sacrifice the "quick asset" value of the conversion men that can be trained. That is, the conversion man must be "capitalized for all that he is worth" and the green man trained to fill in behind him.

The Necessity of Adjustment.—Of course, in all cases, a training department must adjust itself to the situation as it exists. Presumably the Employment Department will deal with the securing of men, but the Training Department will undoubtedly be called upon to advise as to how it can train to the best advantage, hence the preceding discussion is included as one of the problems of a training department.

CHAPTER XLI

APPRENTICESHIP TRAINING AND THE TRAINING DEPARTMENT

Preliminary.—One of the problems with which a Training Department may have to concern itself is the training of apprentices. In many plants such apprenticeship training schemes are already in operation, and are likely to be considered as forming a part of the work of a training department that may be established or developed to meet the present emergency conditions.

The General Aim of Apprenticeship Training.—Whatever the trade, apprenticeship training has the general aim of "passing on the trade," that is, it is a method for providing new workers to carry on the trade from generation to generation. As commonly used the term only applies to what are commonly called the "skilled" trades.

An apprentice is therefore a young man who is under training for a skilled trade which he expects to follow after he is trained.

Ordinary Conditions of Apprenticeship Training.—Under ordinary conditions an apprentice is placed in production work in the trade for which he is to be trained. He may or may not be placed under any instructional conditions. As a rule he is expected to get what instruction he does get from workmen and foremen whose job is to get out production. Sometimes this shop experience is supplemented by a few hours a week in a "school room" where certain general or special technical work is given him.

The "Paying" Apprentice.—Under most conditions an apprentice, to a greater or less extent, "pays for his keep" through the value of his labor. Under these conditions the tendency is always to hold him on work that he can do until he has turned out enough product to more or less offset the cost of his training. This, of course, tends to increase the training time if it is prolonged beyond the point where he has learned to do the job well and quickly.

Conditions Affecting the Length of Apprenticeship Training. —The tendency to unduly prolong a given kind of production training and the fact that, in at least many cases, instructors are untrained, or there are no instructors, tends to increase the term of apprenticeship beyond the point required for effective training under good conditions.

Proper Conditions for Apprenticeship Training.—Where apprentices are to be trained much more effective work can be done if they are trained in a training department whose business is training. An effective instructional order, trained instructors, good instructional conditions, training on production, but with production as a by-product of training, will result in training apprentices not only better but much more rapidly than does the usual present method.

The general principles laid down for training in general will therefore apply to apprenticeship training.

Some Special Problems of Apprenticeship Training.—As already stated the training of apprentices offers certain special problems that do not come up in ordinary training work. These special problems are mostly due to the fact that the time required for training apprentices is much longer than that required for ordinary training and hence calls for the laying out of a much more complicated course of instruction. It is also quite generally true that apprenticeship training is started at an earlier age than shop training, hence the characteristics of the apprentice are somewhat different from those of the average man who comes under instruction in a training department.

CHAPTER XLII

THE "COLD STORAGE" VS. THE APPLICATION THEORY OF INSTRUCTIONAL ORDER

Preliminary.—This section contains a brief discussion of two possible principles on which an instructional order may be developed. These two principles are commonly designated as the principle of training for deferred values, or the "cold storage" principle, and the principle of training for immediate values, or the "application" principle.

Training for Deferred Values: "Cold Storage."—According to this theory all auxiliary knowledge, and all training in general, should be mastered by the learner *before he has occasion to apply it in actual work*. In instruction work organized on this basis a learner is, for example, thoroughly drilled on decimal fractions before he needs to use the micrometer in the machine shop; or he is given board measure before he has occasion to use it in the carpenter shop; or he is informed how to figure resistances of various sizes of wire before he meets that kind of problem in his electrical practice; or he is "taught" how to figure an indicator card before he is allowed to "take" one in steam practice.

According to this theory the learner is first given the required knowledge and later, when the necessity arises, he is expected to be able to apply it, that is, just as eggs can be put in cold storage, kept until wanted and then used, so it is expected that a learner can master the method of doing a technical job, say a calculation, or a piece of auxiliary knowledge, or a safety first item, and can carry it in his head until it is needed. The principle on which work of this sort is based assumes that the application value of the work is *deferred* until some time after it is learned or acquired, hence it is called the principle of deferred values, or often the "cold storage" principle, because the learner carries it in a sort of mental "cold storage" until it is needed.

Training for Immediate Values: "Application."—According to the other principle all information, etc., should be given *at the time that it is needed on the job*, so that, according to this principle, no "cold storage" period should come in between acquisition and application. This principle is known as the principle of instructing for immediate values, or the "Application Principle."

According to this principle a learner would not be given any one piece of auxiliary information or process until he needed it in his practical work. He would then learn the process by being taught on the job how to solve that particular problem. By this method a man would not be taught, for example, indexing, or riveting, or laying off a certain pattern, until he was instructed in actually doing that job, or the job of which that operation was a part. He would then be taught how to make the necessary calculations or constructions, or operations at that moment, on the job, by being required to do that work before he could go ahead with the job.

How the Cold Storage Principle is Carried out in Practice.— In training work this principle is often followed in such cases as giving safety first lectures to green men, in attempting to give organized "courses" in "shop mathematics" or "blueprint reading" to learners before they have come in contact with the blueprint or the need for the calculations in the actual work in the shop. In general such work is characterized by:

(1) Class instruction rather than instruction in small groups or by individuals.
(2) Excessive repetition, drill, and memorizing.
(3) Theory first, application later.
(4) Limited application.
(5) Problems more or less artificial and imaginary.
(6) Little or no application of knowledge to real situations while learning.
(7) Recitations, lectures, examinations.

In apprentice training this method is often worked out by what is called the part time scheme, in which an attempt is made to make the cold storage period relatively small, which, in general, is organized as follows:

(a) Organization of Classes: Classes are usually organized in such a way that a period of shop work alternates with a period of instruction in non-shop work. The two most common arrangements are: (1) the half day period, and (2) the week and week about period.

In the half day scheme learners are paired by classes or divisions. One division goes into the shop for the first half of the day, while the other division goes into the class room. At noon the two divisions exchange places.

In the week about scheme, one division works in the shop a week while the other division is attending classes in related studies. At the end of the week the two divisions exchange. In certain cases the "rotation period" is even longer. Where this practice is followed, the shop day is usually seven to eight hours long, or the usual working day, while the school days is about six hours. In this sort of training the work is often spoken of as divided into two parts, shop work, in the production department, or shop and "non-shop work" in the class room.

(b) Location of Class Rooms: Class rooms are usually located apart from the shops in another part of the building or even entirely outside of the plant.

(c) Teachers: Teachers of non-shop work in this type of organization are generally not experienced mechanics. Usually they have had more or less incidental contact with industry. Frequently they have had teaching experience in regular high schools before entering the service of the training department. Sometimes they are recent graduates of the technical college having slight contact with industry and no teaching experience. Occasionally women are employed in this capacity.

Instructors in "non-shop work" are rarely found to have had a training or experience in teaching that essentially differs in method or point of view from the teaching commonly practiced by the regular high school.

Instructors in Shop Work.—Under the usual type of this organization no regular instructors on actual production processes are employed. In so far as instruction is given in this part of the work it is given by workmen or foremen who are not, under ordinary conditions, trained instructors, though they are, of course, experienced mechanics.

Sometimes regular high school text books are used.

(e) Selection of subject matter: In general two methods are followed:

1. The subject method. Where this method is used courses are given in Arithmetic, Algebra, Geometry, etc., and practically all the subject matter usually given in texts on those subjects is taught.

2. The topic method. In this method the usual text books are used, but the subject matter of the course is selected by omitting certain topics given in the book that have little or no direct bearing upon the practical work, and giving more time to those topics that have. In Algebra, for example, the Binominal Theorem is omitted and additional attention is given to formulas and simple equations. It should be noted that in schools of this type the selection of subject matter is usually from the point of view of the subject to be taught rather than from the point of view of the trade.

Practice of the Application Theory.—As this method is worked out in practice, in training work the auxiliary material is "tied up" to the lesson and needs no further description. Some features of this method would be:

(1) Instruction by individuals or in small groups rather than by classes.
(2) Experience subsituted for organized knowledge.
(3) Comparatively little drill or memorizing.
(4) Comparatively little recitation work.
(5) Real problems.
(6) Real needs to be met.
(7) Application first, theory later.

(c) Instructors: All auxiliary information is usually given by a shop instructor on the job. Sometimes the class room instruction given in more advanced work is given by a shop man and sometimes by a teacher who is not a trained mechanic. Occasionally the shop instructors are assisted in the non-shop work by a "floating instructor." There is a tendency to create a new type of instructor for the teaching of this sort of work known as the instructor on related work.

(d) Location of class rooms: Class rooms and drafting rooms are sometimes built adjacent to the shops. Frequently seats and desks are put into one end of the shops.

(e) Text books: None used except occasionally for reference during first period. Handbooks and correspondence school books are used to some extent for this purpose at all points in the course.

The Cold Storage and the Application Methods in Training the Working Force.—Considerable space has been given to a description of these two methods because both have been to a considerable extent developed in recent years, and so are likely to be suggested for training. The method described in this book as that under which a training department should be operated is the application method. The character of the work in which instruction must be given, the need for rapid training, the type of men to be trained, all demand the conditions set up by the application method. Even in the training of apprentices (where such work is a part of the responsibility of the training department), more effective results will be obtained by the use of training schemes based on application than on cold storage methods.

Summary and Conclusions.—General instructional organization based upon the "cold storage" principle will probably find but little place in the work of a training department under emergency conditions. As a matter of fact neither is it to be recommended for the training for future values, as in the case of apprentice training, although at this time it is the method that has been quite commonly adopted for this particular form of training, and is likely to be that already in use in any apprenticeship schemes that a training department may take over or initiate.

While it possesses certain apparent advantages, these are more apparent than real, it is more costly than appears at first sight, and is relatively less efficient than is work developed on the "application principle."

In certain types of trade extension work it can probably be used to a fair degree of effectiveness with highly selected groups of well advanced men, and local conditions often make it the only principle that can be used under these circumstances, although even here work developed on the application principle would be undoubtedly more efficient.

CHAPTER XLIII

THE RELATIVE ORDER IN WHICH A LEARNER SHOULD ACQUIRE THEORY AND PRACTICE

Preliminary.—This section discusses certain principles relating to the relative order in which theory and practice should be presented to the learner. The discussion is general in its character. The principles set forth would apply in training for some trades more than for others and might apply more particularly here in connection with relatively long training courses for the more highly skilled trades having a considerable technical content, or in apprenticeship training. This discussion bears especially on what is sometimes termed "training in fundamentals." Such "fundamental training" is often proposed as a first step in a training scheme for trade training. Since work of this kind may be proposed as a part of the work of some training departments the matter of its value is discussed in this section.

The Relative Place of Theory and Practice.—Any line of practical instruction requires a training in both the how and why; in theory and in practice. The question as to the relative order in which theory and practice should be taught has often been raised, and, since it is a very important point in determining both program and organization, since it involves a general principle of teaching, it is discussed here somewhat fully.

Instructors recognize in general two methods of procedure: (1) To pass from general principles or fundamentals to definite practice; (2) To pass from definite practice to abstract principles. Thus in training a machinist by the first method a learner could be taught the theoretical principles on which practice is based. He could be taught the theory of cutting speed; the theoretical principles of getting full duty out of a machine; the mechanical principles used in the machine; he could be trained in the mathematics which he would later apply in the shop, on problems which were purely abstract in their character, as for example: he could be taught how to evaluate formulæ, how to demonstrate the various geometrical relations involved in the case of the inscribed polygon and the circle without any knowledge on his part that these particular mathematical principles would be involved in any practical shop work. This method of instruction is commonly used in the regular schools. Algebra, geometry, mechanical drawing, and in many cases science are taught from the standpoint of general principles without any regard to specific application.

An illustration of instruction under the second method would be to have the learner first come in contact with application of theoretical principles through real work in the shop. Here he would learn, as a matter of practice, that certain cutting speeds were used on certain metals and he would learn to use the various devices provided for the purpose to get such cutting speed, in fact he might be taught to cut entirely "by the chip." He could learn the control of the longitudinal, transverse, and vertical feeds without any knowledge of the theoretical or mechanical principles involved. He could learn as a matter of fact that he was expected to take off as heavy a chip as the tool would stand in order to get out production and to know that his machine must be up on production if it is to pay for itself.

The Second Method the More Efficient.—The second method is by far the more efficient order of procedure, since it leads to the development of much greater interest on the part of the learners, and to a much more rapid and complete group of principles when they are presented. The method of proceeding from concrete and specific knowledge to general and theoretical knowledge has always been recognized as the most efficient order of procedure in securing effective instruction.

Why the Second Procedure is Recommended.—The efficiency of the method of passing from actual knowledge of how a thing is done to the reason why it is done, rather than by the reverse process, is based upon a well-known characteristic of the human mind, which is, that the majority of people find it very difficult to think in terms of things about which they have had no actual experience; and hence their interest is not aroused. It is extremely difficult for a person who has no knowledge of baseball to understand a description of the game. It has been found difficult or almost impossible in Porto Rico to give the children in the public schools any idea of what snow is because they have never seen snow. If a person has never seen a mountain or a hill it is extremely difficult for him to get any intelligent understanding of hills and mountains.

In the same way if a learner has had no experience on the job, if he has not actually learned how things are done so that the doing of them right has become largely a matter of course with him, it is extremely difficult to get him to understand the general principles involved and he will not be interested in mastering them. But if he comes to the mathematical principles involved in the work of his trade after having first learned how to practically do the jobs in a great variety of ways, he then "sees the bearing" of them and is interested in learning them and applying them. A general principle may be regarded as a pigeonhole in a desk in which we can place a number of things that we know should have the same label, but if we have not the things a pigeonhole is not of very much use, and we are not greatly interested in having it around. The fact that we can only apply principles when we have a lot of concrete examples which we can bring together under that principle is of course well known to everybody, because we are all aware how difficult it is for two people to understand each other when they are talking about a matter of which both of them have not had some experience. A person brought up in the middle west will find it extremely difficult to talk interestingly about navigation and the problem of the management of a vessel with a captain of an ocean steamer, whereas the captain of the ocean steamer would find it equally difficult to talk intelligently and interestingly with the westerner about the problems of cattle raising on a western ranch.

It has been already stated that auxiliary information

should be given to the learner on the job, so that, in practice in a training department, it is absolutely necessary that the man should first have some real work from which he can get his concrete experience, or the instructional basis, before any attempt can be made to utilize it for instruction in the theoretical principles involved. It is also true that such a foundation must be pretty well laid before any great attempt is made to give theoretical work in any definite and organized way.

The Two Methods and Interest Factors.—When work is developed on the principle of passing from practice to theory, interest factors can be used to much greater advantage than when the reverse order is followed. This is particularly true of self-confidence, curiosity, and the appeal to the vocational aim.

The development of self-confidence, a very important interest factor, especially in the earlier periods of the learner's progression, can only be obtained if, from the beginning he can do his work at least fairly well, and the better he does it the more strongly will his interest be aroused and sustained. Hence his work at first, should be that which he can most easily grasp and carry out effectively. He should be able to do a good job easily from the start, and this condition can be brought about much better if the instruction first deals with methods of doing jobs and he is allowed to concentrate his attention entirely on doing, on the "how," rather than on the "why," at this stage of his progression through the training course.

Thus it is easier, and hence more interesting, for the learner to learn how to set a tool or chuck a job than to figure the offset on turning a taper or to work out abstract formulæ on the functions of angles. He can more easily learn what cutting speed is and learn to set his machine for the suitable cutting speeds for various metals than learn how to figure the speeds or why such speeds are called for; and his interest in learning how to figure speeds or solve trigonometrical formulæ will only be aroused after he has discovered that there are such things and that somebody must know how to use them in order to get out the practical working rules that he uses on his jobs.

Curiosity, so far as it has value as an interest factor, is aroused mainly by the practical side of a trade.

Take the case of a man just admitted to a training department for training as a machinist. He is thinking of a machinist as a person who works metal with machines. He knows little or nothing about the technical side of the trade. Hence his main interest lies on the productive or "job" side of the work. The relation of abstract principles can only become clear to him as a result of his seeing that such principles underline his practice. If his earlier instruction deals with the doing of work which he knows is the sort of work done by machinists he can understand that he is progressing in the line of his chosen trade, and his interest is strongly maintained, whereas if he first gets instruction in principles, by virtue of the fact that he has had no shop experience of how those principles apply, there is required an abstract power of visualization and "far sightedness" which but few people possess.

Conclusion and Summary.—The procedure of working from general abstract principles to special applications in the development of a training course should not be followed in any work in a training department, since it is the less efficient order of progression for practically all individuals who will come into such a department. It establishes inefficient instructional conditions, tends to unnecessarily increase the instructional turnover, and unquestionably decreases speed in training. These conditions should be, of course, avoided in any training work, but must be reduced to a minimum in emergency training.

CHAPTER XLIV

The Short Unit Course in Trade Extension Work.—Mention has been made in these notes of the so-called "Short Unit Course" in connection with trade extension work, and the following paragraph gives a brief description of this form of organization of instructional material.

"Long Courses," Unit Courses and Short Unit Courses.—Trade extension courses can be organized in three ways. According to the first type, courses covering a long period are laid out (two years or three years), and these courses offer simultaneously several trade subjects, as shop mathematics, mechanical drawing and perhaps shop work. Such courses may be called "Long Courses."

The second type of organization offers only one line of instruction, say shop work, or shop mathematics, but offers that subject for a relatively long time, say through one winter's work. Such courses may be called Short courses, since they offer one *unit* or subject at a time.

The Short Unit Course differs from either of the types just described in consisting of a part of a unit, usually a block from a multiblock trade or even a certain kind of a job, or group of jobs. The length of time required is determined solely by the time required to instruct in the short unit in question. It may run as low as six or eight hours.

It has been found in many cases that, with trade extension men, the short unit course best meets their needs and it can undoubtedly be used to advantage in this type of work in many cases.

PART IX

THE USE OF THIS MATERIAL IN INSTRUCTOR TRAINING COURSES

CHAPTER XLV

THE USE OF THIS MATERIAL IN INSTRUCTOR TRAINING COURSES

The original purpose for which much of this material was prepared was for use in training courses for competent mechanics who wished to secure instructor training. The following suggestions are based upon past experience in using it for that purpose.

General Organization.—This work can be carried on under either of four conditions.

(1) *As intensive training*, where the men put their entire time onto the work, being, of course, entirely withdrawn from regular work (production or instruction as the case may be) during that time.

(2) *As intensive training on a part time basis*, where the men put a part of their time onto the training work and a part of their time onto their regular work, (production or instruction).

(3) As *evening*, or "*leisure time*" *courses*, where the men put in full time on their regular work and attend the training course in their leisure time (evenings, Saturday afternoons, etc.).

(4) A modification of (3) is where the work is given in "leisure time" courses, but in short units.

Discussion of these Methods.—Where it can be done, plan(1) unquestionably is to be recommended. The process of "converting" production men into instructors is much easier if their attention can be concentrated on instruction problems and they are withdrawn from production experiences during the training process. This fact, taken in connection with the fact that, during their training, they can devote their entire time, both in class and out, to the work, results in much greater efficiency. The same number of hours under this plan will give from a third to a half more efficiency compared to the efficiency obtained under plans 3 and 4.

Whenever possible the straight, full time intensive plan is to be recommended.

Plan (2). This plan particularly appeals to concerns that are unable or unwilling to release men for full time intensive training. It will be noted that it contains two possibilities.

(a) The men alternate between *production* work and training work.
(b) The men alternate between *instruction* work and training work.

The first modification has all the disadvantages of plans 3 and 4. All the arguments presented in Part I against putting a man on production and instruction at the same time apply here.

This plan is not to be recommended, under any circumstances.

The second modification has certain advantages and makes possible the relatively intensive training of men who are already employed in instruction work. The fact that they are instructing while they are under training gives an opportunity for practice teaching under observation and criticism that can be carried on parallel to the instructor training work. It is questionable however if this plan gives a greater training efficiency than plan 1.

Plan 3, evening classes, is the plan likely to be adopted under ordinary conditions. It is, of course, less efficient than either plan 1 or plan 2b. Under ordinary evening class conditions, given for eighty or one hundred hours during the winter, the time is too short for very effective training, the working power of the men is relatively low, since they come to the work after a day's work on their regular jobs, and time for out of class work is extremely limited.

Plan 4 partially meets these conditions by permitting more intensive training on any unit that may be selected, and, to that extent, is more effective.

Choice between plans 3 and 4 would have to be determined by local conditions.

For men with no instructing experience, probably plan 3, in spite of the fact that only a relatively superficial training can be given, is the more efficient. Where men are engaged in instructing during the day (foremen, instructing foremen, instructors) the unit plan may better meet their needs.

Conditions of Admission.—It is assumed that this material will be used only in training courses for men who are thoroughly competent in their respective occupations. As is pointed out in the text, only such competent men can "hold down their jobs" as practical instructors. Some form of admission requirement should therefore be enforced. In general, the means of determining the qualifications of an instructor as given in the text, will serve equally well here.

Time.—Under plan 1 fairly satisfactory results have been obtained in thirty-six days, eight hours a day, four hours on Saturday, with enough "home work" to keep the men busy evenings. This time includes five days of practice teaching, a total of two hundred and sixty-four hours.

Under plan 2b the "slip" due to alternation is about offset by the parallel instruction experience, and the time would probably be about the same.

In working under plans three and four if the usual school program is followed the course can be run for from twenty to twenty-five weeks. Experience has shown that with men working during the day it is impossible to secure constant attendance and avoid over fatigue if the work is carried on for more than two nights a week, two hours a night. This gives a possible time of from eighty to one hundred hours.

If the unit plan is adopted about two units can be intensively handled in this time.

Where specialized instructors are to be trained the omission of certain parts of the work will of course reduce the training time if that is absolutely necessary. If possible, it is better to put more time onto the remaining blocks of the course.

Instructing Conditions—Location.—Evidently plans 1 and 2 can be best carried on in a plant where the trades of the different men are carried on. This condition exists where all the men come from one concern, or from a group of concerns all turning out the same product. This is by far the most efficient arrangement.

Where the training course cannot be located in the plant itself, for plans 1 and 2 it should be located as near a suitable plant as possible, where such relations can be established as will make practice teaching possible.

Plans 3 and 4 offer very different conditions. In this case the men usually come to their work from their homes and the location of the training course should enable them to get back and forth easily. Under these conditions space in some public building, a school house, for example, is usually available especially during the period that the schools are open for evening work.

Instructing Conditions—Equipment.—The equipment required (outside of that used for practice teaching) is exceedingly simple. The best equipment consists of tables large enough to accommodate one group to a table, chairs, a blackboard, and ordinary writing materials. Since many men who attend these courses use tobacco, spittoons are a desirable part of the equipment where it is considered that chewing is not objectionable.

Tablet arm chairs, when tables are not available are the next best seating equipment.

The use of regular school desks and chairs should be avoided. The less "school" atmosphere there is around the work the better.

Instructing Conditions. Size and Make-up of Group.— Not over eight or ten men should be handled by one instructor. That instructor should handle these men through the entire course. Experience has shown that shifting instructors during the course, or using more that one instructor with a group reduces the efficiency of the work. The work must be so largely individual, so much assistance and supervision is required that effective work cannot be done with a larger group than that given above. As the group size is increased above that number the efficiency of the work goes down very rapidly.

Order of Presentation.—The material on Analysis and Determination of trade content Part II. How to put it over (Parts IV, V, VI). The securing of an effective instructional order (Part III) and Instructional Management (Part VII) have been treated as four independent blocks. The remaining material Parts I and VIII has been regarded as constituting several blocks of minor importance, whose chief value from the training standpoint was appreciative rather than technical, and which would be treated largely as auxiliary information, to be brought in as occasion offered.

Experience has shown that, for the four main blocks as given, the order given above is the most effective. An exception to this statement is that, under full time intensive training it has sometimes been found advisable to parallel blocks one and two by working on one block in the morning and one in the afternoon. This modified arrangement has been found advantageous where the group under training was kept at work for eight or ten hours a day.

Under these conditions, where men used to active work were kept quiet for so long a period, by the parallel arrangement men were brought sooner to the point in block two where practice teaching afforded physical relief. Under ordinary conditions, such as would exist in an evening or part time course the parallel modification offers no special advantages.

The general appreciation blocks referred to will require little direct time in the course. That portion of the material can be drawn on for discussion as opportunity offers or made a basis for out-of-class study, which may be followed by discussions in the class.

Training Specialized Instructors.—Where the men under training are to instruct in one job, or in a group of disconnected jobs (as in many cases of semi-skilled work) the whole question of effective instructional order drops out and that block can be wholly omitted. The chapters on blocking out the trade can also be omitted.

Method of Presentation.—The material was not prepared as a text to be studied or as a basis for lecture presentation or as "lecture notes" but as a basis for discussion and for the working out of assigned problems and practice teaching. The most effective method has been to give a student problems, exercises, or questions on the subject covered by one chapter and to let him work them out with such individual assistance from the instructor as he might need, the material itself relieving the instructor of the necessity of doing much preparation or presentation. The effective work of the instructor has come mainly in steps three and four of the "lesson" that he is putting over. (Roughly speaking each chapter calls for a lesson to be put over by the instructor.)

The recitation is of little value in this work. Questioning along development lines is often of value and the discussion, guided by the instructor, will find considerable place, especially in criticizing practice teaching and in the work on instructional management.

Supplementary Material.—This may be of three kinds. Exercises, problems, and questions. For the work in lesson planning and in the analysis and classification of trade content, certain forms, some of which are suggested in the material, have proved helpful in guiding the man's thinking. Similar forms of an exercise nature (as for the analysis of jobs) have also been of value for the same reason. A number of situations which come up in instructing under industrial conditions can be presented as questions, and, provided that they illustrate actual situations, are of great value in promoting discussion. Use of "supplementary reading books" is not likely to be desirable. If well worked out such problems and exercises can be used for out-of-class work.

Homework.—It is often possible to start a man in the class and after he has "got to going" let him finish up the work at home and then submit it to the instructor for criticism. This is especially true of the classification work in block I, the lesson planning work and the working up of the card catalog of jobs. All such work done at home saves time in the class. Under good management a great deal of time can be saved in this way.

General Objectives.—However the work is carried on it must be remembered that its purpose is not to impart information but to train a man so that he can apply the principles of effective training in actual instruction on jobs. This result will be obtained in proportion as the man, not the instructor, does the work. As a result of this training work each block represents the development of some degree of ability to do certain things. These may be called general objectives. In block one the general objectives are to develop power to analyze and classify the given trade. In block two to give command of the general instructional processes under the conditions of industral training. In block three to train each man to rearrange the jobs that he analyzed out in block one into an effective instructional order based upon the principles of progression. In block four to train him in handling a group under instructional conditions as he will meet them in practice.

These general objectives are, of course, made up of groups of minor objectives, which should be self evident to the instructor.

Practice Teaching.—For effective results this work should include practice teaching. Fairly satisfactory results have been obtained by requiring each man to plan and teach at least five distinct teaching units in connection with block two, and, in connection with the work in instructional management, to require him to take charge of a group of learners for a total of forty hours.

All practice teaching, of course, should be under observation and criticism by the instructor and, in general by other members of the group as well.

Under ordinary conditions such practice teaching is often difficult to secure but its value is so great that every effort should be made to include at least some of it in the course. A poor substitute is to have practice lessons put over by one man to the other members of his group, although this may be sometimes used to advantage in giving a man a chance to "take a few practice shots" before he tries the actual practice teaching.

Methods of Conducting Practice Teaching.—Where the training work is conducted in the plant it should be possible to arrange for practice teaching in the plant, if plans 1 or 2b (see page 351) are followed. In evening or other leisure time classes it is exceedingly difficult to secure practice teaching. One plan that has been followed with some success has been to utilize evening trade schools for this work where such schools have been in session.

Practice teaching should be given in connection with two blocks of the training course. In connection with lesson planning each man should put over to actual learners at least five individual teaching units. In connection with instructional management he should, if possible, spend several days in charge of a group.

Practice teaching is of little value unless carried on under observation and constructive criticism. In the practice on individual lessons indicated above an excellent plan is to follow the Normal School practice and have the work of each man in turn observed by the other members of his group, and to follow each lesson by a group discussion. Full time work with the group must, of course, be observed by the instructor and his criticism made the basis of conference with each man.

APPENDIX

APPENDIX

A. THE USE OF THIS MATERIAL BY FOREMEN

The Foreman and Training.—Although the independent training department is the more efficient organization, as conditions exist in many plants, the foreman of a shop is responsible for the training that is given there. If there is any training by intention, he has to carry the heavy load of getting out production, "running his shop" and of training as well. Whether he carries on the training work himself, or whether he puts the actual work of instruction into the hands of instructors, he should know what constitutes good instruction, if the training work is to be well done. If he gives the training himself, he must know how to do a good instructing job. If he has instructors, he must know whether they are or are not giving good instruction. In either case, he certainly should know the points in the instructing game.

Many foremen have had considerable experience in training help. Many such men, while they know that they have succeeded in putting over the training, are conscious that something has not been just right—they have known that while they knew the jobs to be taught (or their instructors knew them), many new men failed to "catch on" readily, seemed to progress very slowly, were "dumb," and often never seemed to get so that they could do a first class job. Sometimes, a good many of the men in training would quit before they were trained, giving all sorts of reasons, and so increasing the turnover.

The trouble, of course, lies in the fact that, whether whoever gave the instruction was or was not a first class man on his job, he did not know "how to put it over." He may have known his own game but he did not know the instructing game. He did not know the instructing operations, the instructing methods. He did not know how to distinguish between the *learning* difficulties that a green man has to overcome and the *production* difficulties that a competent workman has to overcome. He did not know that a man who is *learning* how to do a job is a very different sort of a fellow from a man who is doing that same job.

APPENDIX

Foremen, who find themselves in this situation, will find that this book gives them a number of pointers on "how to put it over" to better advantage. If they will practice putting into operation the suggestions that are made as to analyzing what is to be taught, using the instruction process in the training work and seeing that the training conditions are the best for the different instructing jobs that have to be done, they will be surprised to find how much better things will go and how much quicker learners will be trained.

The best way to use the suggestions that are made and the methods described, is to work them out in practice in the training work. Simply reading them will not do much good. Put over a lesson to a learner, see how it is done, and compare the way it was done with the way it should be done according to the instructions. Plan that lesson accordingly and try it again. If it goes better, think *why*. See how the order in which learners get different jobs or operations squares with an effective order as determined by learning difficulties by the method described. Make a study of learning difficulties and see if an instructing order based on them does not give quicker training results and reduce turnover. Look at the conditions under which the different training jobs are carried on. See if they are good or poor conditions for training. If they are not good, change them and see if things go better. Of course the general principles described, and the general suggestions made, must be worked out in practice for each shop, or each trade, according to the requirements of that sort of a job and according to conditions in that particular plant, that is. They must be applied in practice in the particular way that will give the best results in any given case. Practice is the only way by which any one can learn to do this.

The attention of foremen is particularly drawn to the fact that the principles of good instruction can be effectively applied to a much wider range of work than is often thought possible. This is especially true in what are often called semi-skilled jobs. Recent experience has shown that there are few of these jobs where training organized and carried out in accordance with the principles of good instruction will not result in training new workers more rapidly, make better workers of them and increase their stability after they are trained. Just as in relatively short jobs it pays to use the best tools, machines, and the most effective operations, so even in semi-skilled jobs it pays to use the best instructing methods. In both cases, the supervisor who can do this, or can get it done, will secure greater efficiency.

It is a mistake to think that the principles and methods described can only be used in training for "skilled" trades. With the exception of the fact that no instructional order of jobs is called for the principles and methods of good instruction will apply just as much to instruction on single jobs (as in a munition factory) as in regular trade training. The jobs can be analyzed, the teaching points determined, and arranged in the best instructing order. All the points in effective instructional management will apply just as well here as in training in more "skilled work."

B. THE USE OF THIS MATERIAL BY INSTRUCTORS FOR SELF TRAINING

The Instructor and Self Training.—An instructor has the direct job of putting over the training. As an instructor he is really following a new trade—instructing. This is a trade by itself. Of course an instructor must know his own trade—that is absolutely necessary, but, if he is going to do a good job in his new trade he must also know the "tricks" of that trade. The following suggestions are made to instructors who may wish to use this book and who cannot take advantage of a training course, that is, they wish to train themselves.

Simply reading the book will be of little help. The instructions, the methods, and the suggestions must be worked out on the instructor's own job. He must apply them in his own line. He must work things out for himself.

This being understood, the following suggestions may be of value:

(1) Take a job on which training is being given. Analyze it (Part I, Chapter II). Now find a good man that is doing that job (not a learner, but a first class man) and check up what he actually does. Compare your "check list" by observation with your analysis from memory. See how near the two agree. You will probably find that your "memory list" was incomplete. Try some other jobs in the same way. Practice this until you can make a good analysis.

(2) Now practice analyzing out a teaching unit. Determine the successive teaching points in one job. See if they are too many for one "bite." If so, determine how teaching

APPENDIX

the whole job can be broken up into two or more "lessons" of about the right length. Try it on a learner and see.

(3) Now practice making out a skeleton plan for instructing on that job. The analysis and the layout as described in Part VI, Chapter XXIX. Try following this plan in teaching this job to a learner. See how it goes. If it goes well, all right, if not, consider what the matter is, make a new plan and try again. Do the same with other jobs.

(4) Now practice selecting the best methods for putting over a given teaching unit, following the discussion in Part V, and lay out a general operation sheet from your skeleton plan (Part V). Try this out, and if, after trial, you think you can improve it, change it and try it out again. Practice in this way until you can choose good methods for the different jobs to be taught.

(5) Now, practice getting out a few detailed operation sheets, as illustrated in Part VI. Try these out. It pays to work these detailed sheets out until you can put in the detail without any written memorandum when you instruct from a skeleton layout.

(6) Now, analyze what you have to put over and classify it according to Part II.

(7) If your work calls for instruction on more than one job, make a skeleton layout for each job, get out a general operation sheet and put in the necessary auxiliary information by the method described in Part III, Chapter XIII.

Now consider learning difficulties, lay out the progression factor table for the blocks, get out the type job specifications and lay out the jobs in an effective instructional order, as in Part III. (It is best to make a card catalogue.) Try this instructional order out in practice. If it can be improved determine what is the matter with it, change it, and try again.

(8) The suggestions in Parts VII and VIII must be simply worked out in practice in connection with the instruction work. Pay especial attention to finding the "economical size" of instruction groups, and to the determination of the best instructional conditions (Part VIII, Chapter XLI).

If you are concerned with trade extension work or apprentice training, the suggestions in Part VIII should be of special value. These suggestions are for the benefit of an instructor who is so

APPENDIX

situated that he must train himself. It is only fair to say that, under these conditions, it would be a pretty difficult piece of work. If an instructor can take advantage of a training course it is of very great advantage, because he gets the assistance of a competent teacher, a man who knows the teaching trade.

C. SOME OF THE MORE IMPORTANT TERMS USED IN PARTS I, II, III

Analysis.—(Trade). Listing out all the things that the learner must be taught if he is to be taught the complete trade.

Assembling Jobs.—(Trades). Jobs that call for the putting together of parts that some other workers have turned out, arranged in some determined relation to each other.

Auxiliary Material.—Information that a man is expected to have in his possession and to use in doing his job, but which he is not directly paid for using. (Safety precautions, trade terms, care of tools, etc.)

Block.—A group of teaching jobs having a common set of learning difficulties.

Block Progression Method.—An order of jobs derived by drawing the instruction line from the bottom to the top of two or more independent blocks in succession. (Used only for independent blocks.)

Block Base.—The determining cause of the learning difficulties. (Operations, machines, construction, etc.)

Checking Levels.—Points on a difficulty scale at which the relative degree of the different progression factors are determined.

Classified Content.—What is to be put over arranged under classification headings, as production jobs, trade terms, etc.

Checking Level Specifications.—The statement of the intensity of the progression factors at any given degree on the difficulty scale.

Course of Instruction.—An instructional operation sheet for instructing a learner in a trade or any part of a trade.

Difficulty Scale.—A layout of *degrees of intensity* of progression factors.

Effective Instructional Order.—An order of teaching jobs arranged according to a difficulty scale so that learning and instructional difficulties are reduced to a minimum.

Forming Jobs.—(Trade).—The stock is formed by some method, but its shape is not changed.

Independent Blocks.—Blocks in which learner can be put through one block without using anything contained in another block.

Instructor.—A competent producer whose job is to put over what he knows.

Instructing by Subjects.—The auxiliary is organized in "courses of instruction" and is "taught" by subjects.

Instructing by Tying Up.—The special auxiliary information and knowledge that comes into play on a given job is given to the learner when he is instructed in that job.

Instructional Difficulties.—Difficulties that tend to prevent rapid learning or cause imperfect learning.

Instruction Line.—A line drawn through an instructional layout to indicate the order in which a learner is to be routed through the different teaching jobs.

Instructional Order.—The order in which the teaching jobs in a course of instruction are arranged. (May apply to a block or to an entire course of instruction.)

Job.—Anything that a man is paid for doing.

Multiblock Trade.—A trade in which the instructional order breaks up into more than one block.

Occupational Dangers.—Dangers that go with a given trade and that no amount of care will entirely remove, though they can be reduced to a minimum. The danger "goes with the job." (Diving, working in a powder plant, working with high tension currents.)

Product.—The result of doing a production job.

Production Job.—Any job that results in affecting stock or in fixing parts in a determined relation to each other.

Productional Difficulties.—Difficulties that tend to prevent rapid production or poor work.

Progression Factors.—Causes of learning difficulties that must be taken into consideration in laying out a progressive course of training.

Progression Factor Table.—A layout of progression factors from minimum to maximum.

Putting Over.—Teaching: instructing.

Real Jobs.—Actual jobs that approximate to type jobs in their characteristics as determined from the difficulty scale.

Related Blocks.—Blocks where knowledge and training in one block will help the learner in going through another block.

Service Jobs.—A job that makes the getting out of production easier, cheaper or more rapid.

Shaping Jobs (Trades).—Jobs that change the form to the stock but not the shape.

Single Block Trade.—A trade in which the instructional order breaks up into only one block.

Spiral Method.—An order of jobs derived by drawing the instruction line through all number one jobs in two or more independent blocks, then through number two jobs and so on. (Used only for independent blocks.)

Technical Jobs.—A job that is a necessary step in the getting out of a production job but which, in itself, does not result in affecting stock. Generally calls for the use of either drawing or mathematics.

Trade Drawing (Technical Jobs).—Jobs calling for the use of blueprint sketches, etc.

Trade Mathematics (Technical Jobs).—Jobs calling for the use of some form of mathematics.

Type Jobs.—Imaginary jobs that correspond exactly to the specifications for any degree on the difficulty scale.

SOME OF THE MORE IMPORTANT TERMS IN PARTS IV, V, VI

In order to facilitate the use of this material in units these terms are grouped by parts.

Aim (of lesson).—The exact purpose for which the lesson is taught.

Application (step 3 in the lesson).—(1) Training the learner to apply what he has been taught in step 2. (2) Locating "weak spots" and correcting them.

Concentration.—Sticking to the particular teaching unit that is to be put over. Not getting "side tracked" during the progress of the lesson.

Conciseness.—Same as concentration.

Content (of lesson).—The teaching unit.

Demonstration (method for step 2).—Showing a man how to do the job with the actual tools, processes, etc., or by the trade methods. Showing him the "real thing."

Derived Lesson.—A lesson in which the teaching base can be developed from things or ideas which the instructor knows that he has already taught to the learner in previous lessons.

Development (line of approach in handling a lesson).—Leading the learner to "get" the lesson, by thinking from point to point.

APPENDIX

Discussion (method for step 3).—The group and the instructor discuss the teaching unit. From this discussion, the instructor determines "weak points" and corrects them during the discussion. He also judges as to whether the men can or cannot apply, from what goes on in the discussion.

Effective Order (in presentation).—The order in which the ideas in the teaching unit are presented to the learner, or arranged so that the learner goes from one new idea to the next with the least difficulty.

Elementary Lesson.—A lesson requiring a teaching base derived from some things or ideas which the learner has accidentally "picked up" somewhere before he is instructed in this particular teaching unit.

Examination (method for steps 3 or 4).—The instructor uses "sampling" questions asked at random or intended to "hit the high spots."

Experiment (method for step 2).—Letting the learner "dope out" the correct method or procedure by himself.

Informational (line of approach in handling a lesson).—When the instructing step is conducted on the basis of the instructor's giving information to the learner or the learner giving information to the instructor.

Instructor.—A man who knows how to do things but is paid to put them over to somebody else.

Job.—Anything that a man is paid to do.

Jumping-Off Point (J. O. P.).—The point in his thinking where the learner "jumps" from what he knows (step 1) to what he does not know and is to be taught (step 2).

Learner.—The individual who is to be instructed.

Lecture (method for step 2).—Passing out the information. Telling.

Lesson.—The entire procedure followed in instructing a learner, or putting over some specific thing that is to be taught (a teaching unit).

Lesson Plan.—A plan for a lesson worked out on paper. Consists of (a) An analysis of the lesson for steps 1 and 2; (b) an operation sheet.

Methods.—The instruction devices or "tools" used to "put through" the different instruction steps.

Operation Sheet.—An "operation sheet" for carrying out the lesson. (Includes line of approach, class of lesson, methods etc.)

Preparation.—The first step in the lesson. Its purpose to establish a foundation. It adds nothing to what the learner knows or can do.

Written Recitation (method for step 3 or 4).—The men answer questions in writing instead of orally.

Presentation.—The second step in the lesson. The step in which the learner is given (presented to) the teaching unit. This is where all new ideas are put over.

Primary Lesson.—Same as elementary.

Production Job.—A job that results in the working up of stock.

Production Lesson or Teaching Unit.—A lesson or teaching unit on a production job.

Pupil.—School teacher's term for a learner.

Recitation (method for steps 3 and 4).—The instructor asks a series of questions in order to find out how thoroughly the learners (or the learner) have "got" the lesson or the teaching unit, and also to see if they can apply it in practice.

Steps (in the lesson or the instructional process).—Consist of (1) preparation, (2) presentation, (3) application, (4) testing or (inspection).

Subject (of lesson).—The teaching unit. What is to be taught.

Suggestive Demonstration.—A demonstration used to secure a teaching base for step 1 where the learner has no ideas or experiences which can be used to get a J. O. P. It may be combined with suggestive questions.

Suggestive Illustration.—An illustration used in the same way.

Suggestive Questions.—Questions asked so as to use "key ideas."

Teaching Base.—The ideas which the instructor uses to get the J. O. P.

Teaching Unit.—The particular thing or job which is to be put over in any given lesson (step 2).

Technical Job.—A job that does not result in the working up of stock but is a necessary step in the doing of a production job.

Technical Lesson (or teaching unit).—A lesson on a technical job.

Test.—A written recitation (method for step 3 or 4).

Testing (step 4 in the lesson).—The step in which the instructor determines by "inspection" that the lesson has been thoroughly taught.

Trade Intelligence.—The power to "use your head on the job." The result of instruction followed by training.

Testing on the Job.—Putting the learner, who has been instructed, up against the actual job (technical or production) to see if he can do it. (Method for steps 3 and 4).

SOME OF THE MORE IMPORTANT TERMS USED IN PARTS VII AND VIII.

Allied Trades.—One which contains a large proportion of trade knowledge and skill that can be used for a given shipyard trade.

Attention.—Attention is a sort of "instantaneous" interest, which is usually attracted by something uncommon or unexpected or startling.

By-Product.—A product which is obtained during the process of producing the thing that a concern is in business to produce.

Checking Records.—Records kept for the special purpose of checking up the work of a training department, in any given line, as when an instructor consults his progression chart in order that he may determine what sort of a job should be given next.

Class Instruction.—A group organization under which all the members of a group are to be taught the same lesson at the same time.

Conversion Base.—The knowledge, skill, and experience in a man's old trade that he can use in a new trade.

Conversion Training.—The training which consists in giving a competent workman in a trade that is not a shipyard trade such additional knowledge, skill, and training as will enable him to work effectively at a shipyard trade.

Coördinators.—Representatives of the Training Department and the Production Departments whose business is to attend to the filling of requisitions for work drawn by the Training Department upon the Production Departments. The men are designated as Training Coördinators and Production Coördinators respectively.

Coöperative Relations.—Relations which depend for their effectiveness largely on the mutual understanding and good will of the coöperating parties but which do not include specific responsibilities for getting a certain job done.

Credentials.—Evidence as to past experiences—trade experiences on different sorts of work, schools attended, written opinion of others as to ability, etc.

Demonstration Material.—Any material or apparatus used

APPENDIX

in connection with the putting over of a lesson by the use of the demonstration method. (See Pamphlet No. 2.)

Efficiency Records.—Data secured for the purpose of improving the efficiency of any piece of work, as when the time required to train for the same job by different instructors is compared in order to find out the best methods.

Elastic Admission.—An arrangement whereby an instructor can take a man at any time and start him on a training course without regard to where any of the rest of the group are on their progression through the same course.

General Material.—Material that is of general use in instructional work, but which does not especially apply to the requirements of any particular teaching job; blackboards, reference books, etc.

Group Instruction.—Instruction given to a gang which consists of sub-groups in which the members of each sub-group can be instructed in the same thing at the same time.

Illustrative Material.—Any material or apparatus used in connection with the putting over of a lesson by the use of the illustration method. (See Pamphlet No. 2.)

Inside Work.—Work that is carried on under cover either in some place specially provided for the purpose, (a "school room") or on the floor of the shop.

Instructional Engineer.—An instructional engineer is an individual who goes at an instructional problem in the same manner as a production engineer goes at a production problem.

Instructional Material.—Anything that can be used in the instructional process: books, tools or models.

Instructor as Instructor.—An instructor looked at from the standpoint of his work in putting over what is to be taught.

Instructor as Supervisor.—An instructor looked at from the standpoint of his work in keeping the instructional work going, with the entire instruction gang.

Interest.—Whatever makes the learner want to learn.

Justification Records.—Records showing whether or not any given piece of training work is worth doing; as, for example, when it is desired to determine whether rivet sorters can be trained to advantage.

Non-Production Instructional Material.—All material or apparatus used in connection with the putting over a lesson off the job, the use of the demonstration or illustration methods as outlined in Pamphlet No. 2, and general material but not that which can be classified as working material.

Outside Work.—Work carried on outdoors in the yard or on the ship.

Paying Apprentices.—An apprentice who to a greater or less extent pays for his keep through the value of his labor.

Personal Interview.—Any sort of a "talk" which will enable an instructor to get a line on a prospective learner's qualifications.

Poor Instruction.—The result of doing an inefficient instructing job.

Poor Learner.—A man who, if all other causes of failure were removed, would still fail to make good.

Poor Management.—Failure of the instructor to meet any or all of the conditions of good management, especially in his relations with his men, bad handling of interest factors, etc.

Rotary Gang.—A group organization in which the instructor always has a group of the same size; this requires that as soon as a man is discharged from the group another man comes in, so that the group consists of men in all stages of progression but is always full.

School Discipline.—This means the discipline maintained in an ordinary school as distinguished from the sort of discipline maintained in a good production plant.

Seminar.—An instructional organization under which the different men in a group, while each working on specified problems, come together with the instructor at frequent stated intervals for discussions and reports.

Supervisor.—A man who directs and is responsible for the activities of a gang; quarterman, leading hand, foreman, assistant, superintendent.

Supervisory Training.—The training given to men to fit them for some form of supervisory work.

Trade Extension Training.—The training given to a man who is already somewhat advanced in his particular work to extend his trade knowledge or his trade skill, or both, as the case may be.

Trade Training.—The training which gives to a man who does not know or who cannot do anything in a given trade, that which he needs so that he does know and can do the things which constitute that trade.

Training Gang.—A group of men to be trained by an instructor or "training boss."

Working Material.—Any material that is used in doing an instructional production job. Example: a bulkhead on which a man is being trained to rivet constitutes working material.

Working Relations.—Relations which result from the necessity of discharging mutual responsibilities.

CPSIA information can be obtained
at www.ICGtesting.com
Printed in the USA
BVHW010923030719
552253BV00005B/5/P